Kerried
Away

KAS Confidential
477 Peace Portal Dr,
Ste 107-153
Blaine, WA 98230

Produced by:
KAS Confidential
www.KerriKrysko.com

Ordering Information:
For details, contact the publisher at the address above.
Orders by U.S. trade bookstores and wholesalers.
Available for purchase in Chapters/Indigo and Black Bond Book stores.
Currently in Libraries across Canada

Distributed to the trade by The Ingram Book Company

Printed in the United States of America

First Edition

Kerried

Away

part one

Kerri Krysko

Contents

Foreword

I have known Kerri-Lynn for over 15 years. As her family physician, I have seen Kerri-Lynn transform from a frightened, insecure woman to one who is confident, self-assured and strong.

Her strength and courage have allowed her to face the challenges that have confronted her over the years. Kerri-Lynn has had the remarkable ability to focus on her self-preservation, as well as the well-being of her children. Her children, Ashton and Sable will continue to benefit from her growth, and they can mature into young adults knowing that their mother fought hard for safety and security.

Kerri-Lynn is truly an amazing person and her journey provides inspiration to all those who know her, including me.

G.P / M.D / PHD

Dr. Lowe

Introduction

"Taking a moment to re-evaulate all around you, with patience only you can acquire - isn't such a bad thing but is something, that can utterly change your very future."

It was the moment in which I knew I was being tested. A moment in which the world ceased to exist and all I could see was a movie and scenarios playing in mind. The outcome was a decision that would change my very existence. My childhood visions of a prince coming in and swooping me off my feet were crushed by a man who used me, degraded me and at times made me feel the very ground I walked on was paved with gold.

I didn't have a moment to mull everything over, I didn't have that chance nor did I have the guts to ask. I was cornered and the only thought I had, in that fast moment, was NOT to allow my own precious children see the violent outcome if I said NO!

I could take any amount of pain in the world for them, any beating and all the disgusting words that were thrown my way, just to protect my sons, from any more volatile situations but I just couldn't see them hurt anymore, I just could not. It was my weakness but also my only strength.

I did know what was right and what was wrong and to me, at that moment, it was the right thing to do. Not many would agree, but unless you were there, in my shoes you may have chosen as I had as well.

I couldn't even imagine what saying NO would do to The Beast's pride, let alone image and I could just imagine what that would mean for us. So in the moment, I said yes.....

I said yes, to protect my children from witnessing beauty and pain together. I said yes, so I didn't have to endure another run for safety. I said yes, because maybe just maybe, I couldn't survive another back-hand or comment, and in that instant my whole world crashed around me like a cold wave from the salty ocean that stung my skin. My resolve and determination I had mustered over the last few weeks were gone. I felt defeated, beyond exhausted, and I knew the biggest battle was yet to come.

I slowly walked towards the door leading into the apartment, our once precious sanctuary, where I was willing to move from, in a split second. But. moving house, would only mean an angrier man who would be more determined than ever to hunt me down until he found me.

As I reached for the door and slowly slid Sable down from my hip, I shook, and that was when my precious angel, Ashton, looked at me, with no longer a smile, but a knowledgeable look of an old soul who knew what his mother had just done.

I felt sick and utterly hideous that my son knew. All the weeks of covering the bruises with our lovely family time away hadn't taken away what he had seen or heard. He knew and during that time he kept quiet so to protect me, even then. The truth was that he wasn't a young child anymore. These last few years had aged him. In that moment my son turned into a young man who raised his chin and put his touch to my skin with a gentleness that only he could give me. He sent me a look of such bravado; like that of a solider going into battle. My son knew and my baby boy officially stepped up as my protector with my knowledge of his wisdom coming full-circle. No words were needed between us, we were a team.

I felt ashamed, I felt disgusted and at the same time I knew I would do anything to take down The Beast if he ever laid another hand to me or god forbid, my children. I used all the street smarts I had acquired to finally put my emotions and forgiving attitude aside. There I promised myself, to always be one step ahead. In that moment, The Beast gained not *"a soon-to-be, trophy wife"* but a fiercely determined mother, teamed with a maturing child who knew the truth.

He gained not a punching bag, not a minion, not a smile-grin- and-bear-it attitude but an adversary that would call him out. A force that would even lay down her life to protect the ones she loved. That little girl, who was once robbed of a normal childhood, that young lady who tried to find a place to belong had indeed turned into a woman now. A strong woman, who would fight to survive, a woman, who would search and find the answers to end the suffering. A woman, who would use her own god given strength to break this horrid cycle that had started and try to give her own children the life she once envisioned.

Those dreams and wistful moments became her salvation, those taunts became her strength, those beatings became her tools and the love from her angels became her only truth. The truth she had to hold to, for the dark days ahead.....

That was the beginning of the end for this "Beauty and The Beast".

A proposal sent the wheels in motion and the thought of being more Machiavellian than him. Outwitting Damien became the very seed, which planted the tree to grow. **Those were the moments following my proposal.** That resolve saved our lives and that moment was a pivotal crossroad, of two trains colliding and coming to a halt.

"I write this, five years later, from that moment I can now put into words. My healing, strength and love gave me the power to search for the answers and the drive to succeed".

Realization

"Life is only hard, if you allow it to be"

He opened the door for us as we all turned to walk in. He scooped up Sable and tickled him to make him burst with laughter as my Ashton and I took a special moment to grasp hands. Then he turned to me again and went down on bended knee. He spoke to me of love and commitment, of trust and companionship. He took my hands as he looked up and said he had had this all planned and chastised me, for not showing up a week previously, in Calgary.

I was shocked that in a blink of an eye it turned into what I should've done as opposed to the now. He never ceased to amaze me. I was instantly rigid. He felt me clench, so I fell into what I had always done. I pulled him up to quickly hide my face in his embrace. I couldn't let him see uncertainty and I didn't have the energy to spend explaining my actions, I just didn't have the strength.

Damien spoke of wanting to call our babysitter Desiree to come over and watch the kids; so that he could take me for a romantic evening away to celebrate. It was all too much, too fast. It had been no more than half an hour since I had been walking down that hallway, to leave our home, to get away from him. In order to save face in front of my sons and stop a sure assault for running as I did before....

I couldn't prevent him any longer from seeing my turbulent emotions and I just couldn't keep them in check. I had to leave, so I just agreed and quickly walked to the bathroom while he phoned Desiree.

I remember locking the door and sliding down the wall as I sobbed. I'd been "had", once again by him and to myself, an ultimate failure. I was not the pretty, happy, beaming woman I should've been, on the day she gets proposed to. I was a mess and I was in for the biggest battle of survival I had ever known thus far. I knew it was only a matter of time before the facade of Damien came crashing down and the humiliation would begin, again.

He came to check on me in the bathroom while he had Des on the phone, speaking through the door in *'oh hunny and love'* tones that made me physically ill. I tried my hardest to speak without shaking. I was ashamed, so utterly ashamed of myself.

Desiree had been staying with me and was only five minutes away. She must be confused and shocked. I knew she would cover it well, as my girl, had also learned to appease The Beast. She was rushing over from what I had heard and I immediately needed to vacate the bathroom before anymore alarm bells went off. He was smart and I could never underestimate him again. I could never upset him on a day he would consider momentous.

Damien wanted me to send the news to family, via text and picture messages, of the ring and proposal. I thought it had more so to do with the diamond that glittered as beautifully as a star. *To me instead, it was a blood diamond…dripping down my hand, slowly gripping the very insides of my gut and wrenching the heart from my chest.*

I knew they would be sick, or was that me? No, they'd be sick, I would be the laughing stock and ultimately I'd once again lose what little support, I had left or had in the first place. I felt humiliated and thought, *"Wow, look at me, beaten, held hostage, running for my very life, interrogated, privacy invaded, children screaming in terror and now? … Hey guys, guess what? We're a happy family and I am engaged".*

What a fucking joke! I beat myself up relentlessly and no one would even think to stop and ask me why, Karebear? Are you okay?

No, I am not, only the closest who had been witness to his tactics, would play the game with me, until we were safe! Only *they* would see the clearly visible lines of distress on my face, only them, and those individuals, who were very far and few between.

I knew then, I had lost the family I had coveted and tried to please. I also knew that the push back I would get from them wasn't worth explaining why I had said yes. Personally, I had enough on my plate. They would never understand, as they had never lived through what I already had. They, as a whole, only thought I deserved everything I got and that hurt more than any fist raised to me. Inside, I still wished they would actually hear what I was saying and just once in their freakin' lives, care enough to understand. I was a disappointment to them and they had come up with their own negative opinions of who I was, long ago, and nothing I could say or do would change that. It was useless and me I was slowly becoming numb to it all.

My family never realized the twisted diabolical way Damien thought and me, well, I was just starting to realize I never deserved the treatment

I received from them or him either. ***No one deserves that***!

I knew what they would assume and I also knew if any one of them had endured what I had; I would never be so callous in their treatment. I would be there with open arms trying to heal their pain and help them. That is and always will be the separation that divides them and me, my heart and their opinionated ways. I could see past the one-two way thinking and envision far ahead into choices, paths, outcomes and even consequences. I was a child, girl and woman who lived far more than most and took the master's degree in people, to a whole new level.

I by now, knew Damien's thinking and tactics. The more brutal the beatings meant the larger the diamond. My engagement ring twinkled like icicles. It was a three karat Canadian diamond, encrusted in a circle with another two karats. Once again, it was bling baby, *"I'm sorry"* and the life. Someone who was influenced by that was them. Me I wasn't, nor was the pain worth any price he could muster up with a present or held a candle to the torment the children and I received when having to run for our lives.

I felt as though the ring was the only thing he was proud of and another thing he could add to his glory and gloat about. Once again I was robbed of a forever, first time moment in my life but, it also gave me a clarity I needed to fight for what I believed in.

I placed no value on this ring. No object that would be taken away or even used as punishment was worth the excitement one should feel on the day of her engagement. It was as if I was embarking on treacherous waters that would one day test the very forgiving, understanding heart I had. It was another long road to failure in my eyes and all those around me. I couldn't even stop the raging emotions that were inside, choking me. Not even long enough to be happy. All that whispered dimly, was *'I'm sorry my babies, one day my beautiful sons, I PROMISE, we will be free, we will be"*. I hated that moment, proposal, and day as much as I now hated myself. No one will ever understand the depth of grief and self-loathing I felt inside. That day is vivid and feeling it now makes the tears fall freely down my face.

I don't want to come off as if I didn't care about Damien. I did. I cared, but he had done so many hideous things I couldn't look past it all anymore. I couldn't put a blind cover over my eyes and pretend. They were wide open and the tumultuous feelings that raged inside me, were crippling.

What was worse was putting on a façade that all was wonderful in my world and not being able to be honest and true, stripped every valuable trait I had in myself. Every fake smile and forced moment destroyed a piece of me. It suffocated and stuffed that little girl with a need to shine, buried deep inside me, from coming out. It was slowly killing me, every single day. I was denied from being me and the only ones who ever saw the real me, were my precious children. My genuine essence suffused the room with light whenever I was with them and Damien knew it.

I couldn't believe the audacity Damien had and his tactics to save face, after what he had done. It was the ultimate humiliation knowing I had just said yes and now had to pretend this beating I received was somehow acceptable. I now had to show his friends and associates that I somehow deserved another beating because of the father's e-mail from school and there is where he controlled me.

I now know as a victim of abuse, one learns to adapt to your surroundings in order to survive, but I wasn't adapting in my own mind. I was overwhelmed with utter chaos and disharmony. I was a mess and I knew in those initial moments, following my acceptance, I had to be smarter, wiser and find any way I could to sever that tie to him. Without having to run and hide in fear for a lifetime, for the sake of my sons, I had to try to do this and survive. But the façade I had to carry, choked me, like a noose.

It was unbearably hard facing Desiree when she sauntered threw the door a few minutes later. I gave her a look and she fell into the same routine as I did with The Beast. She acted surprised but she wasn't thrilled. I believe she was confused, but knew anything could set him off and played along for the sake of me and my children. She knew the truth that the two of us kept hidden to protect her from him. The day he had held a knife to my throat and flung those mentally destructive words at me, she was in the hallway hiding and he could never know. A promise I made to her, which I would never break, for her safety and mine.

It was weird, almost, *The Beast* wearing his heart on his sleeve. I knew he cared and even loved me in a perverse way. It had just turned into a sickness and an obsession with him. I felt wrong, feeling the emotions that were welling up inside and shackling me further to him. I felt rotten to my core and the guilt was almost evident, almost, but my sons kept me rock solid. I couldn't keep it in check much longer. My resolve was slipping away one second at a time. I was starting to cave and let my guard down a little because of the passionate thoughtfulness of his words and actions. He was being the father I knew he wanted to be and the gallant knight he liked to act, all the while I was planning my escape.

Damien was beaming and I was defeated once again but my determination never stopped my silent wishes to take all this pain away. Was it too much to ask for, to have a normal life for the sake of my own humanity? Was it too much for someone to actually love me? Maybe I just wasn't worth it and everyone was right.

I tried to hold onto my faith and hope that the words he had said were true but I knew it was only time before I would feel the harshness of his hate for me return. I also knew with this ring came a heavy price and I wasn't willing to pay it. Let alone could I even survive it?

Desiree was speechless and her face was ashen. This was too much for a young girl to take. She was barely sixteen and had witnessed more, with me, than she should have. I couldn't bear her growing up to think this was a normal relationship and I could only thank the heavens, she had parents such as she had. They were stable, loving, kind and showed a perfect example of a traditional couple, with a healthy relationship.

Desiree was an old soul, her mother and I had talked about it on a few occasions. I knew without her as my anchor, I would sink. But it wasn't right, any way you looked at it, and the shame I felt weighed heavily on me. There is where my resolve slipped further. Each moment, each scenario and person that came in contact. I had to be smart and hold that truth inside in order to survive.

I never had the support network that I believed normal people had. I never had a family who would heal any pain of mine with love and gentleness or even acceptance. I had only myself and my sons. They are _not_ supposed to be the ones, to protect and shield you but the ones, YOU should shield and protect. It was a reality I was only just realizing. I never felt more alone. I knew I had to be held accountable for doing this to them and everyone around me. Perhaps, I was deserving of this relentless pain because I was guilty for living and accepting it. In those moments following the proposal and Des coming over on Damien's command; my self-loathing and ridicule raged within me as I fought with all I had. All the while covering it up with a fake smile and nod of a broken woman and mother.

I spent a few moments in the kitchen in the company of both Desiree and Damien. He wouldn't leave us alone together. He knew how close we had become. I also believed he carried his own embarrassment about his actions and wanted to prove to her he wasn't The Beast, as she might have thought. Like I said, he was smart. Damien has pride and an image to uphold, he is the perfect gentleman around others when he wants to be. He could weave you into his web with a story or a smile. He was like a brilliant stone that radiates an aura of powerful magnificence and I was his chattel. Except to us, we knew his methods and tactics. This weaved web he might've tried on this day, never worked as I watched Desiree hold herself in check, constantly diverting her eyes from his.

He told me to quickly go and pack for the night, when it became awkward. I had no idea he was thinking of going somewhere overnight and I instantly went rigid. I didn't want to be anywhere alone with him. I was terrified. He had only just tried to kill me and even described the murder scene, as he tormented me for hours; a mere two weeks ago. I panicked and went instantly to my children to whisper all my loves in their ears and radiate all I could. I held them, while silently watching him speak to Desiree through the dining room.

Desiree picked up on my terror and started questioning Damien about where he was taking me and when we would be back. She was smart, and she was on it, like my little hero. I didn't want to leave my children, was this a ploy to get me alone with him so he could kill me. It was all I thought when he said we wouldn't be back tonight. I was about to have an anxiety attack when I seen him stiffen his back. I knew now was not the time to back pedal, I couldn't allow him to turn a hand on her, or worse on all of us. I would take whatever he threw at me, alone. Without them around.

He was calculating her demeanor looking for any crack in case she knew what he done, or thought differently of him in anyway but she held her composure well. He leaned in all of a sudden, as he whispered to her and only when I saw her smile at me and wink, did I release my sons and pent up feelings. I never realized at the time that I was learning to read people's emotions and behaviors, it was just second nature to me and my only way to survive the wrath of fury, from Damien. He was capable of such extreme violence that it didn't have a chance to slowly build, he just instantly lashed out, like a deadly flash if you weren't prepared.

My eyes took in the kitchen as he was standing there speaking with my babysitter. My mind was reliving the last incident in full.

"he grabbed the knife he used to intimidate me, taunting me, and belittling me with every volatile word you can imagine…telling me I am going to die, my kids are going to find me in the bath tub. I heaved and my body shook…"

My head swam. I wanted to curl into a ball and call for my mother to love and protect me, but I couldn't and I knew she wouldn't come. I could never put her through that again, I could never run to any family member for safety again, it was over and I could never ask them for help, it had gone on for too long. They only knew of the aftermath, and never the incidents. Nor, did they ever ask.

I knew when he proposed in the hallway and I said yes, I had sealed my fate and I was the only one able to end this madness. I knew none of my family members, ever fully understood the truth of my situation but I also knew they never cared enough to even take the time to listen. I had heard it in their sneers, jabs and comments just weeks before.

Only my mother knew a few details and she was just too weak to handle any more. She needed to find her own strength and had to fight her own personal demons. I cared and loved her enough to know this burden was mine and mine alone to figure out.

I never knew any differently. I never knew what normal was, only in my dreams and there I had to begin, alone, without causalities in its wake. My heart that loved to help others was not the heart of my family. They had no heart to give me, not the care they would give to others. Somehow I had to stop wishing that and fight for what I knew I would give my own children, not a wasted hope that only crippled me.

I watched as Damien and Desiree carried on about the trip he had just come back from and how he had been planning for months to propose to me, but it was never the right time. I heard most of the conversation as I sat there dazed. When my phone started going off, I knew the messages were received by my family. I felt nothing, nothing at all. I was officially numb and in so many words they said, via text, they would not attend the wedding and that I was pathetic. I played along, agreeing just for the sake of saving face and torment from Damien, or a comment that would dig a hole in my chest. It was a sad way to live but my only way. I was used to their words and what they thought, but nothing hurt

15

me more than knowing I wasn't worth their time.

As we headed out for our special evening my fake smile was back on my face as I walked out the door. I listened as Damien putdown my family in a few short words, using it as a benefit for himself by saying, "I'm the one who loves you baby, we are a family now." I knew I was more alone than ever and it stung. I knew it was his way of getting me back after my stint with my mother on the island.

I handed Desiree a few hundred dollars to order anything she wanted and to take the boys out to the mall first thing in the morning. If I was going out for a special night, they were to be treated to an even more special day/night. My mind echoed with the thought that I might never make it home. That was how I always was, and will be, doing anything just to make them smile and create a happy memory for them, just in case something ever happened to me. Damien quickly ushered me out the door as we said our goodbyes and he tugged me close, showing Desiree and myself "WHY HE IS MY FAMILY".

I was apprehensive getting into his SUV as we arrived downstairs. It was dark now and the full force of being alone and stuck in a vehicle with him, hit me hard. He`d seen the panic on my face, so he came fast around the car, just to hold me. Pushing me against the vehicle, Damien wrapped his huge arms around my fragile body and cradled my head within his embrace. He whispered such loving endearments into my ear that I thought, just for a moment; this is the man I could love. This is the man I had wished him, to always be, the one who made me feel safe. I soaked it all in because those were the emotions I needed to feel, those were the ones that gave me the strength to Kerri On…and those were the only ones I so rarely ever received from anyone.

As we approached the hotel where Damien was taking me for the night of our engagement, my mind was reeling about what I had done. I evaluated every action and word he spoke. I was like a super-natural person with senses that were razor sharp and Damien wasn't uncomfortable in the least. He had no idea those taunts he spoke in his heated rages, "I will break you, I will make you bend to my will" were no longer effective taunts and that he had already broken me. He just wasn't going to bend me to his will. It was fight or flight and I was willing to do the battle.

As we entered our room he was smiling and loving. It was that side of him I relished and savoured. The only issue with that, was he could and would bend things to suit him, manipulation at its finest. I often thought he was fighting his own battles that raged within him, but knew better now than to make excuses for his treatment towards me and even others.

The wounds I still carried on the inside were evident and he knew it, but I never realized how deep they truly were until he started coming on to me. I was no longer the woman he could melt into an intoxicating bliss of heaven nor a influenced young girl. Instead I was standoffish and even repelled by his candor and touch. I tried, I really tried to fall deeply into his embrace but I couldn't and when he felt that distance from me, he pushed me away like a rag doll.

I couldn't just shut off my emotions and forget what he had done. I could never forget that last beating I received. I was still traumatized. It was explained in explicit detail what my death would be and how my own children would find me. I was sickened and I was lost. I never knew who I could trust or where I could go. I was losing me, and fighting my damnedest to be false for him, so I didn't wind up dead and instead I froze. The charade gone and my true self visible for him to see.

The Beast thought this was our special engagement night and I was ruining it. Bruises heal, scars are forever and his words cemented into my head. He never once thought about the painfully fresh scars now embedded within my soul. My scars weren't going to go away because of a sparkly present and few sentences of spoken love. He had pushed me to the point of no return and I was now climbing my way to freedom in my mind.

He carried on about what it cost him and how he had this all planned out. He even tried to pull me close and say he loved me and that I shouldn't have done this to him by running away. I should have come to Calgary to see him when he had asked, via text, while I was at my mother's healing from his brutality. He also stated he had the computer inspected and there was nothing on it that raised anymore alarms. He somehow justified himself all in a breath and all the while, he thought he was such a man.

I couldn't stomach much more but laid there silent and tried to be unassuming. If I allowed him to keep going he would start talking in a frenzy and then who knew how worked up he'd become. I just silently agreed with all he said so I could stop his rant, unreasonably hoping that I didn't hear any more agonizing words that would tear my very soul apart. I couldn't stand another moment of this charade. It ripped me apart.

Those moments following my return and the last few weeks were playing over and over in my mind. I just wanted the refuge in my children's arms and did not want to be here, with him, and I sure as hell did not want to be engaged.

I started hating myself and felt the digs he threw my way, even agreeing made my skin crawl. Even feeling that I deserved it all for laying here with him now. I was gross and I was useless, as he had said. I needed air. I couldn't stomach his touch or even him, let alone myself. Instead of running through the doors for fresh air, I stayed put, listening as if I was attentive. My mind taking over as he continued to cascade around the room and then prop himself up beside me. Everything had to go according to what he felt was the night or else….my mind drifting away here and there.

If I did not take this to the end, try this last thing, an engagement, I would never get away. I knew this as fact, but floating in the back of my mind… did anyone else? Desiree did of that I knew for certain and in a shadowed thought so did my precious son…

 No one will understand that if I didn't say yes, it would have been hell for us. I would have been hurt again and then I would never have a chance at freedom. He would have grabbed me by my hair and even knocked me out as he drug me into the apartment, I felt it or was that my fear of him?

No human being was going to understand my reasoning and I knew more than ever, I was very alone in my battle for freedom. I had to try my hardest to forgive and only look at the good but also always be alert and ready in case he struck out. It was a hard way to be, but the only way. I was with a full-blooded, over inflated, powerful Hells Angel, who was a sociopath, a liar. I had his son and another son, he felt he owned. Does anyone or did anyone understand what I was going through? There began my defense against the family that had always put me down. There began my questioning of all things around me. WTF and what was I going to do?

I knew I had a chance of dying at his hands, with how violent he could become. What he'd already done, nearly killed me and I survived. I needed to fix this, and break this cycle I could help my children and maybe, just maybe I could help him too. I was having many thoughts on how to help and fix everyone, but the feelings of worthlessness and belief in all the mean words ever uttered to me had me convinced that what they'd all said; were right.

I never knew being on survival mode, it was actually altering my thoughts and perception. I never realized I was even worth fighting for, only my children were. I was last on any list and I was used to it. In my mind, I already thought I couldn't get away and I couldn't say No.

In actual fact, I could say NO, but if not for my sons I may well have said that two lettered word. Instead and because of their presence and saving grace, I didn't dare stand up to the beast. They were the strength I held dear. No one wanted to come up or against me on that. I would fight with every last breath in me, if any harm had been dealt to them. There Damien did not have a chance and there is where I knew if I couldn't fight for myself; I could fight for them! Their innocence and their upbringing.

I just wanted life to be kind, caring and I never wanted to hurt any more people. I already felt that I had, in my very brutal, harsh reality. I couldn't hurt all those around me anymore. I still felt as though it was my entire fault, from childhood to whom I dated and where I am now. I never fully grasped that it wasn't. I only knew what he does to me didn't feel nice and it was wrong. I needed to now discover if all those comments that the people I loved, said were true. Because if they were, then I didn't deserve to live and I deserved every fist that came my way. I deserved to just accept what Damien was doing to me and suffer through it or die trying.

I looked at him then, laying on the bed after he shut the curtains and was rambling on about all he planned for us and I just stopped him mid-sentence and kissed him. Searching for any amount of feeling I could find. I knew inside this beast was a passionate man and I also knew that if I could just find that elusive feeling I once had with him, I could shut these raging emotions, running rapid within me and make them stop.

"Cease the moment and forever fall victim to what it entails, as I did…the only way I knew how…search until I found"

It worked, in that initial moment and he melted. He showed me the love he did have for me and he gave me an inkling of mine back.

It was astonishing sometimes what this man could do for a woman, with just a touch of care… I couldn't believe what had just gone through my mind and will never forget it or when it happened. I had put this man, who I had just become engaged to and placed him in a category of 'what he could do to other woman, instead of me' and there I forgot, in a daze all the shitty, crappy things he had done.

I couldn't believe it, in my mind, I never thought of him with me. I had become subservient to the fact he was everyone's and was never really, truly mine and I was even okay with it. I didn't care! I was shocked.

I remember digging deeper as he touched me and I imagined that he was with someone else, not me and somehow it made it better than as if he was, with me. I know he felt the shift in me, he was looking for it because of what had happened moments before and he never snapped.

I had ignored him, half listening and not really into the whole fake happily engaged couple.

Now, this was no fantasy for our clothes were still on, this was a mere 'kiss n cuddle'. Who knew where it would go, but it was then; that notion started, him with anyone but me. I discovered something that would allow me to 'Kerri On' through some endless nights that I knew were in store and as long as he wasn't touching me, I was one hundred percent okay with that.

Just like that I got up and walked outside of the hotel room. Leaving him there shocked and perhaps bothered.

I went outside for a cigarette and to also phone my babysitter to see how the kids were. I vaguely remember explaining this to him as I left. I was stunned and I needed anyone just to talk to and it definitely wasn't him. I had stumbled upon a truth that only the broken can accept. I was okay with him touching other woman as long as it wasn't me. Oh, how many times that passed through my mind since that day and still now I shake my head.

When Desiree answered the phone, she was upset.

"What the hell happened? You're engaged after all he has done to you, Kerri?"

I tried to explain where I was coming from. I only had a few moments to talk and was constantly checking behind me in case he walked up.

She was the only one who accepted me for me. Who even understood the capabilities and lengths of Damien's rage. She had once sat, outside in the hallway, as she heard every defaming word he had spoken and every smack that echoed against my body. She knew because she was the one to stop one of the most horrid painful moments I received, when the beast became unleashed.

My explanations and reasons she understood. She got it and to protect the children it was a necessity, for Beast caught me alone and surprised me with his sudden appearance. I had thought he was still gone to Alberta for a week.

Desiree would soon be the only person I had left in this world. I treasured the good, as I treasured her. Knowing that she cared enough to understand meant the world to me. Protecting my sons meant the universe and for that I will forever be in her debt.

~I, to this day, am sorry, my lovely Desiree, for having even allowed you to see any of that. Please know you saved me and my children many times. We, my girl have been through so much together, I shall never forget, as I believe you won't as well. I love you always 'n' forever ~ Kerri Krysko

Desiree constantly kept me in zcheck, on what was right or wrong when my family and Damien would treat me as they did. She carried a voice of reason and a truth I often sought and needed.

Knowing my sons were okay and there was even a little support for me once this engagement made 'The Headlines' from Des, gave me strength I sought when phoning her. I never shared the revelation of my fantasy with regards to Damien with other woman, anyone but me.

Instead she gave me the solid foundation of having someone there when this was done.

I walked back to the hotel room with a new perspective and also a notion that would see me through even more dark days ahead. But I was willing to try this one last time and give Damien a chance. Try my best to forgive him, for his own mixed up diabolical way of acting or find a way to leave for good! When in actual fact I had made my decision to leave long before then but didn't know how. I felt trapped, even stuck.

My family was another story and I had no idea how they were really feeling as I mentally prepared myself for even more of the fallout, but that was for another day. Today was here and I was willing to make the best of it, as usual.....

I was officially engaged to The Beast.

New Awakening

"Lost memories are found when you glance back and feel the emotions of longing deep within your soul"

I had a feeling, of such isolated loneliness and nowhere in this world to belong, it was crippling. My only reason for carrying on was that I was needed to look out for my little punkins and that's all the carried me. They needed me to be strong, and to protect them from the harsh realities of the world. I/We were now facing. I was alone and I never realized how deeply, and truly scared, I already was.

I never knew that each day I sat back and accepted the fact that some of the closest people I held dear, never respected me or properly cared for me and constantly bastardized me at every turn, was slowly ripping me apart and setting me up for failure. I was still quite young in the art of what surrounded you could and can also shape you.

I was determined to sacrifice all, just to survive and thrive but was continuously being held back, by forces I was unaware of. By a cycle on repeat and never truly getting ahead or away.

I never once felt like the life I was living was where I belonged. I never felt that I deserved the treatment I received, but I did feel defeated, deflated and somehow I simply, accepted it.

I knew it wasn't right, even wrong but somehow in my hearts of hearts, I felt as though; I loved enough, forgave enough and bowed to what others wanted, perhaps slowly things might get better and maybe, just maybe, my dreams would come true and someone might actually genuinely love me.

I sure was in for a rude awakening and a cold splash of reality, which was probably exactly what I needed.

I was no longer that naïve girl who rolled around, running in a circle that was deemed *"not acceptable or even criminal"* who once thought along the lines of *"WE ARE ALL EQUAL"* .

I had changed. Life had changed me and those people I once held dear, no longer clouded my juvenile mind or thoughts. I may have had some of the most glorious days of my life, feeling accepted by them, but they also dealt some blows that left me breathless and without air.

Those people had also broke my heart and hurt me beyond repair, those people who were once my 'family of all families' never truly knew the meaning of a good life. There were okay with life as it was, me well I wanted more for my children, so much more.

I did, I noticed it around me on a daily basis, in our communities, at the schools and just the way some people I saw had a glow of purity to them. I saw it and I have searched for it, quietly storing it away inside me every time something or someone softly presented a ray of light to me. I guess because to me those kind gestures or distant, far away moments I noticed in people is what I wanted to one day provide for my sons. I would see how a father ruffled a child's hair, or a mother just strolled beside her husband NOT behind them and most importantly; the self-esteem in others and how they presented themselves it was unique and special to me. I would then share that with my sons and later what I promised them.

This world, and these old friends, speak on loyalty, equality, respect and family but are the first to turn on you when someone higher up the chain disagrees. There is no loyalty amongst thieves. There is only a moment and even that is short lived. It is a roll of the dice and one bad seed can take that away in a second. Like a drug addict can become so high they get suspicious of another, start a lie and there a few weeks later an innocent person who did nothing ends up dead. That's the streets and eventually that's the life....

I still forgave them (not that what I said above happened to me, but I have seen it and that's the game) and cared enough to look past the darkness and search to understand their motives, for dealing such wrong doings to our beautiful world, but they were no longer my main concern. Those people never amounted to what I felt for my sons; they could never hold even a little light to what I felt for them.

I never wanted those people in any way, shape or form in the presence of my innocent children. For fear that even grazing up against my babes, would somehow taint or pollute them. They lived a life I couldn't imagine living forever. That lifestyle was not all it was cracked up to be and I wanted better. Damien was at the top of the food chain so to speak, so he relished in the power. Me, well I felt bad for the weak and didn't like the way that social latter worked in the bottom sector of that crowd. It wasn't all pleasure but pain as well.

I had helped so many of those people along the way and I guess I was feeling, where were they, when I needed them or my sons needed them? It was as if no one would ever stand up to Damien, or for me. I felt betrayed. That was scary, coming to realize it. Those people, I once held so truly close to my heart, as *my 'familia',* would never step up to The Beast, to protect me. Never! He was Lucy and no one stepped towards Lucy.

Without my sons, I probably would have found a way to end my suffering and I most definitely would not be here writing my story.

I was sinking and the only hope I had was to revisit the treacherous path that lead me down some of the darkest roads of my life. I had to search for the answers to solve my problem if I had any hope at all of making sure my own sons never suffered the same fates I did; especially while I still had the heart and fight to do it.

So, as I contemplated my life, my actions, faults, and wrongdoings and the people in my life, my road to survival began. My life took on a new shape, direction and meaning (*Not that I knew that is what I was doing at the time).* Searching for the answers was my only hope and what I was soon to discover; rocked me to the core.

I immersed myself again as I once had as a young girl, in my romance novels and went on being only myself around my children. It was a longing I had, to be accepted. The only form I received that acceptance was from the parents, at my children's school. I loved it and relished in the structure of it all and them.

I had yet to meet with Stella, since my return from my mother's home on the island, and was looking forward to having my friend back. She loved the simplicity of being a parent and I knew in that regard it would be nice to have her around. I had no friends anymore; it was my sons and I, against the world. So knowing I was going to see her soon, made me ecstatic.

I was caught in such a web of insidious abuse, it made me unaware that seeking comfort in an old friend was not the way to go. I was blinded by having her around for security, as opposed to remembering why we weren't friends for so long in the first place, and why I had initially shut the door on her.

Her heart was nothing like mine and her lies could wreak havoc, for years on an unsuspecting or unknowing soul. I had forgotten, or chose not to remember, her mean, vindictive, untrustworthy side.

I only sought the friend in Stella, the one that could make me laugh and smile again. That was who I needed. I always cared about Stella, somewhat like a sister and I always would, but that didn't mean I had to allow her in our lives. Needless to say, I did and at that time I needed her more than anything. My guilt at having Desiree around so much of this horror, was now gnawing at me. Plus the fact that Damien was pushing her out of our lives but I didn't see that either. I was blind sometimes to his corrosive ways.

Once again, allowing the comfort of familiarity to cloud my judgement or perhaps that negative door was already busted wide open, so it just flooded in.

Damien wasn't impressed with us seeing each other. Stella and I had a magnetic chemistry that only two lost souls can have with each other. He was continuously reminding me what trouble she was and that he didn't trust her. He went on and on, mentioning that Stella was even banned from one of clubhouses for causing trouble.

I felt he just didn't want me to be close to anyone, so I carelessly tossed his warnings aside. I needed my friend more than anything and wasn't going to let him take this from me, too. I was so concerned over his controlling ways, that I let it slip from my mind about her very own destructive, cynical juvenile characteristics.

From my perspective, I was not allowing him to push another person out of my life, as he had done with my family. Or so I thought, at the time. I do know however, Damien was a worldly man, he was smart and sometimes he *was* actually looking out for me, or us, but because of the way he sought to control everything I never heeded his words, only tossed them carelessly aside as another putdown, instead of the truth.

That day I was to see Stella, he watched me get ready with an intensity that I didn't realize. Intensity I would've done better than to overlook, but I was very new to being aware of his tactics and my mind was only coming to terms with it all. It was telling myself be smarter than the Beast, be wiser and one step-ahead; instead I was just starting to program myself with regards to how I had to overcome this adversity. I was just way too excited to see my Stella baby.

We were both parents and to me I thought wiser than our youthful days. With the past behind us and this one story I shall share below; I couldn't wait to see her and there was no way Damien was preventing this from happening, so avoiding eye contact and a tongue lashing I chose to stay focused as I got ready and planned the day ahead. But Damien just had to get his two cents in about Stella and instead of it bothering me, it took me back to place of happiness

I had only just received my licence back from getting a DUI. Four years before I had become pregnant with Sable, I was drinking and driving. I had chosen to hold off the DUI for a few years because I wasn't yet ready to deal with it and because of the court system in B.C. Canada. It allowed me to do this and I did have a great lawyer.

"It was the days of me being carefree and young when it happened.... I was just twenty-three years old, flying up the road and a hill with my brand new, white mustang convertible and the top down.

We were gorgeous, carefree, youthful my three girlfriends and I, driving that night. We were all blonde at the time, I mean winter wheat, white blonde. We had make-up to the nines (MAC of course) and music that begged you to sing, at the top of your lungs.

We'd just left the bar and "they" were lighting a joint in backseat and tried popping it in my mouth. I didn't do drugs, other than the incident many years beforehand. There and then I learnt my very hard lesson. But to me it was BC, and if mother earth grew it, it was fine; this never bothered me but I spit it out making them all laugh. Half a dozen martinis, our short skirts and a Mustang 2005, which was a pure white beauty I must say and beige tan leather seats it was smokin. We were having a blast. (This was when I had broken up with Beast and was in love with Chase).

It was a dark, quiet road and my house was just up the street. I never saw the road stop at the bottom of the hill, so I kicked my car in gear and flew up the hill. As approached the top, all I saw was a dark clothed guy jump out of the way. I never realized it was a police officer until I got closer.

So, when I was pulled over and was flagged down, all the while giggling. I quickly said, "I am sorry, here, you should just take my keys" and I dropped out of the car. I was laughing so hard, I doubted I could have stopped. The police officer had to have had a chuckle as I wasn't incoherent but higher on life, as opposed to drunk on booze. It was fun and sometimes fun brings trouble as it sneaks up on you, as that officer did, sprinting across the road hidden as he was.

I knew that Chase was just behind me by a few blocks in his truck so when he pulled up, he tried to smooth things over. It didn't work. I was half-intoxicated and shouldn't have been driving, anyhow. I was getting my, first and only, DUI and there was no way out of it. My car was driven home by someone else and I headed to the police station to get my ticket and blow in a sensor. I blew a 0.9, which was only a point over, but I had intoxication written all over me face and really, truly I deserved that ticket."

Finally free from the clutches of my mother, and falling for Chase. I was only twenty-three and not exactly as responsible as I would've thought. I had grown so much in four years that instead of fighting my DUI and trying to win the court system, I had opted to stand up in front of the judge and own my mistakes. I wanted to show, my then nine year old son Ashton, it was wrong to have done what I had and that people could've been hurt because of his mother's actions.

So I asked the judge, although I could've gotten off to hand me a sentence that was befitting to re-occurring drunk driving, as opposed to a first offender. I did that for my son and I did that to learn my lesson. It's a street thing really, if you are big enough to own your mistakes, only then will you actually grow from them.

I received a year suspension, eight hundred dollar fine and a sixteen day prison sentence. Like any person, I was terrified.

I deserved it and I was okay with owning my mistakes. It helped me grow as a person and it also gave me the drive to never make the same mistakes twice. I only had to do a quarter of the 16 days, just 2 weekends plus a day, to be exact. No sweat, right? …

Ya? Think again. On my last weekend in jail, I made a massive blunder, or one I thought was huge. I pushed a buzzer to call for a guard, because I needed another blanket. It was cold. Their blankets were made of wool (which I was allergic to), thin, itchy and had not much substance to them at all. It was cold and the bed was nothing more than a metal frame. The time was around 4am and I believe, perhaps, that my calling for the guard had disturbed her in some way. For when she came barrelling up the stairs, she had not a nice thing to say, at all. She ranted like a mad woman.

"What the hell do you want, you aren't dead are you?!? You only push that button if you're dying or dead!"

I never had a chance to get a word in edge wise. She went on and on in a manner I would feel sorry for anyone to be caught in. To be talked to like that was wrong, degrading and just rotten. She even took it to the point that on my very last day 'n' night in that place, she had me placed in what the jail calls, "The Hole".

I was shocked. All of this punishment for pushing a button? That button reads 'assistance'. Nothing more. It does not read "life and death scenarios" or even "Emergency". No other instructions than "Assistance". I was now on a twenty-three hour lock down. All because of pushing a damn button that I had no idea had consequences. I was not a regular inmate; I had never been to a place like that before and was only in for a DUI. I was treated as though I was the scum of the earth and worthless. This was a place where it was okay to verbally abuse the minority and I, still to this day, do not think that is right.

I have seen people on power trips, look who I was with. But this guard, with short brown hair and a butchy body, I wouldn't mess with.

It seemed as though it was acceptable to be as inhumane as she was. But, what do I know?

Her words, that she screamed, I can hear and feel with as much clarity as the day it happened. I feel sorry for the individuals/people, that chose jail to be their home or are better known as, 'Lifers'. The ones, that when they have no food or shelter; purposely try to get locked in jail, just for a fully belly of food and a roof over their heads.

I believe it was another instant that showed me that even the lost, need a kind hand up once in a while. I could never use my power to harm, hurt, belittle or bastardize another human being like that, nor would I want to. I was only just learning the ways of different social statuses and I vowed once again, as I had done in my childhood, to never treat another with discrimination.

I learnt my lesson and never would or have I, driven intoxicated again; I barely drink at all for that matter. Those days were done for me, well before I had my second son, Sable. The punishment was worth the lesson I received. It helped me, grow in age, maturity and to quite simply never do that again. It was wrong.

BACK to Stella and our first time back together since the roommate incident. To think I finally had my licence back and was packing up my babies to visit their Aunty Stella after such a long time, was exciting and forgotten were any wild moments that we had once shared (Those above, being one of them) together. But, Damien still had to through that one in as a reminder why we shouldn't see each other, instead I remember it as a memories of fun and learnt lessons, not bad, but instead growth.

When I pulled up to her house, she ran outside and jumped in my arms. It was a reunion I needed as much as, I believed, did she.

Stella

"A cycle shall repeat, but only if you allow it"

Stella hadn't grown; she was still 5ft nothing at all, with baby blue eyes and could pack a mean punch, even while she laughed. I admired her strength and once again *"WE WERE BACK"*. Good, Bad and completely Unbelievable.

She'd had another baby, and was still with her boyfriend who she was with, when we had our falling out. They had moved to Surrey. The place I vowed never to raise my children in just because of the bad memories and days I had spent longing for my own son. This was a place that even Stella vowed she would never move back to but she had.

Her home was small, but nice. She still had the picture of a sailing boat, wrapped with a three inch wooden frame. She bought it from my mother's friend, an interior decorator, only a few years beforehand. It was nice seeing the familiarity of those items she still hung in decoration. I liked the familiar.

We chatted endlessly about people, places and just stuff. It was a reunion that was inevitable and much needed. I was shocked to see she had a little baby girl and sad that I never even knew. I wasn't allowed social media, dating the man I did. Stella was my own birthing coach when I had been pregnant with Sable and I felt somehow robbed of the same experience with her baby. Regardless, her little girl warmed up to me and loved me, as if we had known each other all along. Stella said that she often told her little girl, all about Auntie Kerri, her sister. That touched me, so did many other things but inside there was always a doubt as to which way Stella would turn, act or even lash out. She had a streak that all had to be weary of, a darkness in her that not even I could extinguish back in the day.

Once the comfort zone was finally settled between us, did we turn to each other, sitting on her front porch, in the carport/garage. Only then did we allow ourselves the permission to get deep, personal and in depth. We wanted to know every detail of every second of the last few years; as we both loved to analyze things, people and just everyday occurrences.

She gazed at me, fishing almost and speculating as she does for information. She seen the hidden side that I always kept guarded and tried to stare it out of me with her baby blues.

"You're engaged to Damien?" she asked in her candid manner but loaded with speculation.

Stunned, I knew it was either the time I opened up, as I should've, or put on a façade that all was sunny, beautiful and cheery with me. I had always been the one to take care of everyone. Do I dare show my weakness and would it be used against me? I had only just re-connected, do I even trust her?

Stella was the jealous type and could become spiteful. Again flittered through my mind, do I trust her, do I lean on her, or had she always been right about him? I knew she was right, but do I allow her that satisfaction or would it be satisfaction to her?

I also knew that out of anyone, once Damien and I were together in front of her, she would put the pieces together and see me as I always was around him; Docile, sad and silent. Not myself and that rubbed her the wrong way, every time. But, would she see my pain or would she know I was broken and how deeply shattered I really was?

She would be searching for that bite and humor that I had when around everyone else. The Kerri with strength and fight that would be smart and witty, that laughed when all else failed, even if it meant sitting on the side of the road with four flat tires. I had once been carefree, but now I was chained in my own hell and about to marry the most twisted Hells Angel in Western Canada.

Stella knew this and that is why she stared at me with attentiveness, searching for the truth about Damien and me.

This I believe was the reason it was easy for her and I to sever our bond of sisterhood a year and half previously. She didn't have a kind spirit or heart as I did. I mean she was nice but had no self-control, almost wicked but altogether awesome as well.

It's hard to describe her without sounding mean, but it's the truth and even though we will no longer, ever have that once bond we shared. I do truly only wish her well, with love, happiness and her own kind of peace. I will always love her and if anyone was to ever harm her, years from now or in the present; I would pick her up, drop her somewhere (other than my own home) just to try and help her. She had a hard life when it came to addiction, self-control or the taunts within her own mind. She's my Stella monster.

I remember looking at her, longing to tell her I've been broken by him and I need help, Stella I need help to pick these pieces up and my insides raged with wanting to release the pain I was in. I needed her strength, I needed her support, and I needed her more than she would ever know. But, I couldn't; my trust was already stretched too thin. I resolved to just adapt and my eyes would speak the truth to her if I dived too deep into it. So they quickly shadowed with brightness as I said to her, with all the falseness I could muster, "We needed to be just us Stella; it was so good to have this last year to ourselves. We bonded and now we are starting our family."

I looked away as fast as I could, in case my eyes betrayed my words. My insides were screaming out, "I NEEDED YOU STELLA, I NEEDED YOU, help me get away, please just help me"! I needed her to be strong for me, show me the truth as I had once done for her. But, I couldn't trust her, let alone with something as precious as the lives of my sons.

She turned a blind eye and allowed what I said to be the truth to her. She was happy and so was I, or so she thought. I felt as though I was going to die inside. I needed someone, anyone, to take away this torture I felt. But I couldn't trust anyone, not now that I was fully with The Beast. Not now that he had all the power and I was left to my own devices which were few and far between.

Life as a wife was very much in the near future, and that future was as tainted as the doors that opened and the people who bowed down around them like slaves. To think that I had once felt safe and invincible with him, only now to feel as trapped as a caged animal.

My visit after that became tedious, I just didn't want to leave the comfort of safety but I had to. I knew the questions would come once I arrived home, so I took my time slowly packing up the kids. As I drove back home that day, I was silent as the kids played their silly games in the backseat. I knew all too soon the excitement of the day would lead into the everlasting night.

When Damien wanted to know something or felt threatened in any way, he would make you talk. If you didn't, he would sit you down in the right position, as he saw fit and drill you for hours on all he needed to know. Watching closely for any sign or hint of emotion where he would feel betrayed, often it would mean something completely different from what he thought. It was twisted, wrong and immorally sickening. If for some reason you spoke in the wrong tone, he would make you repeat it until you did it right, recording the look on your face with a camera and showing you your own face to shame you. I wasn't looking forward to his cruelty. I knew what it entailed and it wasn't anything I would wish on anyone. I just wanted to enjoy the moment and live in the little happiness I received from it.

When I arrived home it wasn't what I expected. It was welcoming, peaceful, loving and it made me cry. I couldn't believe that this man, who was the father of my beautiful baby boy, could screw with my mind as he did.

I expected the worst and came home to supper, roses and beauty. Just the way I always loved it. He swept me off my feet as I came through the door. He nuzzled his face in my neck and told me how much he missed me, how much he loved me and that tonight was my night. He even had a book out on my bed, with slippers and a housecoat so I could relax. It was beautiful and all I could do was sob like a fool.

He shushed me in the room and told me all these wonderful things as he confessed his undying love for me. He, in all his many words said that I was the best mother he knew and soon to be his wife. He was so proud of me and because I always cater to everyone and it was my night to be catered to. My Beast was true to his word, that night, as he did exactly that.

Not a word was mentioned the entire evening; for once I went to bed and slept peacefully. I couldn't believe it, right when I thought I had him figured out, he does that. Never once, questioning me, on my reunion with Stella.

This was one bond he could not sever, between Stella and me. I knew he was aware of that fact and perhaps this was his way of coming to terms with it. I would find out much later the truth on how far he would go to ultimately sever the friendships or any loving relationships I had. But, for now, the quiet contentment I felt, knowing I had someone out there that cared, was enough.

I was done being so mentally exhausted and trying to be one step ahead of him, so I let my guard down with Damien, just a little. I allowed the life we were planning together to take precedence.

I was a slave to my lie, a slave to Damien and a slave to my mistakes.

I did have a charade to play now with Stella and everyone else, for that matter. So I sat back as my last hope faded because of my dishonesty to Stella and I allowed the cards to fall as they would.

This was my life, as warped as it sounds; it was a rollercoaster of epic turns, corners and ups and downs...

Coming to Terms

"Oh, what a tangled web we weave when trying to live up to others expectations and not our own"

Not once realizing, my wish could come true or that the power of thoughts can shape you and make your nightmares very real. My wish for marriage and home gained me a very unrealistic reality.

I wanted love and the forever after. I wanted a family and to be married. I wanted to know stability and security. I wanted the lovely life of companionship that lasted forever. My Beast was anything but a family man, I knew that in my heart. I knew I would have to live with watching others and myself hurt because of him. Those dreams I had, never once included having my sons witness this degrading existence or for them to live that life.

I wanted normalcy and love, real love, the love that takes your breath away. Love that swoops in and engulfs your heart with bliss not flames. A love that protects you from feeling hurt and pain. *A love, that lasted, no matter how irritated one became because you would rather be with them, then apart.*

I was sick of pretending who I was, how I cared. The reality of my dreams, and thoughts as a child, were that, dreams. I had never experienced what a real love was. I was starting to doubt that any love could be as pure as what I had once hoped for and envisioned. The only love that I knew, for sure, was my love for my sons.

I was delusional and a wreck. I was useless and no good; even a pig, as he said, with the squeals never once going away. They were still very fresh in my mind and I felt it every time I got dressed or even showered. Mirrors were my enemy; they showed the exhaustion in my lifeless eyes and the shadows that lined my face. Those thoughts were starting to take root after saying yes, to his proposal. I had let myself down, but most of all I let my children down by showing them a weak woman and mother. I was now a desperate woman stuck in a living hell I felt I created.

I couldn't keep pretending to everyone and myself. I couldn't keep this charade up any longer, so I sat down and picked up a note pad and started writing all the things he was doing that broke my heart. Then I started writing from start to finish how many times he had purposely hurt me and the consequences it was having on us and how it was preventing a healthy, functional relationship.

I wrote all that pain down, all my truth and all the effects it was having on me. Slowly the words just took over as I wrote, not once realizing it was my last plea to him to save us, to save me and to ask him to stop. After 60 pages, I understood I was writing to him, begging for mercy, begging for love and begging for a normal future.

I tucked the notepad away and washed my tear streaked face. I planned a time to sit down and read to him what I had written. I needed to release all this abuse and I needed to find me again. I needed to know if I had to be wary, on guard and afraid any longer. I needed to know if he was going to kill me and place me in a bath tub so blood didn't get all over the house. I needed to know if he was going allow my children to find me cut up, as he said, and dead.

I needed to know if somewhere in his heart he did really care and this wasn't some twisted new joke. A pre-meditated plot of his to make me crazy or even kill me, to cover up his wrong-doings.

I needed to live again and be free. I needed so much that I couldn't function properly anymore. I was terrified and sad, defeated and useless. My darkness was here and I could no longer pretend, not to myself, nor my children, or even the neighbours any longer; I was crumbling.

I just hoped he never found my book of writings before I had a chance show him and read what it said. He would kill me, thinking I wrote a statement or was a rat; oh my god how scared I was after I wrote my heart on those pages.

I needed to show him the true emotion I had inside me, so he never thought anything else. I didn't want to be killed for writing my sadness down. I had always written my feelings down, since childhood, they were mine and my way of healing, growing and releasing the endless hours of loneliness and pain. All I knew was I had to read it to him and not allow him to read it or god forbid find it!

After a few days, I started panicking. What if he did find it? What if he thought I was *ratting* him out? The what-if's played in my mind over and over. I knew then, as my mind started playing tricks on me, I had made a huge mistake. The horrific things he had done to me were now, in black and white, on paper. The only thought that soothed my shattered nerves was that if anything should happen to me, at least my children would be safe and would know the truth. It was ramblings such as these, in my every waking moment, that kept me in check after I wrote those events, feelings and emotions down. I thought about burning it but then my superstitious side came out and thought what if I was supposed to write that because I was going to die.

I needed someone to confide in. Not my babysitter, she was just too young and what she had already been exposed to was just plain wrong. I couldn't put her through that any longer.

I called Stella and opened up for the first time since we had been re-united. I asked her to meet me the following day as I hadn't been truthful with her. I just hoped she wouldn't turn me away, tell on me and I had made the right decision. I had no one else to run to. She was my only chance. As I hung up the phone I felt a weight lifted off me for the first time in a month; since my arrival home and engagement.

I had no idea that those initial steps would begin a tidal wave of events that lead me to now writing my true story.

When you have no one, but yourself, that you can confide in, it's hard. It's those moments when you can do nothing but be busy and cover up the aching sadness, that well up inside you for no apparent reason that actually allows you to somewhat heal and keep going.

I often felt so alone, that I would silently seek that quiet place just to weep. It was the beginning of a depression that I never knew I could have. I loved life, people, and nature. I truly relished in the activity that surrounds us all. But I wasn't in love anymore, I was lost, I cared, but I didn't care. I started believing the things that people were saying to me and I stopped believing in what was right or wrong. I stopped believing in life. I stopped believing there was a better existence out there for me. My hope was gone and what was replaced was a doubt so profound that I can't even put into words. I'm sorry.

I started reflecting on the past during this time and tried to gain courage or even find anything to give me the power to endure what lay ahead.

I had never said even a swear word to Damien. Not even a 'bugger' or 'fuck off' to him. He was the epitome of strength. He had an aura of power that you couldn't or wouldn't stand a chance against. He was my adversity and he scared me, no terrified me.

He would squash you and watch you squirm with light in his eyes, as he did it. When he had become part of my everyday life, it was more and more evident how many people he controlled. I was not the only one. There were more and I felt awful for all of them, some of those very people he controlled became my only truth. I started seeing that truth and that alone, in which I couldn't deny it anymore.

This man was a machine and somehow I had to become a fighter for the people who had ever been wronged or hurt. We were polar opposites, him and I. It grated me more and more, their weakness became my strength. I couldn't stand the way he wounded others and somehow how scared I felt kept a shield of protection around me. I don't get it, nor do I now.

I asked him about it one day, as it slowly became a realization to me; his power and utter control.

I asked him if anyone has ever stood up to him. His words were this:

"No one would be allowed to". His eyes danced as he continued "The only time I ever allowed anyone to tell me what to do, was when I was a prospect!" and he chuckled then, going further, "Even when the wives of Hells Angels were around, I would keep my eyes down, Not NOW"! As he roared with laughter.

I believed him.

I had seen it with my own eyes. He would control a conversation, or tell someone how to speak, repeating things to a forty-five year old man as if he was in kindergarten. It was repulsive and he gloated about it. Making him get all puffed up.

But, somehow, it also gave me hope to start believing in myself again and to stand up for the ones who were being wronged. I have always been able to help the wounded that in itself gives me strength. Slowly I gained this courage with his words, but silently of course. If I couldn`t stand up for myself, I could sure as hell stand up for them. It helped to take my mind off a delusional course it had been on for the last month or so, with a clarity of rare hope.

I looked around my home and touched items that used to bring me joy. I looked at the closet full of clothes that I no longer wore. I even thought of my once admired cooking that had lost its flavor and the passion I once used to put into it.

I looked at the man on my couch who took a nap every afternoon, in the middle of the living room, as to stop the regular functioning of home just to suit him. I saw everything I would give up in a heartbeat just for the promise of a brighter future.

I remembered how he had wronged the father of my son, Ashton.

How Damien had purposely sought him out to hurt him, taking a slice of Kane's ear with him when he was done brutalizing him, with bats and intimidation.

Kane was no more than nineteen years old. To make matters even more horrific, he purposely carried on his vendetta by seeking me out and now used me as tool and weapon to continue his abuse. It was atrocious. It was the beast and it was what life threw at me.

I remembered his new-partner, that he had move up from Alberta. *Chucky,* and how he victimized him. Even taking him to a doctor to get help because his partner wasn't doing what he was told. When, in fact, Chucky had exhausted all his connections just to make their company succeed.

He'd had NHL connections that Damien was enthralled with. (I won't name names but this gentleman has recently passed away in 2014). He even sabotaged those friendships for Chucky, using him to gain his own fame and glory.

It was sad and sick. I watched it all from a distance; how he took everything from everyone, right down to the last bone, before he released them from his grip. It was disgusting and I was allowing him to do this to me, to my life and that of my sons.

By reflecting on how certain things had hurt others, how it harmed them, it gave me the strength and courage to find the truth in my own mind. It gave me what I needed to survive and fight for our future; a bright future for me and my sons. My process and fight came from that.

I heard this story once, years and years ago. By a man named Chubs, a man who wanted to become a member but never. He had been drinking heavily in the bar, one night where I was working and he`d caught wind I was dating Damien. He told me in not so many words, that when Damien was a prospect, he in fact used to work for him. This guy went on, that he lost over six-hundred thousand dollars working for Damien. Chubs lost everything because of him. It was why he wanted nothing to do with that lifestyle any longer. Damien had drained him. I heard the vague whisperings of Damien telling me, at some point, that it cost him over six-hundred thousand to become a Hells Angel. It made me wonder if somehow there wasn't really two sides to this story but the truth was there hidden in the great, wide open.

I had seen flashes of how Damien's own family acts with him. They all encircle and look up to him, running here and there to do his bidding. I saw how his own brother laughed at some of the derogatory remarks he made about me, (never helping me in Mexico but truly turning a blind eye) he even shared the same laughter as Damien and the same gleam in his eye.

I always thought his brother, Drake, to be the quieter one, less assured of himself, softer even. But then, I saw the disturbing side of him. I saw the same thing in him that grips a person with the promise of power, gold and status. I saw his brother in him. No longer was I fooled.

Drake threw his own life aside, to follow the promise and footsteps of a brother, who lived on the darker side of life. I saw the truth, the whole truth, with Damien's status in life and how people become fools around him. He has bent the will of many kind and unkind people, in turn, breaking them.

As I put all the pieces of this twisted puzzle together; I realized that I would lose every shred of myself by the hand and mind of this man, if I continued. I also knew that I had to start by being the one person I had never been around him and that was by being myself.

I had to start realizing I was not the words that taunted me all my life and that I was actually worth something in this world. I had to start believing the people who have embraced me and whom I barely knew. The people in our world, that took a moment to acknowledge me, in a super market, at the schools, in my doctor's office and our community. Only then would I see the beauty in life once again, only then would I find the lost girl I had become.

The last person I should've run to was Stella but I did… that gate of negativity was opened and I knew if anyone could handle the perverse way I was abused and find the humor in it, it was her. She would make me laugh. She would hide me if I needed it and only she had that sacred bond we shared together. Sisters.

``*With every seed that is planted, no matter if it's not nurtured with sun and water, it shall eventually grow*``

Those were the ponderings that were continuously on repeat in my mind, on silent, with regards to the unsubstantial world, I had with Damien. I repeated it in my home, on a drive, right down to while falling asleep. I was consumed by all of it. I had to find a way to find peace. I had to find a way to give my sons the life I knew they deserved. This was not me just accepting it, or liking it as my family was saying. This was me trying to find the safest way to get out. I had to try to survive and every waking moment I had was reliving the horrors and taunts of all the people I cared about. I needed out. So I planted my own seeds, and I begged silently for god or my angels to release me from the dark path I was on.

Life may have gone on hour by hour and minute by minute but my life was stuck on the same continuous time-warp, that wouldn't go away. I was in limbo and I was soon to become a wife to a man who was all adored in our world. A new set of rules would be laid. I just didn't know if my body, heart and soul could handle his teachings. *I could no longer "stay sweet"*.

Part 2

"Kerried Away"

Acceptance

"Seeing a new life before me, a tumultuous road behind me, I evaluated all and whoever stepped in my path; as any sane person would do"

Had I just sat back and accepted all that was happening, I wouldn't have found the courage to search for freedom. I wouldn't have fought with my own mind for freedom and truth. I would be dead.

I wasn't a freak. I wasn't bi-polar. I was abused and I was only just coming to terms with all of it. Remember, my family would say I deserved it; that they in fact, would be crack heads if they were with me; I was the problem.

If you're told these things throughout your life they start to take root and you start believing it, even if you say you don't. Sometimes, just sometimes, life has a different plan and there are people out there that instill belief in you, with gentle-care.

I was mixed up, to say the least. Spun in so many circles, I thought I was on a horrific ride from hell. So my mind was my only refuge and because I wasn't allowed to speak unless spoken too, in the right tone; I would have only this, as my source or search for freedom.

I couldn't understand why people, away from everyone, liked me, hugged me and even smiled with me. But yet the people closest to me dictated how I should act, how I should be and who I was. That alone made me start questioning everything and everyone.

I was just a young woman, with a dream and a destiny, I had yet to find. I wasn't the blacked out, biker support chick, covered in tattoos, that is often stereo-typed around the crowd I was in. Not many of us were. There are some really beautiful, intelligent women amongst even the toughest crowds and you wouldn't even know it unless you were told or opened your eyes to it.

I liked some of the wives at the clubhouse, they had courage and strength. Some were treated like complete gold. It was refreshing at times to see them, because it kept The Beast in check. On other times it was humiliating to see them; as I knew, that they knew, what I was tolerating and could visibly see my bruises. Some knew all too well the way I was treated and others not in the slightest.

Some of these wives had children, some were new and some were old, but they all carried their own gift. That, I can say for sure. Some I stop and think of to this day. **Thank-you N.**

I was only allowed around other wives at functions, parties or mandatory events. That was what The Beast said. I had already bonded with a few and often shared private laughs with them, on the way certain people acted when we were around.

It was like we could pick out the cheaters in the crowd amongst these men and we could pick out the girls that wouldn't hesitate to jump into bed with "our" men, just for the taste of a bad-boy. But what got me was, not *all* the guys would do that to their wives. You could tell, and there I gained a new respect for some of the men in patches.

Sitting along the gold plated bar at the clubhouse, in the distinguished hand crafted and carved out death head chairs, is where we would sit. No wife had less than a two karat ring or diamonds that didn't sparkle enough to blind whatever unsuspecting soul, the night brought in. We all had white teeth, Louis Vuitton bags and the best clothes. Our hair was done once a month by a stylist and our nails screamed 'bling bang baby, ouch'.

 Some ladies had short hair, some had long but the common trait we all had was our own type of power; the type of power that comes from being the girl/wife of a member. *(NOT the mother of a member, some didn't have that aura at all. Some of those mothers were discarded, as I soon found out and a member can only truly claim one girl as their own).* It's hard to understand but it is what it is and I will never begin to comprehend it at all.

I know that each Country, Charter and Clubhouse is different and I never realized that at the time, when it came to Hells Angels. Not once did it cross my mind, that not all Hells Angels are rich, or even all have gigantic houses.

The ones I knew, all drove Lamborghinis, million dollar-plus homes and jewellery that a true celebrity/star *could* be envious of. Their pockets were stacked and their credit cards were limitless. It was the way, around me, and the way for most of the west coast.

Not all Hells Angels are scruffy or old. Not all are mean and vindictive either. It depends entirely on the person, as with any walk of life. Just like our mayor in Toronto, not all mayors are the way they should be or have it the way you might think. Members are not all are dangerous, gross or greasy. But also on the flat side, not all members are glorious either or flattering.

People assume too much at times. They would never know if they were sitting downtown in a restaurant with a full patched gangster Hells Angel, having lunch as I heard some politician was once. (Not Toronto's Mayor), just to set, that record straight.

I also think that if someone reads something from twenty years ago, that does not justify their actions towards another human being/organization/government official, later on in life. We all are not cut from the same cloth and in that I promise. See this is where we have to modernize our libraries and thinking.

I liked being around these ladies. I felt a common bond, as they didn't seem to be as flakey as some of the other girls I knew because of who I was with.

One of the things I admired most, was how they took care of themselves. I am finicky on how I represent myself, at school or in public and even at home. I like to be healthy, nourished and well maintained, as they did too. I also knew if there was an event coming up, my soon-to-be husband wouldn't be as aggressive with me; hence, no bruises or broken bones.

Hells Angels have a monarchy of sorts; Rules, regulations and a weekly meeting. I came to enjoy that weekly meeting more and more, as it would allow me time to be with my sons and by myself.

Members all had to abide by a certain code of ethics or they could be fined and in extreme cases, even cut loose from the umbilical cord that attached them. Shunned or kicked out of the club in good standing or bad standing. (which meant you couldn't speak to another member or associated member and had to black out your club tattoos).

They had to pay their dues and monthly costs for being a Hells Angel, but what was different than the democracy that we live by, is as citizens; our political, representatives were paid to work in our government; as opposed to the *members who had to pay to be in it*.

This defies the system and defines who they are.

Now, on the other hand these members also pay their taxes and have jobs or own businesses. They try to stay within the law and a lot of them do.

This is where, once again. I believe society has it wrong on some levels. I am not justifying the behavior of corrupt individuals or condoning any sort of violence or crime by any person at all! I am one hundred percent against it! I am just showing the two sides to this coin. The rules I was only just becoming acquainted with.

This was now only a glimpse into what my life was about to become. My life with The Beast was the polar opposite to some of the finer qualities of it all.

I had a lot to learn when it came to being the right person for Damien. I was slowly being skinned and re-stitched to the making of who he thought I should be. It was tough and it was even tougher to be the perfection that he sought me to be.

I reluctantly started slipping into this person that was a far cry from who I was and I hated it. I didn't want to be in all these tight clothes or have bleached blonde hair. I liked my dark tresses with sun kissed touches of blonde. I liked to be comfortable but classy and I liked a *"Kathy"* purse as opposed to all these high end ones that you had to switch with every outfit. But that wasn't the hardest; the hardest was living with it.

Perhaps with choice it would have been different, perhaps with another member would have been better.

I was being shaped into a mannequin, a 'Stepford wife' and his own personal play thing, by Damien. I don't know if he realized what he was doing, but he was stripping away the very little I had left of me and I believe he did know what he was doing, as he told me he would break me to make me what he wanted.

I silently wished and hoped, that just maybe things could or would be different. But, like any toxic delusional thought that is tainted with ill-gotten motives, *as his were,* there's also a harsh dose of reality and things can come tumbling down without a care. It can also be a silent wake up call to keep fighting for what you believe in, without you even realizing it at the time. Like the scars I still carry from Mexico, recently.

My life was changing at a rapid pace. It went from an engagement, to buying the old rental property in White Rock, to building a mansion on it for us as a family. I was sitting back as all these preparations were taking place, silently, hoping to sneak away and hide the notepad I had written my private thoughts in or get away in general.

The one I was going to share with Stella but still, was hesitant to trust her. She still thought all was wonderful in my world and she had not a clue. But that day was fast approaching and these events/functions were slowing downing. Soon I would be able to share with her, just had to find the courage first.

Those functions became a moment in which I could or would know I wouldn't be hurt for a while and those woman became a camouflage of what I hopefully wanted to be, or eventually have. Strength.

But like any quick dose of everyday events, or Band-Aids, the reality would still set in and became all too real, all over again and I would have to go home, put on a fake smile and silently be scared.

I searched for truth everywhere, so you never know who you pass on a street, flip the bird to driving or talking to a parent at school. You don't know how one sentence and word, can have an impact in their lives, because so many people without ever realizing it, kept me sane and instilled a belief in me to keep going.

Hidden Agendas

"Life never got better, but different, during and after that time. It was as if we were in our own world and our own private hell".

I was finally able to spend a day with Stella and I was really looking forward to it. Damien must've assumed we would only be talking about my upcoming nuptials, not even considering I had yet to even elaborate on our engagement with anyone.

Often feeling ashamed when I was out picking up a few things and a lady would notice my engagement ring and say in a sweet chuckle "Awe, you must be one lucky lady". I would have to mask my enthusiasm and smile, or say "thank-you", never once revealing that they had no idea the price I had already paid for it and what I had yet to endure because of it.

One time I actually spoke those thoughts out loud, at a store called "Home Again" a beautiful boutique filled with designer decorative items and plaques with the most inspirational sayings that left you with a glow. Now that woman's face at the register was shocked. I don't believe she understood what I was saying and most likely went home talking about me to her family, "about what a spoiled woman I was", the gal who entered her store. Maybe, just maybe after I left, the comment actually registered with her but while I was there, it sure didn't and it left me feeling rotten. Not because of what I said; "It's NOT worth the price I paid for it", which was the truth but because she assumed far too much and judged me with her look.

Damien had asked that whatever wedding ideas I had, I was to go over them with him first. He said over and over again, countless times, that he could plan it in less than thirty days, so don't even bother.

Another of his requests was that the wedding party be 'good looking' as in pretty to look at- so nooooo friends who were less than beautiful, are to be in the pictures . I was also only to invite, very few people, as he was doing the majority of invites.

The nerve of what he said hit home, because it was always for show with him/fake. To me you don't have to be pretty, or thin to be beautiful. It was something that bothered me and to this day I still feel ashamed by his request.

The rules of going out with Stella were over bearing and the enthusiasm I had to muster, as he spoke of what is allowed at a wedding, (I wasn't even looking forward to) was hard. He thought I was going over there to look at magazines and have girl talk. When in fact I was going to share with Stella my captivity and get what I had written out of our apartment, before it was found!

I didn't feel special at all, it was another moment in my life that was supposed to be special and a first time ever event that I felt was robbed from me. It hurt and that I couldn't fix it no matter how hard I tried. I couldn't just leave, he would hunt us down. I didn't have family to turn to because I either pushed them away or after a few days their comments would only beat me down as his did. I was exhausted and by the time I arrived to pick up Stella, I just let it all pour out of me that day.

I don't believe I would have been so forth coming with her, if he hadn't hit an artery with his demands and opinions about the one special day; getting married. I had forever dreamed about as a child. I couldn't stuff it in any longer. The charade had gone on too long. I didn't have a day go by that I wasn't insulted or pushed around in some way. I was suffocating inside and no matter how hard I tried to feel those feelings I had once before, I didn't, I couldn't do it and I wasn't able to keep pretending anymore.

I do not know if Stella had ever seen me like that before, pulling up to only get out and fall to my knees in anguish, pain and suffering. I collapsed in her arms.

I know we had already seen some rough times but this was a first. I was so utterly broken inside. I didn't know if I would ever mend. But on these rare occasions Stella just took it all in; my pity, my rage, my sorrow and my cover-up lies, about Damien. I told her about why I was on the island, not it all as my shame was still to fresh. But, importantly, how she was right. I wasn't myself around him.

Her eyes flashed as she watched me, wicked, mad and angry that I was hurt. In a moment I knew I had the other half of me. She would hold me together until I was strong enough to stand on my own again. I knew this, as I felt her tighten her hold on me and followed my eyes, with a defiant angry glare. (She was upset with him, not me) She my little hatchet, Stella didn't need to be convinced, she knew I was telling her the truth and in a grip she showed me I had her for support...

She never said, "I told you so" or "I deserved it". Not once. She unfolded in a way only Stella could do. With heart and a bite, that would make anyone feel better. She said how she always knew he was like that. Some nights she would hear me through the walls, of our old place, asking him to stop! Many times, she had wanted to rush in and help me.

She mentioned sitting at the lounge that day; while I was 9months pregnant and how he only offered her food; I wasn't' allowed any because I was "Too Fat" being pregnant and all, with his son at the time. She went on and on reminding me of the little things that led to these more horrific incidents. She gave me what any friend would do, truth and facts, which allowed me to be an outsider looking in. She gave me the missing pieces in a puzzle I was stuck in by hard-talk and truth!

I never told Stella "all" about the last time, a month and a half earlier, that he had almost killed me and was going to do it in a bath tub. I only told her about running away to my mother's. I don't know if that was me hiding my shame or I was still trying my hardest to understand it. But Stella didn't need to be told. She knew what he was capable of. But did she really know the half of it?

If not for her holding me up at that time, I would have fallen and for that she will always remain in my heart as a *once* sister, and how my real sister could've been.

It took a lot to open up like I had and admit my wrongs, admit that I wasn't okay and that I had chosen to stay. But Stella understood how hard it was to really shake a guy like that. She knew that I couldn't just leave. That meant the world to me, her knowing; I had a person out there that understood, that if I didn't take this to the bitter end, I would never be free.

My once distrust of Stella left me in a wave of truth; my heart, forgetting the garbage, from a couple years beforehand. I had a euphoria of renewed strength and conviction. I had a friend and most of all I felt as though I had family.

We laughed after that release, we sang and we did things together on a daily basis. She never truly left my side unless she had to go home. It was as though we had never been separated in the first place. I loved her and she owned a part of me that I do not know if it could ever, truly be replaced.

"We all have difficulties, we all have problems, we're not perfect but sometimes, just sometimes, we find a person that accepts us for us. That my friends, is a grand gift."

I was unified; I felt a weight had been lifted and I felt I could accomplish anything. Damien felt the shift in me after that day and was even more so watchful. But even he lay off me, for a while.

We all fell into a routine and it wasn't so bad. I noticed my son Ashton more at ease and for that I was thankful. Sable was constantly protected from the goings-on's, as it was an unspoken truth between Des, Ash, Stella and I. Ashton and I made sure of that. We just knew, it was just something we had to do.

I believe Damien was so wrapped up in building the house and running around for supplies, errands and his regular hustle that it gave him less time to really notice too much of a dramatic change in me.

But there was.

He honestly has a side of him, which is captivating, intelligent and at times funny. When Damien laughs it lights up his eyes and can really give you a moment to admire his true self. I believe Damien did love me in some perverse way but I had allowed him to get away with so much already, that it had become a disease, a sickness and a habit to fall into when things were stressful. Also, being a full patched Hells Angel just added to the power he already wielded or felt he had.

I didn't want anything to do with the house being built. I don't think Damien wanted me to have anything to do with building it either. I was happy right where I was. I didn't need flash, or in normal terms money, to be happy. I just needed stable emotions and feelings of love and tranquility to keep me satisfied.

I watched all that went on around me. Still, with my defense mechanism and my acquired skills from all the upheaval and abuse; I was ready to jump at any given moment and flee if I had to. I was on edge and knew in a blink I could be toppled to the ground with a fist in my face. No argument, no fuss just one wrong look or tine and that's it. So I was still on my toes, waiting and ready.

I learned that Damien had set a date for the wedding it was supposed to be good luck and good 'Feng shei' to be married on this day. He wanted it to be held in our new home/mansion and the now called "Shangri-La". A nickname his brother Drake had given it. It was a house, big sure but just a house.

I do not know if Damien was only marrying me for the status of being married, 'happy home, happy life', image or simply because he really loved me, still however I always knew it was just about image. It left me perplexed how he could spew such words of hatred and inflict such pain on someone he truly cared about. But if you asked me at that time, I would've said, 'Image and Status'. Or at least that's what I said to Stella. We would often be brutally honest with each other so that it helped soften the blow of reality. In ways, it was also healing the little, which could be healed. I was now slowly becoming subservient, to life.

I truly loathed living like this but I had no choice. You often hear people say that everyone has a choice and it's up to you to decide where and how you want to live. But, I didn't. Or I felt I never had a choice at the time.

I knew I was a screw up and I knew only I had made the choice of being who I was with and running in the crowd I had. I know that and I am okay with it. I have come to terms with accepting all I have done and I would only wish no one followed the road I did.

But to me, I was caught in a plot that was so dangerous. I felt I had only to survive day by day, trying somehow to sever the tie that kept this bond intact in the first place.

I was grasping at straws and even my own sanity. I was reliving certain moments that I felt were detrimental to the place I was now at, in my existence. I knew what I wanted in life and how I wanted the future to be for my sons and me but how to get there seemed to be the problem.

I just didn't know how….. I didn't know who I could trust and I sure didn't know which way to go. I felt that if I hid anywhere I would always be found.

I had to find out where I went wrong. Seek the truth and find out where this all began, or if this was this my fault? How do I fix this? I would, perhaps have to travel down some familiar dark roads I had once followed but I would have to search for the good, the answers, AND THE TRUTH.

I was a slave to every mistake I made and yet no matter how dark, mean or corrupt a person was; I could still find the good and beauty in them. I will never change that for a second, nor would I want to. In my mind I could do this and, no matter what, try and set everything right. It was these thoughts that kept me kind and not bitter to my living-life-horror.

It was who I was and only a fraction of one piece of me, that no one could ever take away. I would continuously tell myself that every day, over and over, filling my own self up with who I was, as the taunts were beginning to become all too real in my self-loathing mind.

With renewed hope and resolution, I did just that; I carried on in my daily activities searching for the answers. Not once thinking it would honestly send me on a quest to actually find them.

Rage

Time, in the midst of craziness can calm even the wildest of storms

It was sunny, bright, and beautiful. It was early spring and I was getting ready for the day, as I was once again going out with Stella. My son Ashton had a friend over, named Tristan and Desiree was coming to Stella's with me.

I was parked by the front door of our apartment building. It had huge trees that left a shady spot at the entrance so that the sun couldn't melt you away with its glare.

I had never lived in a high end condo building but on the lower income scale. My apartment was 1150 square feet and I had done a few renovations in it already, to bring it up to my standard of living.

My rent was only a thousand dollars per month, affordable and I had one of the biggest units in the complex. I loved my apartment. I had put so much love into it and it had always felt like our little sanctuary, plus home.

The walls were a nice mocha, with dashes of Chocolate brown to offset the room and to add dimension. My furniture flowed from room to room and my beautiful super-king cherry wood/mahogany bed, looked stunning in the master bedroom.

When Damien had *"just decided"* to move in and never leave, it became our own (or mine) personal hell. That was a hard thing to swallow and still bothered me.

The kids and I were already loaded in the vehicle when he came barrelling into the parking lot. I knew by the way he slammed his vehicle into park and the look on his face something was wrong. My stomach did a flip as I knew I was usually the scapegoat and would feel the brunt end, of whatever, or whoever; pissed him off. This day, that was not the case.

I had already told the older boys "don't worry, everything will be fine" as he stormed up to the car. You could clearly see how he pulled in and crazy dramatic way he parked; that he was mad! Having Desiree there at the time, helped me to calm down as he fast approached. I had to stay calm for the children's sake and god how I tried.

He rushed up to the vehicle and threw an envelope at me. Roaring!

"What the fuck is this?! What the fuck is this?! You're suing me? You're fucking suing me"! There were plenty other profane words I'd rather not mention. However I had no idea what he was raging about, but looking at my son's ashen face I tried to smooth it over with Damien.

I felt Desire tense up, as she slowly death-gripped my hand, as I was about to exit the vehicle.

Knowing he was stark raving mad and something had set him off, I was reluctant to go inside, but I had to quickly defuse the situation. There was nothing other than that to do. I had to keep this away from the boys. I had to.

I couldn't let my children see any more of his outrage. I couldn't let Ashton's friend witness Damien's violent outbursts. I just couldn't.

I tried to calm him for a second. I asked him to go upstairs where he could tell me what's going on and so it wasn't in front of the kids. I didn't want them to witness any more than they already had. I refused to allow it!

He wouldn't go upstairs. Instead as I was opening the door to get out and smooth things over, which was second nature to me by now. He instead barricaded me back inside the car, almost slamming the door shut on my body. He would've broken half my side for sure, if Des didn't rip me back inside at the same time I was lurching back in.

Standing and spitting mad, right in front of the driver side door. He tried reaching for me, to yank me close, so he could hurt me and that's when the kids started screaming. I pulled back in time not to feel his hand, whip out against my chest to grab me. But that only made him madder.

I had protected Sable from 85% of the abuse but Ashton had seen/heard the majority of it. Ashton froze, going white but then gaining courage, I think, because his friend was there. He focused on Sable trying to calm him down, as his friend cocked his head shocked at what

Damien was doing and knowing it was wrong. There is where Tristan gained respect from me.

I tried again to calm him down and say, "let's go upstairs". I still didn't know what was going on and kept pleading over and over, " Please stop, please stop, the kids, they're scared, let's go upstairs, whatever it is we will figure it out, please…"

Tears had started falling from my eyes. My resolve had quickly faded when he made the first attempt to grab me in front of all present.

He had me now, by the arm, pinching and digging his fingers into my skin so it hurt, and his manly grip had my arm weak. He released me only to rip open the door, to yank me out. Then grabbing me by the arm he dragged me upstairs. I could see the door wide open and the car was still running, as I looked back while being forced up the elevator.

He was shaking with rage but kept looking at me with disgust, silently shaking his head back and forth as he intimidated me and pre- pared me for what was to come when he got me into the apartment. Spitting in my face in the elevator. He pushed me down that hallway, over and over, almost making me crash into the floor with his aggres- sion. I was absolutely terrified. When we reached my door, he smashed me into it with such a force I saw stars.

"You fucking, dirty pig! Trying to sue me for money?!"

I couldn't think and went into shock. I was so scared and had no idea what he was talking about, none at all. I would never do that, ever. He must be mistaken and I had no way to make him understand as I was useless when he released his malice on me like that.

He shoved open the bedroom door with my body as I crashed into the floor. Grabbing me by my neck he started dragging into the bedroom, where he forcefully tossed me aside. I slammed into the dresser and screamed, "Please Stop, Please!" and then I blacked out.

I came to against the dresser and the bed, him on top of me, choking me. My precious son Ashton and his friend were dragging him off, screaming at him. I don't know if it was my son's voice that bounced me into reality but I do know, those two boys, if not for them, who knows what would have happened.

Tristian gave Ashton the ultimate power that day to step up and fight The Beast for the right reasons. Those two boys were able to pull him off of me, just long enough, to snap Damien out of it. He shook them off and stormed out of the apartment.

Those two felt the adrenaline that came with a fight, as they bounced around high fiving, from my recollection. *You would have to ask them but I am quite sure that was their reaction.*

I tried to get my bearings straight. Ashton leaned over me saying, "Don't worry Mom, I love you, he's gone". Feeling like the hero he was and fully one hundred percent sincere. Both boys gave me a hand up as my head swam in confusion.

Tristian went off, "Guys don't hit woman, that isn't right Mama" and a few profanities the boys felt were okay. They were okay and deserved to release however they felt they needed to at the time. To me they were heroes, that any police officer or community would be proud of.

All at once, I felt sick and I felt so sad for what they had to do to keep me safe. I asked where Sable was and then I rushed to him. No time for pity. "*OMG what if he has taken my baby as punishment!?*" I ran out the door, oblivious to the blood coming out of my mouth and my brain pounding with a headache.

Sable was fine. The car had music coming from it and as I approached Desiree made a hand signal and mouthed, that Damien was across the street; walking away. I later found out that Desiree sent the boys in to check on me, as she calmed Sable. The window was open in my room and they heard Damien yelling, and the boys went flying up the stairs.

I jumped in the vehicle to just hold my baby, and made sure I swept him with enough hugs and kisses; that no tear was left on his face. I, being the mom I was, always had treats and candy in the car. I reached into the glove box and gave him a lollipop. He was my little ray of light, my own sunshine and the good that Damien could never be.

I looked in the rear-view mirror and wiped the little bit of blood away from my mouth and saw Damien coming towards me, again. I was now trapped in the backseat and there was no way to avoid him.

I tried to scramble out as he pushed his top part of the body in and said, "Hi Honey". No words can describe the utter shock I felt.

I allowed him his moment and just sat there numb, not looking at him, but Sable. I knew then I hated him, I didn't like him and was just utterly appalled. How can anyone just shut themselves off like that and change, in a blink of an eye, to normal and sweet?

I looked out into the parking lot and watched the trees swoosh with the little wind and calmness came over me. I now knew his game, his tactics and mentality. This, my friends, is where I knew I had to be smarter. This is where I knew his cards have been played and this is where I put all emotion aside and did what only I could have done; find the bravery to *Kerri On*.

I asked him to "get out" – in a demanding voice I had yet to ever u and so I could have a cigarette, to calm down.

I asked then in a sturdy voice if I could see this letter, he had mentioned. He switched just like that and a too demanding voice of mine to show me who was boss as he pulled me out with enough aggression to show me he was fuming, but not enough to alarm Sable.

I quickly switched my panic state, just as fast as I came to be disgusted. I showed him he couldn't scare me and I knew what he was capable of. He didn't like that at all. But if my son and his friend could be strong so could I.

Inside I didn't know if I could do this and I didn't know if my legs would indeed carry me. I was rocked to my inner self and I had to now deal with the mentality of head games and trickery, the worst abuse I believe anyone can suffer and by the beast.

The kind that makes you quiver inside knowing you're alone. The kind of abuse, where you're screaming out the truth and no one hears you or believes in you. The kind that takes away your soul and leaves you blackened and broken from the inside, robbing you of all the beauty you have left. The kind of abuse you want to fight against with every fibre of your being, in order to not become like your abuser.

"As I look back I know I did the best I could do during these times and I know that I am lucky."

I couldn't begin to understand his tactics, but I could now visibly see them and acknowledge them. He needed the control like a drug, if I kept allowing him that he would keep bending me to his will.

So again, I asked to see this letter, just so he didn't see or feel my fear. He threw it at me, landing on the ground by my feet. I remember thinking before I picked it up, is he going to boot me in the face? Instead, I courageously picked it up to read what was inside.

I had only a moment to glimpse before he ripped it out of my hands. He wanted to control what I was reading and how I interpreted it, I am quite sure.

My two young warriors were eying him, as they stood off in the distance. I was in the shady area under the tree outside. He put his arms around either side of me and barked the reason he was upset. I was only now, after all that had happened, hearing the truth behind this madness.

"You are suing me for child support and with family maintenance?!" I was stunned, not really understanding any of it.

"You just want money don't you, you fucking pig?!" his famous word, he always used freely when addressing me. I clammed up inside, my strength fading away as fast as I allowed it to surface; his words tore at me. I was standing there like a fool as I allowed the tears to fall freely from my eyes.

It hurt me more than anything in the world when he called me names and taunted me like that. But, I didn't run. I didn't hide and it took all I had inside me not to look over at anyone who was present for strength.

He didn't just leave it at that, he leaned in ever so close and bite my ear. An excruciating pain, unlike any other, ripped through me. It was his way of looking like he was being amicable, while still inflicting pain. This was the beginning of him allowing what he thought I deserved, to now be demonstrated in public.

I tried to talk, but couldn't. I cried out but he stifled it beneath his collarbone. I was hurting from the inside but I couldn't allow any of these children to see the latest violence he was signifying with his control.

My back to the vehicle, I silently pleaded with my eyes for him to stop. He never gave me a chance to speak or address anything, he just continued as if it was my punishment, for something I had done to hurt him, within society.

He pulled out his phone. I inwardly cringed that he was going to take another picture of my face. To humiliate me, he would show me how ugly and disgusting I was. But he didn't. He started punching numbers in as to make a call. He then turned on me before sending the signal to ring and told me, "It's the courthouse; you will tell them, that there will be no hearing and stop all this now! Won't you?!"

Of course I would, in a heartbeat. I had no idea what this was all about but if I had a few moments peace, I would figure it out. I had no problem with that, but I was never granted even a second to think about it, let alone the consideration a normal spouse would give by trying to work this out nicely. Or maybe just help another understand what it was all even about. That was not my life and he was not normal. I was starting to think that neither was I normal and maybe I was a lost cause, this type of treatment wears a person down to the point of breaking or dying. I was close to both, if not already there.

I was shaking and hurt, reliving what he had done once before, forcing me to call my family and say I had mental issues. All the while, being held by gun point; a knife pointed at me, with his hand in his pocket imitating an actual gun that he was going to use to kill me if I didn't do his bidding.

He pressed send and passed me the phone while hovering over me. I had tears sliding down my face, silently of course as not to cause the boys to come running as the courthouse picked up the phone and I was patched through. I don't know why I clammed up but I tried to be and say exactly what he ordered, word for word, but couldn't hold it together.

The lady on the other end asked if I was okay, leaving me wishing she was right here, right now holding me and chasing this demon away.

I tried again to say what he ordered me to, "Please I do not want to go to court for money or maintenance". She paused a minute longer, trying to ask my name so she could look this all up, asking again "if I was okay".

I broke down as I often did when someone seemed to care. I cried and tried to stop but couldn't. Damien just threw his hands up, cursing as he stormed away.

With him not hovering over me, made a world of a difference. I was able to answer a few of the questions the clerk was asking. She asked me if I needed help, if I was okay and if she should call the police. She had heard him dictating how I should speak and what to say. The Beast was caught being the one thing he never wanted anyone to think, abusive.

But at the sound of her saying police, I got scared and told her, "No, please, you can't do that".

I was always polite and mindful when speaking with people. I never was that rude, ignorant person some can be. I didn't have that in me.

At times when I was being putdown and belittled by people, like with my family, I could eventually have a bite to me with regards to tone and stick up for myself. But only when it became too much.

I was rarely rude to people who were nice or people in our communities. Once, while driving, I flipped the bird at someone who had cut me off and then saw that it was an old elderly, lady. I was ashamed. So I pulled up where she had parked and got out saying, "I am so sorry, just so sorry". In the end, her hugging me saying it's alright sweetie, it's alright. That was my way of making sure I never hurt another's feelings.

I cared about humanity and I was watchful of making sure I was always respectful, even teaching my sons to always shake hands with eye contact or stop to help another.

When the tears and uncontrollable sadness had subsided somewhat, I told the courthouse clerk that I would be fine. Only then did she explain what was going on. It was not me that had filed a lawsuit for maintenance (which I knew) but it was Family Maintenance themselves that had filed in the same year as Sable was born. It had only just landed in the court system. I couldn't just call and stop it, as it wasn't me doing it.

It was her that told me why Damien was upset, not him. That in itself gave me clarity knowing he never would hear a thing I say or give me the respect a normal person would automatically do when addressing a situation.

It had all started was when my 'baby boo' Sable was born. I had needed assistance, due to a high risk pregnancy, stress and just being a single woman *already raising a child on my own, with no support.*

WOMAN or People who need financial help, "Please know there is nothing wrong or shameful with that"

When I had gone to research and acquire resources available to me as a pregnant woman; I had signed a form that had to do with who the father was and they were connected to the Family Maintenance Department, which in turn went in pursuit of payments from... low and behold... the father of the child they were helping to support! Damien and that was 2 and half years beforehand.

She was so kind on the phone, explaining everything and I honestly value others who take their own personal time to help another. Again an angel that walks this earth.

The woman was a lifeline for me. She showed me, once again, how wonderful people truly are in our community. She said to me, "You do not deserve to feel as scared as you did honey, and you can get away". That lady wanted to help me and she had no idea that her care, did indeed help me. It showed me a world outside the one I was living in and that little ray of hope went a long way.

Damien was, *who knew where. When* I got off the phone, I gained a new found empowerment and also a few moments to gather my thoughts, just to hash this all up and put a brave face on.

I asked the boys to get in the car, as we were still going out for the day. I put on nice music and allowed them to feel at ease, as I waited for The Beast to show himself; I had his phone. I just wanted to be civil.

He sauntered up with Slurpee's for everyone, as if nothing happened or his walk away calmed him. It was the weirdest thing. I waited patiently as he handed them out and watched as his glance landed on Ashton and Tristan. They were fish out of water. Damien had a way of stopping you in your tracks with just a look. He shook their hands like men and then leaned in the window as if nothing had happened.

I casually handed him his phone and went to explain that this could be figured out and it was not really a big deal. He just leaned in and said in a weird fucked up way, (no other way to describe this).

"See *why* you don't make Daddy mad? Love you baby! Have a good day." And off he went. Just like that, as if all was great in his world.

I or we, were left there stunned, shocked and silent. I put the vehicle in drive and shakily drove out of the parking lot. The boys in the back seats started bursting out in a nervous laughter and chatter.

"Omg, I was so scared when he came up! Omg, did you see how he looked at me?" and "Ya bro, ya bro ya".

I allowed them the time to release any emotion they were going through and get it all out. It was enough to break the silence and shock in me, as I pushed my rear-view mirror to face them and told them how proud I was. No child should ever have to do that and I will talk to your parents Tristan. I am sorry.

Ashton sat back and realized for the first time I believe, he had a true friend in Tristan. He wasn't as timid as he would've been if that happened without him there. My son was growing up and he learnt a valuable lesson this time, that even others know its wrong to treat a person the way Damien does, not just him alone in his own private thoughts. I was proud of my son and in a way proud in myself for raising him to know right from wrong..

As I looked at my little baby boy Sable, I knew then I would never allow him to witness and live through what his brother has had to. I had to protect him and show him, that was not how a man behaves or how they should be. I had one chance to make this right for my son and I was going to do it. No matter the cost.

I would never allow him to be the product of his father's careless character or world. I would only teach him the good in life and how to protect, conquer and overcome the title that Damien placed on him. I would teach him how to be a hero, a real hero. That vow and promise was made that day.

Desiree just held my hand silently and squeezed it. We were all coming to our own private realizations.

That was the opening that Damien needed to end his charade of doting fiancé and the wall came crashing down. He was now once again justified in the way he treated me.

False Personas

"The beauty in life, is in the way you and you alone,
perceive it to be"

It was still early spring and the sun was bright; a day where you want to just relax and for summer just to be here already. But, there was still school, work and daily routines in place.

Ashton was at elementary school and it was just after the noon hour when I heard a knock on the door. Damien was sleeping on the couch as usual and baby Sable, was also asleep for his mid-day nap, all tucked in on my bed.

Blake (my old roommate) had long ago moved out and I still missed him regularly, always wondering why he moved in the first place? He had known I never wanted Damien in our home and even that it wasn't safe for us here alone with him. It left me wondering on many occasions, countless times just why he left.

I had only come to the realization that perhaps or maybe he had his own life to live and I couldn't hold him back just because it didn't suit me. I found that reasoning and that reasoning alone to set my mind at ease. But, my best friend, I missed terribly and oh, how often I thought of him. Theses peaceful moments to myself I always thought of my good life and friends or things I loved.

It was such a quiet day and getting that knock right on my apartment door was out of the ordinary unless someone had a key for the downstairs entry, hoping Blake was visiting, I quickly jumped to answer it. Thinking and still remembering how ironic that was, but these things always seemed to happen to me so when I opened the door, I was shocked.

It wasn't Blake at all, but two very well dressed people. One was a woman with dark hair and the other was a man about the same age as Damien, late 30's, with dark hair and a massive frame. The woman just looked at me; we were all silent, eerily silent. I asked how I could help them, hoping to cut the awkwardness.

The lady, {I will not mention the name} quietly and discreetly said that she was with Child Services and she needed to come in and speak with me. My heart plummeted to the ground. I was breathless, shaking, and completely horrified.

I quickly allowed them in, as I had nothing to hide and started rambling things like…I am a good mother,   you can look around, I don't mind at all, please, I have nothing to hide. I carried on repeating myself and stumbling all over words. Even opening my fridge so they could see as I offered them a refreshment. The man just gently closed the fridge door and said, "No we are fine. I am only here to accompany her". As he pointed to the woman.

This lady looked at me with such care; taking me all in. She was so silent and quietly nice.

The man spoke up at that time and said he was "Gang Squad" and that he was required to accompany her to my residence. I asked if they wanted anything to drink, he again, declined. Needless to say, I was still in shock. I then asked him if he wanted to sit down while the woman and I spoke.

I directed him to the living room with a hand gesture as I was rooted in spot, with utter bewilderment. She put her hand on me, just as I heard Damien's voice echoing throughout my home.

"Why HELLO 'so and so', what the fuck is Gang Squad doing in my girl's house?"

Damien knew this guy by name and, apparently, they knew each other well, from what I heard because two minutes later there was a chuckle.

I rounded the corner with the lady, into the living room in order to see that everything was alright and I felt perhaps, she wanted to as well. The police officer from the gang taskforce was now sitting on the chair comfortably and Damien was sitting up, definitely not sleeping like he once was, but wide awake.

"So, I am going to ask you again (whatever his name was) what's going on and why are you at my girl's house? Don't fuck with me. I know what you guys are all about." Damien spoke with amusement, not anger.

They both seemed to be smiling, as if all was okay. Anyone would be taken aback and even shocked. It was like two guys, in a change room talking politics and crime. Like this is nothing new, and all but, to ordinary.

The agent said, "Child Services needed to pay a house call, dude, and you know protocol, don't you? One of us must attend." Somehow, from there, the conversation took a different turn and they were chatting about sports.

You couldn't have fathomed how surreal it felt. My very heart was crumbling around me and all I could do was stand there like a mute. The woman took control as my resolve was fading and asked if I could show her around. I quickly jumped to accommodate her as we left the guys to 'shoot the shit'.

Once we were at the far end of the apartment, she ushered me into the master bedroom and gently shut the door. I started explaining, as fast as I could, in a complete panic, "I keep a good home, you can come over whenever you want, but please my children are my life, the very air I breathe, and don't hurt them by punishing me." I pleaded with my eyes.

She never allowed me to say another word. She shushed me as quietly and as gently as she could. Handing me her business card. She then, once again, very quietly, but firmly, whispered, "I am not Child Welfare, Kerri, not at all". She watched my expression change before she continued.

"I needed to speak with you and had to bring him (she nodded her head toward the door to indicate the other agent) to make sure Damien was safe, while I was here and or if he was around at all. I came to speak with you, privately". Again she waited to see the expression on my face before continuing.

"You cannot tell him, Kerri, who I really was, okay. We do not have much time. This is important. Please call me at this number, leave a message, we will meet. Do not tell him who I am. This is of extreme importance." And quietly with a serene look she said, "I am not here to hurt or harm you in anyway".

She quickly opened the door and allowed me to walk through ahead of her, as she rubbed my back soothingly.

She and I walked into the living room and she spoke to the agent, "Everything appears fine here. We won't have to come back. Nice meeting you, Damien."

I walked them to the door as quickly as they had come in. As they walked out she turned and looked at me one more time. Then held her fingers to her lips, as if to signal our silent promise of secrecy. Holding my gaze, she seemed to be saying so many unspoken things with her eyes and that she contacted me for a reason of pure, purity.

She then turned to leave. I smiled regretfully and grabbed her hand to shake it, hoping she had seen the genuineness and compassion in my eyes because I couldn't do anything to help her; I couldn't possibly call her.

There was no way I could talk. My life and that of my children were too important. Whatever she had to tell me or what kind of information she wanted from me, I would never know.

This event would play often in my mind over the years. I knew whatever it was, it wasn't some small thing. It was deadly. Of that, I was certain and I felt bad.

I waited for a few minutes at the door, taking deep breathes, trying to take everything in. I needed a few moments to myself but Damien came quickly behind me to wrap his arms around me. Still facing the door I leaned back, as I allowed all the raw emotions to subside.

The turbulent feelings came from opening the door and being told Child Services were actually at my house, to visit me. I knew I had stayed too long with Damien but what the system doesn't know is there are special cases where some don't understand or actually have choice!!

*Children should always have a choice and they shouldn't EVER have to live in certain surroundings, that jeopardize their own well-being and that is the truth. So shame on the parents that are to messed up to see that sometimes their children have to be removed until a parent is big enough, healthy enough to protect them. **NOT that this happened to me,** but I do see where that needs to happen for many children who are too young to know they deserve better than the surroundings in which they are accustomed to; that are not healthy.*

That rocked me right down to the core of my being. It is a moment of knowing the abuse could not be around my sons, a wake up call; but to find out that it wasn't Child Protective Services but an undercover agent, from the Bureau Of Investigations who had actually visited in their stead; cloaked in disguise, as if to help me or gain something crucial in return, was something entirely different. I was inwardly, reeling.

I had taken one beating for a father at my sons' school e-mailing me an innocent 'Happy Mother's Day', who just happened to be a police officer. His younger son, a "Little Buddy" to my older son, in the school's Buddy Program.

THIS was one event that I was not willing to repeat.

Did they think I was stupid or that I wasn't already defamed enough by The Beast? Did they really think I would talk to them, already truly, fearing for my children's and my very life?

I assume they knew the danger my children and I were already in due to the continuous surveillance I was quite sure we were under. Whatever they wanted, I just didn't have a need to know at that time.

I had enough of my own problems to sort out and this was one that I didn't have the strength to go up against; where not even they could help me.

Nor, did I have it in my blood to share anything of a criminal or corrupt nature.

I took another deep breath. His arms were around me, while barely listening to what he was murmuring in my ear.

"It's okay baby, they can't touch us, we will fix this, and no one will ever take your babies away, again". (Referring to my mother's past actions} It was reassuring to hear his consoling and not his accusing, defaming remarks. He got off on the crazy, it was Damien but not always in a brutal manner, sometimes in a gentle protective one as well.

I had no idea, if and when they first arrived, until that moment where his arms came around me in a embrace, whether I would somehow be blamed. I felt relieved and was even more convinced to speak with him, when normally I couldn't. And there was no way I was taking the risk of letting him find that card the woman had given me. There was no way. My life depended on it and they (police/gang squad/Investigators) all had each other, I had only me to watch out for my children and mines safety.

I was still facing the door, when I finally said, "It wasn't Social Services Damien." I uttered it quietly, barely above a whisper, I didn't want him to go off and start freaking out. I also wanted them to be gone from his wrath. I still will always protect people, it's my nature. How can anyone blame a person for doing their job? I was not a petty thief or such a loser that I couldn't see that. I couldn't stand by and watch someone be dehumanized or belittled and I didn't like seeing him do it to others, either. To me I didn't have the notion or mentality that because you're a cop you're a goof! I just didn't. I like people for who they truly are, on the inside.

That is where I would use my title … to help victims of pain/abuse. I would set a person straight even if it was the middle of the day at a grocery store, at a concert, on the street or even within my community. I would not allow a person, no matter who you were to victimize another and I still won't.

He didn't' get it and tried to say, "don't worry that was 'so and so' from gang squad, we will fix this." I turned around and said in a clearer voice, "It wasn't Social services Damien, it was cops. He couldn't grip it or understand, still believing I was talking about only the gentlemen. He led me to the living room to sit down; probably to calm my nerves because he thought I was in denial. They really were convincing, at least to him.

I just didn't know how much to say or how to say it, in case he started drilling me, in his interrogating manner and it escalated to violence.

Carefully choosing my words; I then explained everything, from answering the door, to him waking up and me doing the introduction to my home.

I explained being in the bedroom and the lady handing me her card and I also explained the quiet gesture she shared with me at the door.

I couldn't, in anyway, be implicated. She had a team to back her and I had no one. I am sorry but for them to contact me, in that manner, knowing the fatal consequences I would face, wasn't safe nor was it right.

He was stunned. I swear he almost choked on his own tongue. I still laugh as I visibly see his expression in my mind! His eyes were saucers and instead of immediately jumping into rage, he sat speechless. Which wasn't very often. He was blown away.

The implied threat of Family Protective Services strolling through my door and then, just as suddenly, no threat…I was on a reeling moment myself.

I was a woman who would die for her children and couldn't live without them. Oh dear, please, I wish they used any other method than that: the implied threat of me losing my children. Approach me at a grocery store and hand me a card or even a playground but please do not portray Family Services to a mother who was already barely surviving and was fighting her own demons for self-hell and persecution. But do not come into my home where you may think was safe, when in fact it was the worst place for me to be approached.

I was shocked and still numb. He was floored. I had showed her my fridge, walking her throughout my whole house, down to my children's rooms and taking at least ten minutes before she told me the truth. She could clearly tell I was terrorized over her supposed title and the assumed threat. I was completely unsuspecting.

Damien's green eyes twirled, as his mind took everything in I was saying. He just pulled me into him, placed a few kisses on the top of my brow and said, "I gotta make some calls". He rose to his feet in a hurry and walked out, but not before shaking his head in shock.

I had to pack up Sable and pick up my eldest son from school as Damien tore out of the parking lot. When he returned he stated, "That what they had done was illegal and it would be taken care of". Simple and matter of fact.

This was how he lived and was used to the constant watchful guard, but to me I wanted a place it didn't matter what others saw, because I had nothing to hide.

I felt honestly rotten for maybe getting this woman in trouble, I didn't want anyone to get in trouble but I also never wanted another mother to feel or go through what I just did. It's an odd situation and an even odder lifestyle.

Damien was still going off about it days later, sharing private jokes about it with me and his friends. I, once again, turned inward solemn and quiet, always private within my own mind. I didn't want to hear what he thought it might be, or what it was about. I wanted to know nothing. I had taught myself well, from when I was younger, to vacate the rooms where any uncomfortable discussions were taking place. I sure as hell didn't want to hear him demoralize another human being, who wasn't mean in the least but more than likely covered her own ass in case he was indeed there! Which he was.

There wasn't much talk in close quarters, anyhow, there never was. Because of wire taps and other gadgets the government might have installed. So in that regard Damien was brilliant and intelligent. He was, as I have said before, a man of many substances and none of them were weak; except perhaps the private punishments he dealt humanity.

I couldn't be involved. The less I knew the better. The way I grew up in my teenage years, I would leave the room if anyone was in a deep conversation, that I wanted to be no part of. I didn't want to be stained with evilness or even meanness. I just wasn't that person; I always enjoyed just being nice, loyal, and respectful, the simplicity of life. But still solid to the core. I stood for what I believed was right, just not against him.

People around knew me and anyone of them could come to my house for a safe haven. I was trusted, but I was also no part of anything that could ever harm my sons, or criminal and I was proud of that.

That is why, what Damien was doing to me, with control and violence, was epic on so many levels. He was breaking the one person "most" loved and trusted. The one any street person could come to for warmth, help or even food. I gave them shelter when they had none.

Even then, no one could or would step up to help me. Although I had given their own children and even them a place of safety, or food many times before. How could I not feel betrayed?

You see, anyone who is not a Hells Angel but runs in the crowd of underdogs, thugs and hustlers will state openly, "I don't give a F*#! About HA" but in front of a true Hells Angel, you would see that very person, polishing the members shoes and doing their bidding.

If any girl or guy is reading this, who perhaps is in the life, you will all know that being abused by a man or woman is wrong!

That does not label you a rat. It just doesn't.

Even the most straight up thugs will beat down a guy who is laying a hand on their girl, and especially abusing a child.

In most gangs or with street level thugs, it's wrong and heavily frowned upon.

And so, I ask, "Why if *that was* the case, didn't anyone help me? Or help my children. No one? Why?"

I will tell you why, because I was with and attached to one of the most notorious, craziest, high ranking members of all. Yes, Damien's nickname on the streets was "LUCY".

Some people were so envious of that fact, that they loved me to my face and hated me behind my back, not realizing the torture of having someone like that so enamored with you and ultimately paying the critical price; with my very own humanity.

All those girls who flung themselves at him, could have him for all I cared by this point, but instead they hated me behind my back and to my face they sprinkled me with sugar. It was endless and again I state the life.

Where is the realness in that?

Needless to say, I NEVER called the cops for help, nor that lady. They couldn't help me, as was just proof, no one could, and it was up to me get away and me alone.

Courage

"The love of a mother should never be tested on the grounds of a battle field, where even the mightiest can and will fall by her hand".

It was spring and the summer wanted to be in full bloom. The house we were building, better known as "Shangri-La", was structured, framed and well under way. I was to be married in 3 months' time.

It didn't look as if the house would be completed for the wedding and we hadn't yet done any preparations or planning for the upcoming nuptials.

Damien would tell me repeatedly, "I can plan a wedding or any party in thirty days". It wasn't said in a humbly confident way but a factual dominant boastful way.

These were the days all leading to our marriage.

August 8th, 2008.

I was continuously asked by people when it was, where it was, what was going on, and so forth. People who asked were being genuine and sincere. So, when my own mother asked about it and warned me that I had to get the invites out to family or they wouldn't be able to make it; it set the wheels in motion and also set up another battle between Damien and me.

Now I know, this was not her intention, as she wouldn't want to upset him; as she still cowered around him, since Sables 2nd birthday; when he had sent her to our room, as if she was a child, and made me sign over my car.

You have to understand the control this man wielded. It was nothing short of power and corruption mixed with sadness and defeat and sometimes highlighted with blood and glory; if you catch my drift.

People loved him, bowed down to him and even felt good when he gave them the time of day, bragging about it to their own family and friends. It is the life {*The life of hustlers and gangsters*}.

My mother was not like that, she wasn't influenced by his bling or charm. She sensed defeat and even loathing with the aura of power that he inflicted upon us. She was not fooled but also not stupid either; she understood one word, could mean devastation for us (the children and I).

She knew this and was starting to become like myself around him, timid. But with her thoughtful caution, she gave something valuable to me; a truth and understanding. When the mental, delusional moments of self-doubt set in, my mind would anchor itself to that truth and it helped my overwhelmed brain not feel so crazy.

It was the things that were said that screwed me up, the innuendos and twisted head games of Damien's. I was starting to question every word, action and instant with him. I felt that at any time he could turn on me, yes, but it felt more ominous than that. It was as if something was planned or something was up, that I was unaware of.

I do not believe Damien wanted anyone to be too close to him; he didn't trust easily but appeared to laugh and embrace people whole heartedly. He had secrets and he had what he wanted most in this world. A club of brothers, which gave him the euphoria of power, anything else was last.

I guess when you're fighting with a truth inside so profound and know that your living a life that you do not want or think is right, you start to question everything that brushes through your everyday life, as I was now doing.

It's what makes my accounting of my life easy because all I had were my own private thoughts. It's hard when you know the capabilities of someone and yet you're stuck with them or stay. I know my only real strength came when others that were loyal to me, were around; only then did I actually feel safe and only then did I feel a little confidence.

Like I have said before fast cars, bling and money meant nothing to me. It was a joke and my eyes were wide open. It's just, when would my mind tell me to do something, my body wasn't capable of? When would I become strong enough to fight for what I believed in?

Not only stand up and defend others but myself and my own children? When was enough, enough? How much more does a person have to go through before they crack, crumble and leave or die, trying? When!?

I couldn't understand why, if I knew it was wrong, did I stay? Was it fear, was it loneliness, did I love him or was I so caught up in having a family with the father of my child, that I just sucked it up and dealt with every blow that came my way? Did I feel so alone and felt I had no one that he was my only option, was he right?

I believe it was all of the above combined, no support system in place or anyone strong enough to show me he wasn't as powerful as the image gave him. I knew by then that my family didn't support me or even like me. Not knowing me for the past fifteen years, not being anywhere close to them and they still just thought I was the delinquent teenager, I always was or had been.

I knew they had no idea how to genuinely love me or respect me, because I have seen how other families are with loved ones and it was not cold like that. To me their barbs and comments had a way of sticking inside me. Only to make me feel worthless; no matter how hard I tried with them.

I knew that I had a doctor who understood only a fraction of certain parts of my life. So that, god forbid, if something happened to me I felt confident that my children would be safe. But how can you fight for something when you can't even fight for yourself?

Is it when he says that one more rude comment or belittles some-one you care about? Or is it when you watch him treated as if he sits upon a throne and you almost choke on the sickness of it and see the way falseness and dishonesty surrounds him?

Is it when your own dreams have been crushed and ground below his boot heel, once too often? Or after you've been extorted, beaten and violated in your own home? Or is it when you don't have a dime to your name because you're not *allowed* any.

Or is it, when you have to dress up in the finest brand name clothing, with a ten thousand dollar purse when all you want to do is buy a Christmas tree, go look at lights, bake cookies, and sit around the fireplace with love, hope and a future to look forward to.

I didn't want another Christmas where I wasn't allowed to shop for presents until Christmas Eve and then to find out he had done it, without me.

I didn't want to quietly borrow money from my step-father for that exact Christmas tree or food. I just wanted normalcy, that's all I wanted, all I ever wanted. I wanted memories of goodness, I wanted a future and I wanted that for my beautiful sons. I didn't want another fake smile or a man who dictated how I sat, or walked, how I spoke and dressed. I didn't even think I could survive another hand of abuse, let alone stomach another memorable event.

I couldn't take it anymore; my mind was constantly on alert and seeking the solace of refuge for my sanity and in figuring out what was real or not. I was on overload.

So after I had been asked again, over the phone by my mother, about invitations. Then he nonchalantly said whatever he said in a careless manner and a, 'I don't have time for this and you aren't getting a dime for it' tone of voice … I cracked.

I tilted my head at him because he was once again laying on the couch in the middle of a beautiful day and said from the dining room (*we had an open floor plan*). *With no filter and no cautious demeanor, I spouted what was first in my mind and then out of my mouth before I had a chance to draw it back in.*

"Fuck You!" In a disgusted, no good and snippy tone of my voice.

Like, why am I walking on eggshells? Why do I have to carefully plan the tone of my voice or my approach to this man, why? I refused and I rebelled.

After watching, for so long, how others had bowed down to him, I just couldn't stomach another day of doing it myself. I couldn't, and boy did it feel good. It was a huge release, of so many pent up emotions the very first time I talked back and it felt good, no, it felt great; being real and being ME.

I just didn't care anymore, if he charged at me or hurt me. I had finally found my voice and that in itself made me very, very proud. It released a whole lot of those tumultuous feelings raging inside.

Damien sat there, eyes popping out of his head, with a look of shock. He re-grouped fast, though and sneered at me in a tone so deadly and cold, it could have frozen ice.

"No one ever, *EVER,* speaks like that to me! E*specially* not **my** Bitch"!

He went on as his eyes darkened with such hatred, it is hard to forget. Vivid green to dilated black in a snap. "You're lucky this time. Next time, I will smack that ugly look from your face and wipe that tone from your voice, exactly as I would do to alllll (he allowed that word to linger) my Bitches, or *anyone* who speaks to meeeee, like that!"

"Alright hunny", I thought to myself, as he said the last two words, *"the fight is on."* I was shocked by my rebellion but too repulsed to even stop myself. I couldn't allow this guy to carry on like such an egomaniac.

I was disgusted and finally, all the moments of pain and anger by his hand clambered up within me. I had enough.

I glimpsed the rude awakening of life as his wife, his girl and the mother to his child. I looked him dead center in the middle of his eyes and repeated it.

"Fuck you!" came out of me in a nature as fearless as his. In tone that never shook or altered in any way what so ever. I was in loathe of him and every fiber of what he stood for. He was now all my pain, all my bruises and all my anguish.

I yelled for the boys in a voice that meant 'hustle NOW' and ordered, "Let's go!"

I scooped them up as they ran towards me and we walked out my front door. I never looked back over my shoulder once but I stopped, only briefly, to place *his* ring on the table.

I hated him, I hated that he took over my home and I hated seeing how many people had suffered, at the hands of him. I cracked. I`d had had enough; he was the pig, not me!

My adrenaline was too potent to feel fear, my reservations were too strong and the mother in me was deadly, at that moment. I felt invincible and surer of myself, than ever before.

I didn't run down the hallway in fright, I walked with my head held high in utter determination.

He never came to the door, nor did he chase me down the hallway, and he didn't even scream obscenities off the balcony. I had left him speechless or he was just too lazy to care, or maybe, perhaps, he was even planning my very demise.

I contacted my step-father and asked him to book me a hotel for a few nights. I only told him that we had an argument and I needed to get away with my sons.

My step-father booked us at the 'Pink Palace' and for the time being, we felt safe. When he/ my step-father arrived, he left us money and just gave me a quick hug, passing on hope for a brighter day.

My step-father could be a man of many words or none at all. Today, it was none and it wouldn't be until tonight that the true ramifications of what I had done would settle in and grip me.

As the darkness of night was falling over the sky, the boys were contentedly playing on their Nintendo DS`s after spending time in the pool.

Thinking they were on yet another mini vacation. They had no real idea, of what had transpired at home nor would I allow them to know. I was not going to let them witness or be a tool on the days that The Beast unleashed his fury on me and more violence occurred. I couldn't further destroy their already broken image of what life was about. It wasn`t right and I was becoming more and more aware of it. My reality was setting in.

I tried reading my novel. Reading would usually take away any of my criss cross thoughts, but it wasn't working tonight. I was afraid of the night, it left me feeling anxious and trapped. I do not know of what exactly, I was terrified of, but this night I felt petrified. This night was my worst nightmare and anytime I saw a light shine in our window or heard someone passing by our door, I would jump.

My mind was swimming with all the threats I had heard from

Damien over the years, and even others, who would put things in my ear, like, *"You can never get away"*

In the whispers of the night, *I* could even hear Kane, Ashton's father's voice, warning me, *"They are a worldwide organization Kerri, you should be scared. You're never going to be able to live a normal life."*

It was as if they were all right. Echoing into my every thought and I was very much alone. Seconds seemed like minutes, and minutes those were hours.

My anxiety spiked even more so, when I heard a loud noise after the kids had fallen asleep. I jumped and my heart started racing. I panicked, unlike any time before.

I tried to call Desiree but her phone was off. I tried to call my step-father but he never answered and the full wash of fear hit me. I was struggling and gasping for air, when I started saying over and over in my head, *"I can't die, my kids need me, I can't die, my kids need me"*, trying to quell the wave of anxiety strangling me. Using that once tool to stop my anxiety, with a sentence meant for strength, on repeat. It never worked.

I called the front desk to let them know if anyone, anyone at all, was to inquire as to if I was staying there, to immediately say no!

I wanted no one to be able to link where the kids and I were staying or what room. I felt better knowing this room was under my step-fathers name, but Damien would be able to figure that out.

I started skimming the phone book for safe houses and anyone, just anyone I could talk to.

I needed someone, anyone, to help me feel not so afraid. I was very much on high tension alert. This is when I started realizing how extreme and unique my situation was; how even a transition house for women of abuse couldn't accommodate me. When I phoned a few, they turned me away. I was in grave peril.

I realized then how very, very, lucky I was. For every minute I was to be alive, others surely fell. I was on my own and this night, I felt it more than ever.

I knew I couldn't call the police. They would ask what had happened. I, in turn reporting that I had said "*fuck you*" to my fiancé and now I think I am going to die, was NOT abuse by him.

But it was and his hands could kill. I knew this….How ridiculous that would sound even to an officer, a person or as I say now to me.

I would be back at square one and even more screwed then when I had started down the hallway. I should've filtered my mouth but I just couldn't anymore.

No one knew more than I, at that moment how vicarious my situation was. It was the same questions, over and over, from the few transition houses I did call and each one said to try another number or to try this number.

They, or these supposed safe houses, did not understand! I needed someone, now, with heart and compassion ready for immediate action with regards to the safety I sought.

I knew on the streets you were not considered a rat if you were being beaten by a partner and police were called. I knew that I wouldn't be labelled a rat by any thugs, but Damien played by a whole different set of rules than the rest of the individuals I knew. Like many things, somehow, that didn't apply to him or was not in the equation for me.

I knew more than any other time before how royally I had screwed up my life.

I remember, when I was young, and there was this 1-800 number for children to call for help, so I started looking in the back of the yellow pages frantically and I found a 1-800 number for emergency safety issues and suicide.

I felt unsure of myself calling but I was desperate. When a lady picked up with a soft voice and asked how she could help me, I broke down like never, ever before. I didn't feel interrogated like the transition houses made me feel or like a drug addict searching for a bed for the night. I felt cared for and a genuine appreciation for waking up (or that's what I thought) whoever answered the number that night. I felt safely connected and that was all I needed in those moments.

I spoke hesitantly, at first, about my life, my pain, my choices. I spoke of the adoration I had for my children and my hope and belief in family and love. I spoke of every mistake I ever made and the heart I do have. I spoke for hours to this woman, every now and then; she would set my mind at ease by assuring me, that what I was saying, was actually okay and confidential. No one would ever know.

She promised me more times than I care to remember that no authorities would come, unless I was going to kill myself, which I wasn't.

She was beautiful in every sense of the word when it came to human nature and experience. I opened up like I do, when I feel at ease, respected and valued. Angels do come when you call for help, they do....*and if you are living through what I am describing, I promise there is help and you can share.*

When I finally felt comfortable and safe, I opened up about where I was, (Not the location) but who I was actually with and how I really had no one.

I freely told her all about the abuse by his hands and the indescribable, useless way I felt about myself. I told her everything. She was my anchor, this dark, lonely, sad night and I needed her.

I told her I didn't want to kill myself, I just wanted to learn how to live again and how I was spun into so many webs and circles that I didn't know who I could trust.

I knew I shocked her. I could hear her sudden intake of breathe and the tone change in her voice. It almost made me regret saying my fiancé was a Hells Angel. I didn't know if that would mean I just inadvertently spoke aloud a statement I shouldn't have and now I really had to run.

But she surprised me, she kept my secrets and she told me of a place I could go to and who could help. She said I had to be really, really, one-hundred percent sure when I made that call, though. She was preparing me for a granted wish, I had wished so many times-a truly safe haven.

She waited to hear my voice and calculate my tone, then she said the ray of hope that has stayed in me all this time.

She told me how I could go underground and have my name and the names of my children changed. I would be able to live in another country and start fresh. A whole new life, but no one would ever be able to make contact with me again, nor could I ever be with them. I had to be sure though. There a seed was planted and she watered it just enough to take root. *For that I thank her now today~*

She gave me the numbers I needed and we talked for many hours. She told me stories of other people she has spoken to and none were like mine, as none are ever the same but all were unique in our own ways and that she was a volunteer.

I held onto that phone for dear life that night and into the early hours. She was the friend I was looking for, the one I could trust and open up to.

I went over scenarios with her on how it would work and how long it would take to happen. She gave me all the answers she could give me. When I finally hung up on that phone call, I felt safe and I fell asleep clutching those precious phone numbers she had given me to use only if I had to.

I knew I finally had the true hope of a brighter day and my quest for the answers was about to begin before I made the most colossal move of my life, a fight for *Freedom~*

When I woke the next morning, I knew I had to call Stella to let her know that I was okay. I had left quite the message on her answering machine the night before. I called everyone else I had contacted and saved her for last. I was desperate last night.

When we did speak she said that Damien was searching for me and the kids all night; even showing up at her place. Knocking on her bedroom window late into the evening.

I was shocked, but not really. She told me how all he wanted was for us to come home and that it has been hard building the house and planning a wedding, all at the same time. She said she actually felt bad for him and that he seemed broken. I said the boys and I would come over and we would visit.

When we arrived I had a few thoughts and worries about whether Damien might show up or what if she called him. I didn't have to ask because she immediately assured me she would never call him; Stella could read me. She told me how her boyfriend had to console "big tough Damien" half the night, reassuring him that I would come home and we were safe.

Stella was laughing at the mental picture of it all. That is why; when I had first called her phone, she had hit the mute button. She knew that to answer my call, might alert Damien to where I was.

She said she knew I was fine and that she couldn't sneak away to call or the guys would know. She said that Damien was caught sneaking around in the backyard and throwing rocks at their window thinking they were asleep, when he had come last night. I was again shocked, as the quick description before didn't tally the picture she described now with gestures and facial expressions.

It was nice having her in my corner and I did have to laugh at it all. I felt amazing and surprisingly well after my panic spiked night, the evening before. I felt better than I had in a long time and more at ease. Thinking about it, I even felt good to finally swear at The Beast and really be honest about what I felt with his behavior. It gave me a new confidence and backbone I never felt I had before.

Stella and I made jokes and mimics of his unique instances, tone and just of it all. It was our release, or more so mine. She was proud of me for finally standing up to him and being the normal Kerri, she knew I always was.

She asked when I was going to go back home.

I wasn't going home yet. I had another night at the hotel paid for and the boys were on a mini vacation. I needed to sort my own thoughts out. I had to learn how to stand on my own two feet and not allow Damien to crush me.

With my new found strength I chose to no longer cower to him or to show fear. I had to be solidified on my stance or he would prey on me, as he would a victim. He liked my weakness, it gave him something I would never know or understand.

My lovely lady from the night before, also gave me such courage and a gift from above I believe. I was not going to ill-use the knowledge she gave me but allowed it to instill a true belief in me. I knew what I wanted and it wasn't this.

I never told Stelly about my call, or my resolve, just touched on the basics of things and circumstances. She would never understand my true inner chaos, no one would, and I was only starting to barely understand it all myself. My heart was different, unique and very, very kind.

My resolve never faded, it became stronger by the moment, and I knew that the feelings I once had for Damien would never be the same; he had pushed me too far, spoken too harshly, and laid one hand too many on me, for once and for all. The damage was done. I couldn't *Kerri On* as I once had with a blind eye and that grin-n- bear it attitude. I had changed, not just last night but overall as a person these past few years.

I spoke to Stella of my newly formulated plan, finding a way out with actually starting at the beginning and breaking the cycle where it started.

I shared with her about what I had written and how writing all the things he has already done to the boys and I, was somewhat healing but also my last attempt at fixing a wrong that had been done.

I shared that I wrote those thoughts on paper, not to sabotage him or hurt him, but to heal and find a way to reach him. I wanted him to see the pain in my face and hear it in my voice when I read him my truth. I needed to see his reaction to know if he really did care. But, Stella gave me a word of advice after she took the time to read all sixty-two pages of my notes.

She said, "He is going to kill you Kerri. He cannot find this" as she held up the hidden binder I had previously stashed at her house a day not so long ago. In no way can he find this!" She was very adamant about that and I felt it to my inner self- she was right.

Here is another time when I once allowed another person's opinion to cloud my own judgement. How can writing how I feel be so wrong, or used against me? I wrote with the purest of intentions and to hopefully salvage what little I could. Even that was wrong, but I could see her reasoning and chose to hide it at her place for a little while longer, until I determined what to do. But her opinion weakened my self-confidence the lady had given me the night before, because of her solidifying the fear in me that I was trying to wash away.

Stella and I had a very deep conversation that day; it was the furthest from butterflies and rainbows. I told her something that had been nagging at the back of my head for a while now.

I told her how I wanted to find 'Action', my first boyfriend. The first to ever abuse me. I needed to ask him if all this was indeed my fault, and if I was crazy or if I deserved the fists and remarks that came my way from the guys I dated. I needed to start from the beginning in order to fix my life. The beginning to me was him; at that time it was him. I had been told it was me and the guys I dated plus friends I had, so there is where I started.

I never realized the dark, twisted journey that it would require me to walk and perhaps if I knew this, and that it would lead me to such gut wrenching pain in the future, I may have stopped what I was about to embark on. I don't know if my resolve for answers would've been this determined… or this path chosen, so firmly. But after all the pain, I say it was worth it.

I needed to know if what Damien was saying "That I needed help and to visit a doctor, I needed to be broken and rebuilt, re-invented as he put it, again" was true. I needed to know if I was the problem.

I knew the way he would say those words, was in a repulsive, unciv-ilized, ignorant way, but it played havoc inside me and tore at my very heart. It was breaking me and now to actually hear those abusive words from my family, as a grown woman was a completely different type of pain altogether. The invincible teenager was gone and a lady/mother stood in her place.

It was embedded in me now, all those words and careless comments thrown from every angle and by all that I truly and dearly loved. I needed these answers and I thought that was where I needed to start, to stop this from happening in my own children's lives. I had to start with Action, the axe wielding cave-man who had once protected me , then harmed me and had me fleeing across two provinces and into the bosom of not family but friends.

I had to search for the truth and I didn't trust anyone close to me to tell me the answers I sought, I just didn't. For the sake of my sanity and my children I had to find out if I did deserve this life, if I did deserve the beatings I got and if I was the problem everyone said I was.

Hopefully it would help me either bend and mold to The Beasts demands, or fight for what I "think" I believe in; myself and truth, with a dash of justice!

There began my journey. I didn't want to run and hide. I didn't want to change my name and cause anymore tumultuous feelings of upheaval in my sons lives. I didn't want to look over my shoulder the rest of my life and I didn't want to continue being part of this side of the tracks that just didn't have the heart I did.

The very same world I once thought was rock solid and real; had given me a hand of distrust and disloyalty. I had watched so many people, with good hearts, burned by that lifestyle. A lifestyle that wasn't as awesome as some may believe it to be.

I also thought and saw the other side of life, in regards to my family and the way 'they' thought normal was or should be. To me; I couldn't fathom how so much hate, gossip, and opinions that circulated in their lives was somehow the normal way to live. But of course maybe that only had to do with talking and referring to me? It felt toxic and it felt mean. So was it really right?

What was normal to me ???

I had to search because somehow and somewhere, I lost the truth I always had, my heart cared about others, but why did I feel as though no one care about me? If they thought the way they treated me was caring, then I was way out to lunch with thinking; that's not how you treat people you love.

I held on to this grain of truth for my sanity- I would never talk or treat my own children this way, nor would I allow my sons to do that to each other. No matter how life can be, good or bad. Mistakes made a feats had; we were to be there for each other. To build up not squash down.

Like I said I was either going to become hardened or I was going to stand up and fight once again for what I believed in. Except this time, with my kind of justice!

Love, compassion and a 'fudge you' attitude! {As in leave without a word and a trace}

It was weird feeling like I was cornered. I had never had to fight from within before, or maybe I had; but without the years of wisdom behind me. I was always a free bird, a gypsy girl and I felt trapped.

I had a man who was potent, intoxicating and just plain lethal! I was marrying a man who hated me, the way I looked and who I was. Yeah, life has thrown me punches and curve balls but this was on all whole new level, this was just erroneous! I couldn't help thinking if the fates had punished me, or perhaps I was meant to live like this; I was every chaotic emotion you could feel but most of all I was lost in the midst of a hell I was starting to believe was my doing. But I seemed to be fighting that notion, when really the easiest thing I could do was cave to it and accept it.

I felt so alone during this time and yet I was surrounded by people, but they weren't my people, they were his. Even the ones I thought were once mine, were in actual fact; his.

I had no more trust to give, not even for my Stella.

She now in this instant, stood before me and played both sides from the previous night. It was when I heard her say, "I felt bad for him Kerri". That I knew to be cautious now.

I have seen how she can manipulate and be manipulated. I told her only so much. And seeing how her boyfriend genuinely looked up to Damien, left me feeling unsure and uneasy. I've seen that in others before with him and that is a warning sign as to the feeble loyalty I thought I may have with her family. I knew that in any given moment she could turn on me. Call it intuition; that's all I had left now go on, so I did. It was my way of deciphering the good from the bad.

I am not saying that her boyfriend was bad, he was a hard working individual that enjoyed the outdoors. He worked to provide for his family and I believe it's also what he lived for. I also know however, that somewhere inside anyone of us, often lays two sides, one that can stay dormant and handle life. Then another that can rise to the occasion and cause destruction. I didn't want to find out nor know which he was.

I had also seen how Damien can make anyone feel confidant and worthwhile, promising the world and then taking it all away in a swoop of his arm. I believe he had seen the fire in Stella's boyfriend's eyes and knew this man would or could be a good addition to his team. It was the quiet, calculating demeanor he had and let's be real, Stella wouldn't date some who is a square-head or a hundred percent law-abiding normal, would she? Yes, I wasn't fooled.

But I can say this about her boyfriend, he was a great guy because I knew the values he had for his family and they were a lot like mine. I didn't know during this time who I could trust, as I barely trusted myself these days. So I stayed cautious on divulging to much and from sharing everything with these people.

I kept Ms. Stella in the loop with the general goings on, just not all the details. I had to, I needed to and if I didn't, I believe I would've succumbed to the tortures and pressure of Damien. I loved her and that I can say for sure, but trust was feeble for me, to say the least.

I wasn't allowed on Facebook, Twitter wasn't that big yet and quite simply any social media for that matter was taboo for me. Stella, I left looking online for Action, but sharing the information about changing my name for plan of disappearing was not for her ears, or knowledge.

So I asked Stella to try and track him down and I would call her later. I left her with the room number, in case she had any luck. As I packed up the boys to leave and depart with at least some of the confidence and resolve I had from the night before.

Love Of A Mother

On my way back to the hotel, while driving down the freeway; I felt good and even content. Like for the first time I knew my way or had a path to choose, even follow.

My sons were laughing and giggling away in the backseat. I felt, free. Something felt right and real for the very first time in my life that I started weeping, as silently as I could.

My phone was off and today was our day to enjoy, laugh and just be us. I knew in these moments that this was the beginning to our life; I just felt it and the dark cloud that stayed hovering above us was slowly being lifted, because of awareness.

I no longer cared if he followed through on his threats. I no longer cared if I was alone, because somewhere, something found me and I would never be alone again.

I had my sons and a life we could look forward to, a life of hope, and that was all I needed in these moments, was hope.

The number tucked away in my purse to go underground gave me a new found confidence, unlike anything anyone, could've offered me.

The woman I spoke to, gave me that hope and of course her precious, soft spoken voice.

It wasn't a cops number or card that would get me in trouble, beaten and re-broken. Nor was it a false friend who would turn on me in an instant, it wasn't my mother who just couldn't handle any more stress; this was a person who wouldn't ask me questions, would take immediate action and who would lead us to safety, if I so desired. It was a way out, a new life; it was my own golden ticket away from it all. To me, it had all started with nowhere to go and searching for the answers.

I felt like I had the drive and the time to figure out where I went wrong. This simple need, so deep, I had for the sake of my sons and a good life. I wanted to know if I was the problem.

I was okay with accepting the fact, that if I was the issue maybe I could now accept what was being said with grace and acceptance. Because once you are aware of something, you can fix it. I could fix me if it was me and I was okay with that. If it wasn't me then I had to build that courage I seen in so many others and stand up for myself or even flee.

Tears stung my eyes and just flowed freely down my face knowing that all was okay and I was finally having a chance at true freedom.

The laughter, bubbling from the backseat, stopped cold when my Ashton, noticed my face, instantly putting his back up. He had seen too many of my failures and too much of my pain; it wasn't fair to him.

I quickly pulled over on the freeway, no matter the cars whizzing by and jumped in the backseat. I held them both saying over and over, "These are happy tears *my loves*, happy tears". I soaked in every waking moment I had with them and they were my rock; a rock that they should've NEVER had to be. Or carrying me in the first place. That was my mistake but everything was going to be okay now because their mother just realized the power of her own god given strength: Herself, hope and a way out!

Sable grabbed Ashtons hair in that moment and pulled him away from me, just to have him all to himself. It was a cute gesture and one that reminded me of the innocence he still had inside him. I was more aware than ever that these boys deserved to be children, they deserved to have security, safety and a good-life with good people. I vowed to give it to them.

By the time we arrived back at the hotel, I had come to the conclusion that I didn't want to run and that I was no longer going to be the coward I felt I had been. I had finally shared my voice that had been stifled with Damien. It was a habit from the early days that I seemed to just fall into, probably because of who he was and our first encounter.

He was older than me by ten years and I had to be accountable for giving him the right to control me in some ways. I knew I had left for a reason this time and because of the viscous tone, he'd directed at me. I didn't tolerate it and I never ran away in flight, I walked down that hallway. I needed to remind myself of that.

This was to get away and re-group, maybe perhaps gain a little stance against him; but this time I was not running. This time I was slowly learning how stand on my own two feet again and with validation from a person who was trained in their field. A person that will never know who they talked to or how they actually did help.

Hearing from Stella that he was over there the previous night begging for me to come home, was a good thing. It showed me that, firstly, he wasn't on a stark raving mad streak and, secondly, that I had made a point.

So instead of keeping my phone off, perhaps I would turn it on and when he called, not answer a few times, delete the texts that came in right away; so that I wasn't tempted to answer them or become timid. Then on my own time, phone him back when I wanted to, not when I was being forced or cornered into it.

I had come to the conclusion that I was going to search for answers, and no matter what I found I would deal with it, and try to fix anything I could, even if it was me. I had to break this cycle and god damnt I was going to try.

I say this, again, because after so many years of being told how horrible you are and being hit, beaten and abused you start believing the things that are said about you. It's a brutal cycle that *sometimes* a person can never break.

I wanted to give my sons the best life possible and I knew, all too well, the painful existence I had and there was no way I wanted them to feel even an ounce of what I did, or live their lives in it any longer. Hence, giving me strength to stand up and fight for what I felt the only gift I could give them at that time, "a good life", even if it meant it wasn't with me. Those were the dark thoughts that had me constantly wiping tears from my eyes. I was in a very solitary place.

I turned on my phone as we headed down to the pool, leaving it purposefully on the night stand for when we returned. We splashed and played for hours. It had a rain forest atmosphere, surrounded by rocks and a hidden hot tub, enclosed in a cave. It was beautiful there but the rooms had a mildew feel, because it had an indoor pool, with carpets throughout the building.

I promised the boys pizza and a movie, our usual, after the pool experience. Then we could just relax together and the night approached I didn't feel panicked at all. My anxiety didn't spike to the deathly terror it had the night before.

I went over to my phone, it was on silent mode, and sure enough, my inbox was full, allowing me to delete the messages and make room for new ones.

I didn't even have to view them, nor did I. That in itself was strength and worth the delete. My phone had half a dozen missed calls.

I waited for the pizza to come before stepping outside to make the phone call that was expected by Damien and determine my fate.

My children gave me strength and knowing what they wanted and needed gave me an unfamiliar power I had for myself. Believing in just that; is the main reason I am here today.

I didn't know if this was his tactic for saving face in front of his bros, showing up at Stella's house, in case if I left him for good. I didn't know if he even cared at all or if this was his way of luring me back in, just to stomp my face in for defying him so blatantly.

I had no idea what was going to happen if I called him or went back to our house. I had no idea if he was tracking my location, once I called; but I was not going to lie down and let this bully take our home, or push me around any longer. I really by this point, had enough. I also had no where to go unless I chose to run away and take on a false identity somewhere else.

So instead of cower and take it, I had to put my big girl pants on, face The Beast and learn to speak. I just couldn't be that person who took it any longer yet and knowing I had a contact number for a chance to get out if I needed to, gave me enough of an edge to do this battle and fight for what I believed in. My children's and our very lives.

I grabbed my pack of cigarettes; I had now started smoking more regularly; never before had I smoked like this. A pack of cigarettes lasted me a month, now however they lasted a week.

I left the boys cuddled together in our room. Only when I stepped outside in the cool air, did I start to feel a little apprehensive. I didn't like that someone could be hiding in the bushes with a gun ready to kill me on his demand. I didn't like that and I didn't know any more, if his rants were true or false. I was now officially living hour by hour and had to find some way to keep going.

I know, right? Not so much the limelight and star studded life I lived, that everyone thought. Peaches and crème and anything I wanted, was far from the actual truth. But, hey, people have their own assumptions and I had the truth.

The costly extravagant presents do not make up for the soul that gets lost; it's one of the deadly sins ★Greed★ that tests your morals. I had none of that, I hated the presents, often giving them away (to this day a $8000.00 dollar Louis Vuitton sits in my garage in a bin). They weren't worth the price I paid for them and they sure as hell weren't worth a damn for what my sons had to live through either.

When he picked up the phone and answered right away his voice was quiet and sounded sincere. He was genuinely worried and just wanted the boys to come home, to 'their-proper' home where it was the right place for them to be.

But, it was in the way he said it and the underlining insinuation, which raised the hairs on my neck. Yes, it was nicely spoken but it was as if he did nothing wrong and only cared. That was weird and had me concerned immediately. He spoke as if I had just taken the kids in haste and ripped them from their home of stability for no reason and he was concerned about us and even more so concerned about me.

He spoke so gently, quiet and soft. He spoke slowly as if there was something wrong with me, or my hearing. And then after he had done that and said those words he said, "I love you honey, you can't do this all the time. Just come home." He paused and then went on to say, in a soothing voice, "We are planning a wedding and building a house, things are like this, when there is stress but everything's going to be okay. Everything's going to be just fine, honey, just fine."

I hung up the phone instantly, the last part of his innuendo sinking in. My stomach had risen to the back of my throat; I almost puked, right there, in the parking lot. I needed a minute to think and I didn't have that minute, all I had was now. The phone rang and I reflexively hit hang up. By the next one I had a grip on my bearings, enough to know this was his newest and deadliest way yet of being the "good man everyone thought he was". He was up to taking my very sanity.

It was twisted, it was wrong and it defied logic. It was perverse and it was the new mental game he had just started and now more than ever I had to be on my toes and sharp as a whip.

This man who said he loved me and his children was sick! This man had just done god knows what in the last forty-eight hours we were gone, he had spoken and spewed his bullshit to who knows who and all the while the boys and I were formulating a plan for a healthy life.

This time I knew his tactics and I had seen them in vivid living color, and there was no way my children would ever suffer at the hands of this monster. Even if I did find out he was right, this was all me and I was crazy. I had been sharing with a certified doctor all that has been happening so that my sons would be away from him, if something did happen to me.

It was like I had mustered enough courage to speak out about his treatment towards me and was ready to speak adult-like with him about it. Then when I had called, he made me look like I had a problem and it would all be okay.

We never once spoke of what he said, or what I had done. He simply spoke as if I was a child in need of guidance and it threw all my built up courage off of kilter. It was highly intelligent on his part but absolutely mind blowing and perverse on mine.

I didn't even have that chance to speak of the issue at hand, none, but I did have my intelligence and this time I was on top of it way ahead of time.

I knew I couldn't allow anyone to think I was actually unstable and it rocked my world knowing he had somehow come up with this scheme to spout his nonsense; to whom, I would soon find out.

I mean the derogatory comments and raised hands you knew were coming, but the twisted, diabolical way he just tricked me into sounding like I had to calm down, would raise hairs on anyone's back, as it did mine!

This was the similar discrediting way he had engaged in with

Chucky, his business partner, and how he made him look as if he was mentally unstable over time. The minute Chuck didn't do as he was told or had countered with a different idea or even debated with Damien, somehow it would be turned into Chuck's an idiot. Chucky needed help and, guess what, eventually Chucky was low enough, and so belittled and degraded by Damien's constant harassment and ridicule that he was eventually convinced that there was something wrong with him. He sought medical help and medication.

I watched as a grown vibrant successful man, a father, was demolished by the hand of my fiancé, because of his mental games. Damien even sat in a doctor's office with Chucky, sat right there, while the doctor prescribed anti-depressants to his partner and tranq's.

I couldn't believe the irony of it all. I couldn't believe he was now trying to make me out to be *"in need of help and that he just cared"*. He may not have said it, but his tone and manner said it all. I had just been served by him and I had no clue this was going to be his manoeuver. It caught me so unaware and blindsided.

But what he didn't know, behind my quiet demeanor and self-servant attitude towards him, my mind, brain and heart took in all he did to others as well as myself.

So instead of falling prey to his newest tactic, it brought the fighter out in me. For I had already witnessed many victims fall and I wasn't going to be the next. I had already witnessed being administered by him with mental games and seen him do it to others. I was very aware now. I was smart, not a trophy to rest on your arm, but intelligent. This is where it became no problem to step up to The Beast and no problem to finally see the truth.

I shut the phone off again for the night as I let it all creep in. I lay down on the king-sized bed with my sons and whispered sweet nothings to them all night. It was revitalizing for me to be around their innocent glows. It was as if they could glance at me and fill me back up with love. I didn't have a hateful bone in me but I did have a determination and a power that even others noticed, but it was never mean and never meant to harm. If I could stand up for the weak, I could sure as heck start standing up for my sons and their security.

I was actually fuming mad, not scared or timid that he had the audacity to insinuate that I just ripped my sons from their peaceful home. Beast our home was a joke!

I was choked; you should never come up against a mother (or the person raising them) and her children. No one should do that.

He knew dang well that he spewed his ignorance and I was not going to tolerate it. I made a mental stand against him and he now took it to a whole other level by this trickery. I didn't want to marry him and he knew it. I never did and this brought me back to the hallway and his again mental delusion of fore-play.

As for the house we were building, he was building it, not I. I had never once been included on the structure, framing or design of it, nothing. I had once tried to make a suggestion at a breakfast table in "Ricky's" when we were out with a few of his friends and Stella one morning. When he looked at me across the table and sneered, "Don't fucking speak unless I tell you to!" All of the colour drained from Stella's face. I was ashamed and sat through the rest of the meal in silence.

It was just another moment of humiliation for me . He carried on after that as if nothing happened. Stella left, saying at the end of breakfast that she was so disgusted she couldn't spend the day with me. I knew it was because of him but it was my weakness that she couldn't be around. I was starting to reflect on how truly weak I was and Kerri Krysko the fighter for others, couldn't be weak!

The house he spoke so freely about was a nightmare to me. I never wanted to move out of my apartment nor did I want to live in this fortress, he was calling our new home. It was terrifying knowing how close it was becoming until move in day, let alone the wedding date.

When the boys and I left the hotel the next day, I was determined to ask him to move out of our apartment. I didn't want to be with him; by the time I rounded the corner to my apartment building I was gnawing at the bit, just to get him out. I asked the kids to play outside for a few minutes, before they came upstairs.

When I walked into my place however, no one was there. It was so nice not to feel his dominating presence, that I just soaked it all in and laid claim to my home once more. I told the boys to come up and called Desiree to come over.

I needed to take a few moments for myself and to think. I would often take long walks at the beach overlooking the Pacific Ocean and use that as a way to clear my thoughts. I needed just me time. I needed it more than ever. So I called her for that reason and that alone. Gone was the weak woman and now stood a supposedly crazy one...

I never did get to take that walk, though. I never had that moment to just unwind and re-evaluate, without being on survival mode because when I rounded the corner into my master bedroom I heard a noise. I peeked into my room and looked over at my big screen TV and saw porn playing in the background. I snapped.

I was repulsed, disgusted and knew he had done that, set it up just for my full benefit; in case I came home. Not once caring if the kids had seen that. Not once thinking of them, but teaching me another lesson and showing me how a man marks his territory.

I quickly unplugged the TV and started packing his bags. I couldn't stomach him any longer; I couldn't handle his tactics, mentality, his mean and utterly mortifying character. I just couldn't. I didn't want to raise my children with him. I didn't, I didn't, I didn't and I wouldn't.

But, oh, if only things were that easy. Like a normal person when it was over, it was over. But not for everyone, it just wasn't that simple. I had his belongings all ready for him to go when he came busting through the door, knowing I was finally home.

He took one look at the bags and charged at me, slamming my head into the door of my room. He whispered in a vile tone, so close to my ear, that would it have set anyone over the top or peeing their pants.

"You fucking cunt, YOU ever disobey me, or talk to me like that again, I will do as I promised and the kids will find you dead! Do you understand me!? Now get your fucking ring back on and be happy to see me, do you understand!?" and then "hunnnyyy unpack my bags" in a very distinguished way.

Baby Sable was just rounding the corner to come in and Ashton not far behind him. Damien pushed my head back with his face, as he tried to seal it with a kiss, putting on a show and I couldn't even respond or push him away. I was becoming numb to his threats and I just didn't have it in me to pretend.

I was stuck and the tears welled up in my eyes as I allowed him to show my son the pretense of our reunion and homecoming. His threat won, for now, but only because my sons walked in and for that reason alone.

My eyes lost their light that day, I know they did because after that people would always say that I looked hollow or was gaunt in my face and tired. I even heard that someone claimed I was on drugs, when I wasn't. I had no more fight in me, I had nothing I just had nothing left.

It was hard to hear him after that on the phone, making jokes about how I packed his bags to all his friends, even making me as he watched unpack them. It was sad knowing that even they were laughing at me, never once knowing the full truth of Damien and me. Never once considering how I felt. Never once realizing he forced me like a slave to unpack those items as he glared at me, telling me what to do.

I started becoming sour towards his minions and followers, seeing how they carelessly laughed at me and even in front of my kids, now. How he treated me, they were allowed to. It made me feel even less of a person when they thought it was okay. I watched the change happen around me and I watched how suddenly it was okay to talk to me the very same way he did; just without the brutality of it, which was reserved exclusively for him to administer.

As for my family, they even started treating me as if I was nothing more than a mule to carry their pack of tales and endless comments. It became a very heavy load for me and I seriously started wanting to kill myself. But the only thing that saved me from that, was my sons because I couldn't leave them to face this lifestyle alone. I felt I created it and I alone could only fix it. I stayed alive for them and that purpose alone.

I would catch my oldest son looking at me with compassion when the joking around me or about me became too much. It was sad and it was hard.

I tried once to stick a sharp pole into my leg, from the drawer in our kitchen that I ripped out of its spot, just to stop me from wanting to lash out at him and his friends. He watched and laughed as my anguish came to the surface and the pain to heavy in my heart was laid before him in that instant. I just cracked under the pressure and wanted to die. To me it was safer to hurt myself, then him.

I was hurting inside so deeply that I was slowly losing sight of who I was and my fight for freedom and truth. Damien laughed at me and said "see how crazy you are, see?" It was tough, it was sick but it was he was right.

Stella and I would sneak away sometimes and drive down some of the rougher sides of town still searching for Action, stopping the transients on the street asking if they knew him or where he was, and leaving my phone number to pass to him if they saw him. Promising them money if they found him. I needed Action and it seemed as if he was my only hope to find the truth. I truly believed it started because of who I associated with.

But even that hope, was fading. Stella thought it was fun and cool, not fully understanding how much this meant to me and that was okay. But this was my last hope to find out the truth about myself. I was barely holding on, gone was that number from the lady in my mind, in its place was a useless pig who needed help, me.

Stella was losing that charm she first had when I thought having her in my corner would be good for me. It was becoming evident she was in touch with my sisters and they were talking about me, I could tell.

I knew they were mocking my upcoming nuptials, my decisions lately and me as a person. It hurt knowing that and only made me feel less of a being. My wedding was soon and all I wanted to do was run away, hide and die.

Damien was winning and I knew now he wanted me to look unstable, because he had indeed made me that way. He had ripped the light from my soul and now used what was left just to control. I was losing a battle I didn't even have a chance to fight for because I allowed it to get that way. Because I thought I deserved it, and because I was broken now into tiny pieces, littered on the ground for all to walk on.

Bella

"Looking at the qualities of a person can in fact help you stand stronger, and be a stepping stone in your own self-growth"

I had heard that not one of 'the girls' that were invited to be in my wedding party, wanted to even attend. That was my sisters and even now Stella. It was all a sham and only made me feel more trapped. I felt as a nobody and alone in my horror, that was soon to face me.

Do you have any idea how hard it is seeing those shows on TV, with family, weddings and sisters? Knowing you never had anything remotely close to that. It broke my very heart.

The only one I could even open up to, was a bridesmaid that was also with a Hells Angel. She was a beautiful Russian girl who'd just had a baby with a member. I clicked with her and even admired her strength. To this day I believe she is a remarkable person.

She was crazy and she gave me a spark of truth when we conversed. Her boyfriend was a "known man-whore" with the ladies and she never tolerated it, even burning his clothes on the front lawn and spray painting his garage with profanities about him.

She was cute how fiery she could get but what was different; her boyfriend, this Hells Angel- wouldn't beat her or demoralize her, like mine did. These were two full patched members that treated their girls two different ways. Her boyfriend was Damien's best man at our wedding. *He is a notorious Hells Angels and to me she was Bella; a beautiful person.*

Bella told me she didn't trust Stella in the slightest, but never once did she belittle her either. It was nice knowing that she could see through certain characters, like I could; without being spiteful. I loved this Russian lady. She would become a fast friend of mine, even an ally of sorts, for a short while, anyway until two worlds drove us apart.

The full swing of things, were well under way for the wedding and I was anything but the blushing bride. I couldn't even fathom how wonderful planning a wedding was, because I didn't get the opportunity to. So hearing my Russian "Bella" talk about what her wedding would be like and what dress she wanted, made me wish I could have choices like that. Our relationships were opposite to each other, even though we were both Hells Angels girlfriends and mothers.

She wanted a big, poufy red velvet, wedding dress. I could see how stunning that color would look on her and I lived some of those dreams and moments, vicariously through her own idealistic visions.

Bella had a thick mane of healthy, long, almost black hair that touched her bottom. She had brown, almost black eyes that looked like dark chocolate. Her doe like eyes, were full of strength as opposed to mine being weakened by the storm. Her lips were swollen to the perfect proportions of big and perhaps succulent; not that I was into that.

Bella had been on the cover of Playboy Vixens recently and also a dancer, at the infamous "Brandi's" in downtown Vancouver, B.C. The place where Ben Affleck was caught with a dancer/entertainer that made the headlines. I knew the girl who ran to the tabloids and exploited that story, for money. That twinkie was later fired from work and lost a few friends because of what she did. This was a world I knew, even though I was never a dancer some of my close friends, were.

She was a stripper, yes. Unlike the stereo-type that follows certain labels, she was but a whore, slut or someone who slept around. She was, who she was and she had a confidence that I never would have and that is something to be admired.

A lot of people do not have confidence or pride in themselves and no matter how big, tall, skinny or even what color your skin is, we all deserved to feel beautiful and exude that air of confidence. It was something I searched for in others. In her I found that.

I never judged her at all. I had heard through the grapevine that people had thought I was a dancer at some point, but that was the furthest thing from the truth. I know that Damien's first wife was once a dancer/stripper but she was young at the time and I also believe that was how she met Damien. I, on the other hand, never was; nor have I ever been. If I had even tried to swing around a pole, I would fall flat on my face with my two left feet. But I didn't care if people thought that of me, it was a lot less humiliating then the pig squeals that constantly screamed in my head or the little way I felt about myself.

Bella loved the father of her child relentlessly, passionately and fiercely. I do not believe she would've ever given him up. I thought for sure one day they would get married, and she would be planning that wedding that she 'oh so wanted'. Those two are matched perfectly. They were two separate sticks of dynamite but meant, I believe, to be together.

Bella was one of my bridesmaids and I even wished she was my maid of honor. She made things fun for me and she made me feel human with regards to what I had to live with being with Damien a Hells Angel. She understood the crazier sides of being with a guy like that and she didn't have the two faced genetic of talking with the "family" that only bastardized and doubted me at every turn, nor would she agree with them. Like Stella had been doing lately.

She was the only part of the wedding I could be excited about and with her around Damien wouldn't speak smack to me.

Like I said, she was strong and her strength was admirable. She lived by her own set of rules but also understood the traditional side of family and home, like I did.

Damien, I could sense that he was becoming more and more attached to me lately, possessive even in a non-dominant way and would behave proud and caring at least in front of others, but when it came to his crew or immediate family he didn't hold back to much- (only the raised hands and choking spells he now liked to administer regularly).

I believe it was from being around certain functions and mandatory events at the Hells Angels Clubhouse, we'd been attending. So he started being a little more convincing he was a newly engaged, about to married guy. With Bella and I being friends, it made him want to treat me nicer, or it was seeing how the other wives were treated, perhaps was slowly rubbing off on him. Or, it was the fact of me carrying constant bruises and abrasions that weren't reflecting too well for him with the guys. Whatever it was, he was either too busy or just allowing me more leeway. It allowed me to somewhat breathe with her around and the others. That I enjoyed.

I would grasp any amount of time that I was allowed to smile and be myself that I could get, but the wedding was starting to choke me and I knew if I thought it was bad before, it was going to be much worse later-married. I couldn't shake that foreboding feeling I was having and I couldn't keep putting a fake smile on my face forever, it was wearing me out.

It's embarrassing when everyone knows you get smacked around and they just shake their head or chose not to acknowledge it, but it's even more shameful for the person who has it happening to them, knowing they have to look you in the eye and pretend. As I was now forced to do. The wives would whisper to me and shared with me they knew and that allowed a little of the embarrassment to lift away. Knowing I had them, made me swallow my pride and shine once in a while.

Bella was getting a monthly paycheque from her spouse and one day when they were all conversing about it, she had asked me what I get for groceries and living expenses. When I told her that I get nothing, she was shocked and it left Damien embarrassed. He looked guilty but he also tried to cover it up. "Look what she gets! She gets Shang Ra la!" making it sound as if I was lucky to be in a huge house. That in itself was a joke as I was borrowing money from my step-father regularly, just to keep food on the table. It was sad. Damien controlled everything right down to how I spoke and the way I carried myself and the funds. I was allowed only what I was given.

My mind was continuously going back in time reliving events and analyzing my own life. I couldn't help it and I couldn't stop it. I had only myself to silently be with and I could never just be the regular person who could freely chit chat with others about my life. I was ashamed.

I remember during this time, thinking of when I was friends with everyone and people liked me around the clubhouse. How once I even thought of them all, as my friends. Now, anytime I had too much conversation or one too many laughs when we were out, he would remind me later, "how none of them were my friends and that they were only nice to me because of him".

He would tell me, when I tried saying I really like Bella and another wife I thought I was becoming close with, "That one word for him, and they would never talk to me again".

It left me robbed of feeling anything close to normal and left me very isolated and afraid of communicating too much with any of them.

Sometimes I would even get a discreet comment from a wife while we were out. "He doesn't have us fooled, stand up for yourself." It gave me a little courage and even brought a little life to my eyes and helped me enjoy our nights out a bit more.

But I could never stand up for myself like they said. I didn't want to live with the repercussions of what *would* happen later, when those very wives and people weren't around. I was slowly being driven from any part of who I once was and anyone that may remotely become my friend.

Some nights I would lay with my sons and speak about how they could never follow this road. It isn't cool and when they were old enough to leave, I would send them to UCLA and they could study whatever they wanted to; as long as they didn't follow in their daddy's footsteps, as long as they were far, far away from here.

Damien was getting upset with Bella's constant mentioning on what she gets and about how lucky "we" were, that we had our own pay-cheques from our men. (She had no clue and I believe that rubbed on Damien's nerves) Damien had put on a persona to cover his own em-barrassment and that bothered him. It was mentioned a few times and me I didn't say a word, because unlike her I received nothing. I could only wish I received something to live off of, so I didn't have to be hu-miliated asking my father for food and money all the time. I hated it and knew it wasn't right.

I also knew my older sister never has had to do that. I knew the husbands or boyfriends she has been with over the years and married to, they had taken care of her and their children; it was the normal way to be as a husband, father or even co-parent.

But his control over money was just another thing that mounted the shame inside me. I wasn't allowed to go to work, I was only allowed what was dispensed to me and that was only the scraps of leftovers of what he would give me. That was nothing and when I say nothing, I mean it. Sure I had nice clothes or food, but that was my step-father giving me his card to go to Costco, me taking that to get clothes for the kids. What Damien had was his, simple and how he would say he did all this and acted like he paid for everything, was in fact a lie.

The pressure of the date was fast approaching and there I was even blamed. I just agreed and privately mimicked him behind closed doors. Thought you could plan a wedding in 30 days…

Damien and I had to find a place to host this wedding and we had to do so fast because there was no way it was going to be at our 'Shang ra la', it just wasn't going to happen in time and our house was not going to be built to his satisfaction, in time. I knew he wanted to show off his newest creation or toy with this house but it wouldn't happen. So we picked Hazelmere, a golf course by the USA border.

It was a lovely spot and the managing lady in charge there had it all under control. In no way was it up to The Beasts expectations. He wanted helicopters and bling; he had this idea of 'fan-tab-ullous' and this wasn't it. I had no say, so I learnt early to just to be quiet.

I knew his family was coming and his charter but I still had no clue as to mine, or my immediate family that is. I still heard when I did speak to anyone, they didn't approve, nor were they coming. I had yet to hear from my little sister about attending and these girls were supposed to be my bridesmaids. It was just me and who I was I thought. Their casual treatment was the normal, so that feeling or the feeling of promise and care was not there from the beginning. I just stopped caring or pretended to, but secretly inside it actually broke me down.

It should've been more thought out I thought-this wedding and even planned, but it wasn't. Nor did my voice or dreams really matter even though I knew I would bear the brunt of blame or be at fault somehow.

I mean, c'mon, we were building a house worth 2.7million dollars. He had just ordered, from my understanding, a ten thousand dollar bidet toilet, for our bathroom. We couldn't afford a proper wedding? Or did everything he was doing, all on his own become just too much? The house, oh dear heavens, the house became the root of all excuses and mishaps from this point on. It encased him in a vice grip unlike anything I had ever seen done to a person and that worried me.

I honestly hated the house we were building, or he was building. It was cold and it had an air of darkness to it. It had the elements of home missing and a corrupt feeling that comes when you know there was a shady way in which something was acquired.

I was terrified to move into this fortress, absolutely terrified. I felt the evil that lurked behind these corrupt walls, which were being built. I felt it was built on blood money and I couldn't shake that feeling. I tried to explain to Damien that I didn't like it and he couldn't handle that I was not as enamoured by it, as he was. Stella and I knew the feelings I had were true, we both mocked it and thought it was only building his ego even more so.

All the Beast would say to me, is "Your such a lucky girl aren't you"/ and in front of anyone listening , like I was somehow privileged to be part of this dark house, of cement, rocks and coldness. Or was it married to the man who built it, because it became more married to him than I would ever be.

Life carried on as this year before the wedding, turned into months and soon to be only weeks away.

Shattered Hopes

"Toxic opinions, will leave a damaged heart"

Our house wasn't going to be ready for the wedding and I had to get a wedding dress still. This was one thing I thought I could do and feel beautiful.

My mother and Stella went with me, to one bridal store. I had wanted my sisters to be there, but this was spur of the moment really, not a plan that was well thought out nor the way I envisioned. Nor were they putting in any effort to make this memorable for me. Not that I could blame them. But I wanted my mom there, I really did and at least she showed up. I loved, love and to do this one thing for me, would mean the world to and she did come. That in itself helped me.

I tried on one dress and my mother broke down crying. She couldn't even stomach seeing me in a dress, with the bruises that sprinkled my arms, it only amplified her tears and made her face go grey.

I just wanted a good day, one moment to feel beautiful and like a bride but even that was not to be. Give me something to look forward to was all I wished. Not that it was her fault at all, if anything, it just added to the list of reasons not to marry him. But what choice did I have? He would just hunt me down again. I was not his spouse but his property!

I was grateful that I liked the one dress I tried on, so we bought it. My mother exited that wedding shop so fast and caught the ferry right back home. We didn't have lunch, we didn't look at magazines and we sure as heck didn't get all dreamy. It was a joke and it cut me to the core.

I remember looking at her and crying as I said, "don't worry mom, it will be okay". Trying to make her feel better, when I needed her to make me feel better. She just hugged me and held onto my shoulders; almost like a graze but more like a distant hug. She knew what I was up against, she knew and this was the hardest thing for her to do, for me. Stomach her own determination about regards to Damien; that she choose to run, as I have done countless times.

Stella just wrapped her arms around me in the parking lot after my mother made her hasty exit, while I continued to cry. I cried for all the times I wanted a special moment and never had a mother to share it with. I cried that my sisters were not coming to my wedding and not knowing what was going on, as even that was up in the air. I cried over every beautiful moment that was somehow ruined. But most of all, I cried to release the gut retching humiliating pain that was inside me about my family and my embarrassment to them. I cried because I was joke.

I was really alone in my own private hell. Sure I had a step-father that bought us food and got us a room when we ran for safety. But I couldn't help all those times thinking if this was any other daughter, she would be shipped off and safe to another country. Not begging for a few hundred dollars for a night in a hotel or begging with a look of utter loneliness for just one hug and hope of praise. I got what I deserved and that beat me further down. Everyone was right I heard the snickers and felt the taunts, I deserved this.

I cried and in between sobs I would say, "Stelly, if this was Sam's wedding they would be doing this and doing that. When it was Sabrina's wedding (twice) they flew here and there or planned for weeks and months. In no way have they done that with me about anything or any one of my special moments; from the births of my children, to graduating college(s) did I ever get even one moment of praise. I knew then that no matter the bruises on my arms, with my mother definitely, more than any other time before, that my family never loved me the same as they loved each other.

I knew my heart that ached for them to care about me properly but it was me they didn't like and with such conviction my love for them was one sided. I knew no matter how well I did or what I accomplished, they would never be proud of me, ever.

I also knew the way they gossiped about one another and that they talked just as viciously about me like that. They only heard the bad things and never took the time to acknowledge all the good I do. How could they make their judgements about me, when none of them lived even remotely close to me and haven't for fifteen years. Not once did any of them come to visit me, or hug me or even protect me. Not once did they ever take the time from childhood to now, to ever get to know me. That day will never be forgotten and it only alienated me from my family more than any other time before and Damien's words once again echoed and haunted the inside of every part of me, "my family never loved me or wanted me". He was right, I was a joke.

I know that I wasn't happy about the getting married, nor did I want to but me expressing that only led to the backlash, "THEN WHY ARE YOU, KERRI!" never taking a moment to know the full truth or the time to heal a wounded person in me, instead they didn't get the fact of who he was and the power he wielded.

I remember trying once to explain to my older sister about how Damien had planned this with me, before he ever knew me. Because he had a vendetta with my Kane, my first sons father and all I remember is hearing my sister say, "Your fucked Kerri!" and then "Go get help!!" like I was crazy and she hung up.

That day has echoed inside me for many years; doesn't matter what I say, it was always the same to me. Your no one, your nothing, we don't like you and stay away. Not that all that, was said by all of them , but the casual way I was discarded felt exactly like that. Each tone, each comment carried its own weight and I was alone.

I believe that was the intial moment of understanding that I had always been the blacksheep. I had always tried to say and do the right things to try and impress them, in some positive way. Even be accepted by them to no avail. Even if somehow I did get their attention and if one thing happened that wasn't right in their eyes, I was once again a loser to them. I would hear those exact words from their mouths; no matter what I did, who I helped or what I achieved, I was always going to be less in their eyes than anyone else. I was Kerri Krysko, the bad seed, the ugly one and the troubled sister. I was taboo in their eyes, not human in the least.

Their words hurt me and their disappointment dug just as deep as any word or bruise that I ever received from Damien. They were tearing me apart and I was only coming to realize this. Their abuse came in a volatile way, a hurtful way and one that hit the much wounded center of me.

Damien was happy I was going on this outing with my mother and Stella for my wedding dress; he had even kissed me as I walked out the door and said cheerfully to have fun and not to spend too much of my father's money. He appeared to have pure intentions, on this day, with me and for that, it made going home so soon all the more harder. My make up was smeared and my day had lasted less than thirty minutes, minus the driving and drop offs.

I walked into my apartment only a few hours later, after dropping Stella off; she had gotten a babysitter for the day for her children but the day was ruined by again my mistake. I just wanted to be alone, where I belonged and I went straight into my room, feeling more deflated than ever before by these people I loved, the very same people only I was proud to call family.

Damien, who stayed home with the children, came in expectantly looking to see how my day went and surprised to find me in tears and hurt. He had asked what happened in such a kind way and when I told him about my sisters not coming, (that I had asked to be in the wedding party) and my mother's reactions, he came unglued. He defended me like any devoted man would do; he defended me with such a passion that I could only wish he was always like this. He cared when he seen my true hurting heart and the tears washing down my face.

"Your family treats you like garbage! You should write a book about your mother! Look what they do to you! Don't worry baby, we are your family now. They are jealous of you, they've always been jealous of you.

You are living the life they want."

It was a surprising clarity that when he ranted those words, my automatic response was to stand right up and defend them. I became numb to it all and what had happened. I knew my mother just couldn't see the bruises he had caused, but I also knew my sisters never liked me and, in that regard, he was right.

As for holding me and caring about me in my sadness, it was in the way that I believed any doting husband should always do and for that I was grateful. But when he had said certain words about my family, I couldn't help feeling like it was only okay for him to hurt me; all of it just made me an emotional wreck. But I still inwardly defended them with might, I loved them wholeheartedly, they just didn't know any better but to always treat or talk to me like that.

Thinking back on it, it was good in a way because it helped me see that any special moment I did have in my short life thus far was never celebrated or commemorated by the people I cherished and held above all else.

Not many people who live through what I have get that type of clarity perhaps because they are so beaten down they're too numb; that I understand. Our strength and wisdom come from places we do not expect. I had lived so long already trying to be a pleaser to so many that it was second nature when good things did happen for me, I never expected any type of celebration or congratulatory fanfare turned my way and when it did, I didn't know how to receive a compliment. Even being told I was pretty, I stand there shocked not knowing what to say, hiding my teeth or thinking their lying. Still, even now.

I knew, more than ever, that I would never be treated the same as my other sisters. That was okay because I had my own family and that was made up of my sons and my sons alone. Not my husband, no folks I was not fooled. I tried relentlessly to leave, so many times but where do you go when you have nothing? And what do you do if you expose the one safe place, a woman with a passionate heart told you about because of a world-wide organization of Hells Angels, that you're very own soon to be husband threatened you with? Do you use that escape route to put others in jeopardy, or do you take the mental anguish and brutal beatings begging to the gods just to die? My baby steps were made to freedom, and where others may have thought they were to slow, they were extraordinary to me.

Damien's behavior soon stepped up and became even more like a soon-to-be husband. He started saying he would like to give me a paycheque every month. So, all those chats with his best man and my bridesmaid had obviously made an impact; when you associate with certain people you can pick up their traits. Damien did that and said that he was going to start giving me twenty-five hundred dollars a month, to do with what I wanted. I was shocked but it sure did feel nice and made looking to the future at least a little brighter. Right then and there he walked back in the room I was crying in with a cheque.

I still however couldn't shake the hurt from him putting my family down to me but I did see the truth in them as well and that is why it hurt, because he was right. They didn't really love me and they didn't want to keep me safe. They made me feel as broken with their words as his were to me.

I chose to open a private account at the TD bank and save the money in case of emergencies. And that is exactly what I did, for a few months anyway. It made me feel so secure and was much better than being desolate with nothing. *I'm not saying the abuse stopped but if I wrote every instance down, you would likely wonder why I am alive or how I survived.*

I had no choice but to fall into the role of fiancé and just lived with the fact of this is all up to me now, as an individual. I never once gave up but fell into a Stockholm syndrome role, where I didn't accept what was going on, but lived with it. I knew there was a very small cushion for me to run with now however, in my bank account and that relieved some of the pressure.

"Search Kerri for the truth", whispered in my mind regularly, when manipulation happened or comments that threw me backwards. I told myself all the time on repeat, "hold on, you know what's right, you know what's real". To him I couldn't say if that was the case at all. I can say however it made things a little more bearable and sustainable, knowing I had a quiet mind all to myself, with the truth...

I was going to my doctor's office more frequently just for a place to rest and know there was someone out there I could trust. I told my doctor only a portion of certain things, because I know if he knew all that happened, the certain nights that Damien became enraged, he would have to follow protocol and call the police. But he never pushed, or prodded. He gave me someone I could trust and the reasoning I needed, to assure myself that I wasn't going crazy.

I needed to hear that from a professional authority because after I had been pummeled with mental abuse in that type of form, I was getting so twisted and confused, I began to doubt my sanity. Even you would wonder if you are going crazy with some of the control that he unleashed. So, my doctor's words soothed me and kept me aware of fact and fiction.

I even explained how my family treated me and started relaying that emotion and the offensive way they talked to me, which often played havoc inside of me. Their words hurt and I was starting to see that in itself, wasn't right. They had no filter around my children and the way they treated me in front of them was clearly wrong.

It was a realization, even perhaps an awakening inside of me and a clarity that was only slowly starting to seep in. They cannot do that in front of my sons, they could not, and I would not allow it. I never wanted that toxic opinion to taint my sons. They don't know me, and in no way possibly could, after this many years. It was a true eye-opener to realize how far and long I had allowed it to go on. But this was a process of awakening to the path I had choose to follow and the life I chose to live or ultimately wanted to truly live.

There was something with the way Damien worded things, there was a subtle change in him happening and tiny shackles were being raised up my back again and that left me anxious. I felt it and my radar was going off. I had no idea if it was the money that was changing him, the toys, and the power or if it was just him. Everything was a foggy blur around this time; my life and well-being were being tested. I had a hard time forcing myself to be as he dictated, I should be. It was making me, breaking me and I knew it was ruining me.

Then shit hit the fan one night and the reign of terror started on the streets of the lower mainland we call, Vancouver. The organized gangs rose, the money became thick, and the community got a taste of the violent life on the streets that flooded into their quiet neighborhoods.

All else aside, it was time to make sure my own stay protected, everything else was tossed aside as the strategic lifestyle took precedence.

Glorified Hearts Of A Soldier

"Not all who live a certain way are bad, mean or brutal: some have more heart than even the most law-abiding citizen"

Damien was at his weekly meeting and the boys and I were enjoying our evening at home in the apartment when there was a sudden knock on the door. It was always alarming to me when someone would just knock on my door; you have to ring the buzzer to get upstairs, so whoever it was I must know or maybe someone who lived in the building.

I looked through the peep-hole this time, as before it was a strategic couple pretending to be something than what they really were. This time however it was Damien's super good friend (who was not an HA member), Big E, standing outside in the hallway. I quickly let him in.

He said that 'Boss' had instructed him to come over and sit with us until he got home.

I knew it was something serious because of the way that Big E

worded it and how he just showed up with no warning. I was okay
with serious; I could handle anything like that as long as it didn't hit
me where my heart was. I tried to probe him for information but he
wouldn't budge. I liked Big E, I could be myself around him and knew
he was a good guy inside. He had a heart of gold and that's how I have
always seen him; one big gentle oaf who could stand his ground with
the sheer imposing size of his great strong hulking body; but truly he
was as gentle as could be.

He told me that even if Damien took all night, he would be sleeping
here on my couch and was *not* allowed to leave. I was okay with that because I trusted him. Whatever had happened it was serious and I knew
that then without a doubt.

Damien did however show up a few hours later and was as bright
eyed as could be. He was cool and confident as he assessed our apartment. He said he had to chat with Big E outside for a bit and then
would come back upstairs to explain a few things.

When he walked in he swooped me right into his arms and showered me with kisses. He was a man when he wanted to be and sometimes all I could do was truly fall into the wonderfully gallant side of
him. I cherished every moment of that side of him, especially when it
came out as protector as opposed to beast. I soaked up every amount of
goodness I could when it shined through and just maybe it was the not
knowing and tonight of all nights. There was no flakiness, nor was there
an underlining trickery to this man in that moment. It was Damien,
Lucy and the beast all rolled into one.

Like I said his eyes were dancing and bright, like he was getting off
on something, an adrenaline high. He was The Beast and he will always

have a "Lucy" inside of him, of that I am sure! This night was one of those nights and this night I could handle it because his venom was not directed at me. I waited until he was finished groping me with his ardent side of lust and when he put me down he said the words that I knew eventually, as any wife/girl, I would have to deal with.

"You might have to go somewhere with the kids to hide and be safe until we get this under control, but we will see, and anytime I am gone Big E will be here. Some of the wives are packing up right now and flying out of town. Places are being shot up and it's not safe here for awhile, until things are back under control"

I knew it was serious but I also knew somehow we were going to be fine. I knew nothing would happen to the boys and I, but I didn't know about Damien. I never knew what pockets he was into or the people he played with.

I have a sixth sense about me and right then all I could relish in was the protective side of Damien or somehow I thought I could protect us. I felt safe with him when he was like that and I knew he wouldn't cause me harm tonight; he was on protection mode. It was rare. This side of him showed itself on few and very far and in between occasions.

I believe it was the first time, in as long as I could remember that I just wanted to snuggle right up into his chest and hold him. It was more so now than ever and it was because he genuinely showed me he cared and because he needed me, he actually needed me.

I didn't want any harm to befall him and I still don't. I didn't want to have to get a knock on my door one day and have to tell my children that their never going to see their father again. I wasn't that ruthless and I never would be. Nor would I wish that on anyone.

Like, what was wrong with me? I was willing to go down in a blaze of bullets as long as I knew there was love and protection. I was even more warped then I thought. But it's a part of what and who I am. Make me homeless, but with love and I would be okay. Just don't hurt me, don't hate me and don't change me and I, Kerri Krysko, in return, would protect all that mattered with my life. No matter who you are or if I was with you, or not.

In that exact moment I got a little piece of me back and it offered me a thread of hope that maybe one day it would always be like this; without a life-threatening reign of terror to bring it out. I wished for that more than anyone will ever know. Not about me with the beast but me as whole and as a person. I got Kerri back and it took me by surprise. It gave me a boost of true genuineness that it filled what had been missing, my own soul back.

I also knew whatever he was jumpy about, I wasn't, and it just didn't scare me. I understood the black-sheep and I understood the weak, because I was one as well. How could I not? Look where I have been and what I've also gone through.

As with any city there are gangs, street thugs, crime, chaos and corruption. There are rivalries and there is also a code of ethics you followed; honor amongst thieves if you will. It's how it always will be, since before we *all* even existed.

DO You Follow me?

You didn't harm a child, you didn't steal from family and you didn't cause trouble in another's territory. That's usually just the basics, but every now and again there was someone or another who wanted what the other had.

They would use their status or minions to start trouble, fights and in the end innocent people suffered, our communities suffered and even the criminals and their families suffered, it's a no win situation.

It's also why there is Gang Taskforce and why there are gangs, its life and it's the true divide between the people who lived within society's rules and people who didn't. It's the way, and it is fact.

I am not going to tell you the why or the dramatics of my opinion or what I may know, but I can tell you the gist of it and the scope of danger, that this uprising of thugs in our streets caused.

A lot of people, like the cops, think they know, the how, the who and the why. But do they really? Do they only try to figure out a crime scene to draw a conclusion? Or do they dig deeper and try to find the root of the problem and perhaps start from there?

No one is ever going to know the real reason behind something and when the lid is sealed shut and mouths are closed you *ain't* getting nothing out of a thug, gangster or likewise. It's the law of the street. It is called solid, real or even top left but when its spoken, old school follows and real school knows.

We can go around every day nabbing criminals, putting people away and solving crimes, but it is inevitable that it will happen again and the revolving door will continue; one crime solved and dozens more go on. So you have it, the core problems are never really truly solved in the first place, are they?

We end up seeing a few infamous people, a name in the papers, a face behind the crime and the victims that are left in its wake. No one wins and people hurt, all the same way. That pain never goes away, that crime is never truly solved and those memories stay on, haunting all of us who've had to live through it.

In turn our experiences, plus opinions labelling the next fool that steps up and rises to the occasion. To rape, pillage and kill another; it's sad, its wrong and it's the truth.

When someone can't get a job, because of their looks or background how are they going to eat? Or where are they going to rest? Well they become creative in finding a solution; they become thieves and they become criminals. Sooner or later they become invincible; or so they think…

Ask yourself this; what were you like at sixteen or what were you like at twenty? Ask yourself that. Then remember the times you put the pedal to the metal and roared down that street, unbeatable, carefree and innocence not yet tainted with your first broken heart or your first real taste of being an adult.

Think of that for one minute and then add the fact that these street kids, most likely came from a broken home and the struggles they face actually come from within. Their scars and damage are invisible to the naked eye, the scars that are so deeply embedded inside that only they carry the sheer weight of them, only they carry the hurt that accompanies them.

Now add a friend that gives you what you wanted most in this world, acceptance, promise of family, laughter and you become stronger, bigger and more self-assured than ever before.

Now that promise arises, the promise you waited for all those nights as a child, lonely, sad, afraid and wondering why these police that you heard about didn't save you or protect you and didn't help you. Why all those times you wished to be helped and no one came to rescue you, or answered your prayers, wishes, hopes and even dreams and still there was no one to trust.

But your new friends now do and your new family of friends promise you these things that you only dreamed about and had yearned for with as a child, when everyone else had this things. That it left you empty with a yearning and endless ache.

The only thing you wanted was to make something of yourself, be someone, but you'd been dealt a shitty hand, early, on with no hope, knowledge or promises of a brighter day. Only the haunting memories of all the times you continued feeling that you had no one, lost, lonely and afraid.

What do you do?

The only thing you know how to and you embrace it, you revel in it and you allow yourself to feel great, fabulous and now even successful. But most of all, you belong, you finally belong and you're *someone*. You are actually a someone. You have a family that would die for you, never to turn their back on you. You have this thing you have been missing called; solid, real and loyal.

You're all of a sudden, a *somebody*. You're strong and no one can hurt you anymore, no one can hurt your mother who was abused, no one will ever in your mind hurt anyone close to you again, because now you have a real family and friends.

Now it is YOU who is big enough to protect them and stronger. Now you're a somebody who everyone wants to be around and never

ever, to feel that alone again. Its feeding you and inflating your ego even more.

That promise and status builds you up tenfold and all that flash and scratch your making screams success, validation and having all you only dreamed about as a young child.

What you're making is what a person working a traditional nine-to-five job can only dream of yearning.

So now you're invincible, you're omnipotent, you've made it and you're a big important someone, or so you think. ......It messes with your head and it's become a new level of stressful.

All of a sudden inside, your heart is saying other things, like maybe this is wrong.

No one may be hurting you now, but shit man, you're hurting other families and it weighs on you something heavy, whispering silent guilt. You're tired but you keep going and going, never really stopping. Its become hard living the only way you know how; because no one gave you a chance, no one gave you a taste of the good life, the normal life and the stability you needed. But, they gave you a gun, they taught you to never ever be taken from again, they taught you to be strong. You've got a family now who cares, like really truly cares; they've got your back now that's all that matters- then your conscience kicks in...your growing up ....

The money keeps you dressed in all the finest, top of the line, name brand clothing. Your ride is what all the guys dig and the chicks that throw themselves at you now, become just as fast as your life, ever revolving and ever flowing.

One day you will crack, you're not balanced, you're going too fast and there's no brake on the ride you climbed on willingly; there's no way to stop and **BAM!** Someone's dead and by your hand, by your words, by your gun.

Now you live a nightmare but you aren't going to let anyone see you weak again. You aren't going to fall, you can't feel like you once did, so you toughen up and keep going ..... until one day that saying comes back to you as your laying there, all alone, everything gone, likely dead dead and before the lights go out you remember the code ... "Live by the sword, die by the sword"...and you wonder what it would've been like to just have been loved, as you say your prayers and beg for forgiveness for becoming the kind of person you never dreamed you would become.

Now, that's the life of a thug, that's the inner heart of a criminal. And where we as people go wrong every day is by judging too severely and not embracing the one that got lost inside their mistakes and poor choices; by not giving them a chance when they needed it, before it got too rough and before all those lights were extinguished.

This is what happened on the streets of the west coast in 2008, when all hell broke loose because a bunch of kids, who happened to be brothers, became gun happy and bloated with the greed for power. But who got hurt by this?

Everyone! Everyone did.

The crimes have never truly been solved, have they? Not when every last one of those brothers, but one, is dead. Now how did that work out for these kids, huh? Not very well, indeed. Countless victims along the way were hurt, killed or robbed of their loved ones because of the association. Nothing stopped the madness because it's still happening, new ones rising and old ones falling, it's an ever revolving and constant evolution.

That result, to me, hasn't solved anything but only gave us countless grave sites. That, to me, isn't life; that to me is heartbreaking.

I can't judge and I can only thank everyone and even the gangsters who did their best to stop the violence and reign of pure terror that was happening to others in our communities. I have no harsh judgements for these people, because to me they were only lost- without anyone to just stop and give them hope, when they needed it. Before it was too late, at their own- crossroad; not yours, not mine but at theirs. Only they will or you as someone living through it will know…….

But you know what? These kids looked up to the big guys, the higher up gangsters, and thought hell If I can't be like you, I'm just gonna kill you, be bigger and be better.

This attitude is new school and guess what, countless innocent victims lost their lives because things got too heavy and the people they should've been able to turn to, when they were young, were the ones that were nowhere in sight. The people who should've shown them the right way or guided them a little better, didn't. I ain't going to be like that for my sons, and I ask you whoever reads this- are you?

It goes both ways though, doesn't it? Because, in that crazy world, they in return, have chosen labels for the society around them. It's the divide that will remain, until the bars and blindfolds are lifted and a little understanding is given.

Like I have mentioned before, out here on the west coast, there is money and the money is thick. Armoured cars were being driven by twenty year olds. The guns were rampant, mayhem ensued and tempers were ready to flare, egos inflated and no one could stop the collision course that train wreck was on. Lots of people died tragically. Some of those people I knew.

I don't pick a side because no one wins in this kind of scenario, no one, and there was no way I was going to allow my boys to live this life.

I wasn't going to run either because I knew I was solid and if anyone could talk a person off the ledge; it was me. I knew the rules, the game and I also knew the good life. I had watched it from afar and I liked it, now I just had to figure out a way to get there.

So this night I held onto the one person I normally wouldn't have and hoped by dear god above that somehow he could be saved, woken up and healed. I would hold him tonight and give him the solace he needed but I knew more than ever that I couldn't carry on this way, I just couldn't.

My loyalty was to my children and that's what a real mother offers, protection, safety and that chance at the good life. I just hoped that maybe their dad would wake up and realize this too before it was too late. Sometimes a wake-up call is in order and I did gather my courage from helping others, so here is where my formulated plan begun.

The understanding of it all, this life, this lifestyle surfaced and I knew then that I would stay true to everyone I had met along the way, but I would give my sons the life I had never be granted. I would embrace all people, all life, all backgrounds and all ranks but I would not walk through the fire with them any longer.

It was time to use this as a chance to be free. It was time to show my loyalty to my sons. It was time to be strong and fight for what I believed in, even if that meant waking up and taking on The Beast......

In memory of the countless victims who gave their life, lost their life, a child, friend, mother or father to the streets ~ may you always rest in peace and know that you were loved ~ Kerri Krysko

Lustful Power

"Stepping stones to fated destinies or hopeful dreams"

I was watching Damien a little more closely, now, paying more attention to exactly what he was getting into. Something felt off. It had nothing to do with this rivalry on the streets either. It was watching how the money was changing him, it was hearing how every conversation was about what he had, what he was building and what he was doing.

It was shady. I couldn't understand or even get over his partner Chucky. It bothered me watching this grown man sacrifice his very life to Damien and I didn't like how Damien treated him, nor did I like how all of a sudden Chucky's long-time friends were getting chummy with Damien. I had seen that before, it was exactly what Damien had slowly been trying to do with my family; it was sneaky, wrong and very manipulating actually.

My heart constantly wept inwardly or even cringed for Chucky, but I couldn't say anything because I knew he would just shoot everything right back to Damien and tell him. I watched closely at Damien's stronghold over him and knew somehow I would do whatever I could to get Chucky to realise maybe the medication he was on wasn't by his choice. It was just exactly how to accomplish that which left me lost.

Damien had the construction mortgage of 1.2 million going with the restructure of our house, he also had the income from his excavating company and the ambulance service (he owned with Chucky) in the oil patch, out in Alberta.

It was a lot to manage, so when he started getting phone calls from Mexico, I knew it was only a matter of time before I caught the fallout from his stress. And again, I would wear the marks, more so in my heart and to follow on my body.

I also knew he was getting his hands dirty, being greedy. I watched it with the very house he was building and then down to his "crew". I was very, very well aware of this. I didn't like it and I hated it when people got hurt or burned along the way. I trusted his suave business sense, but I didn't trust how much he was throwing around numbers, demanding on the phone with Mexicans and just the audacity of how he portrayed himself. Or demanded they do this, or that when clearly whoever was on the phone needed time or just wasn't into it. Maybe, just maybe things do not happen in a day, but take patience, perseverance and actual knowledge. I knew or could only assume they were back-peddling on the phone as he would become dictator in a convincing, demanding sort of way. It was different and that's all I knew.

Now I have been around business owners my whole life, know them well; as I watched my own step-father run a multi-million dollar company for 15 years. I seen how he managed things, when there was a good year and even a bad one looming. But comparing the two, my step-father didn't have conversations so brazenly open about money, nor did he spout that off in a demand: secretaries handled it and when cheques came in, they were put in a drawer until there was a deposit. If there was late payments, it went through the proper channels and those cheques were substantial in amount. My step-father never once dipped his hands into those funds, he received his own paycheque, properly and some months he wouldn't take one as he wanted his own company to thrive. The money for jobs he was doing, went towards his company and I felt my fiancé was dipping and using his own personal accounts, as opposed to a legitimate company, that had payroll-without cash and a secretary, banker, office ect....

I also know it doesn't always have to be big numbers, fat cash and large amounts. It has to start first with just a thought, then a piece of paper and so forth. A gradual implementation of an idea that then needs to be brought to fruition. Even leaving a person broke and falling down. Things take time and for the Beast, it was always now, now, and now.

Something felt off and if I had any say in the world, I would've had it stopped. But again, my soon-to-be thought I was a mere trophy and not smart in the least; when in actual fact while in college my class determined me most - to be CEO of a major corporation. There my friends he had it wrong. I would've made it better for everyone but was never given a chance. I would have succeeded where he failed I believe. Because to me you need to have class and that was something that just couldn't be bought!

I could never do that and this bothered me in more ways than just the obvious.

I worked ever so diligently to not upset him that it once again, started making my skin crawl. I couldn't take being fake, I wanted to scream. I found myself mimicking him, when his back was turned, almost indeed making myself sick. I couldn't understand how he could have his hand in so many pursuits and so many people's pockets. I didn't like it;

I didn't like it at all.

He may have been giving me a monthly stipend now for 2 months but I was banking it away, for emergency use only. I knew a time would come and I would need it. I knew that if he found out, he would take it all away from me as well. It was the way of him with me. Anything that was remotely mine, he had to own it, or have it.

I watched him spend like crazy, from ten thousand dollar toilets; to travertine tiled floors that only made the house feel even more unwelcoming and cold. That it was in fact, ridiculous. It may have been every girl's dream, but I was not fake. It was my worst nightmare, I swear. My eyes were being forced wide-open to watch this charade of perfection, when in reality, if you cannot afford it; don't buy it. I grew up from rags, to a steady healthy family home once my step-father made something of himself. I knew the way truly successful people live and it's not house-poor, nor is it like this.

I was ready to implode with trying to suffocate all the emotions that raged inside. This falseness was waning on me. I started comparing to everything around me, and it was something that wasn't honest or even real to me, it was as if I was in a constant foggy haze and I would get tiny glimpses of sunny days.

I wish I had realized sooner, that I was a very empathetic person and could feel emotions other people couldn't sense or feel. I didn't know at the time, that my whole life I had been slowly building one of my greatest traits, born from a great sensitivity. I am most proud of this trait that allows me to connect with people on a deep level. I was learning the art of reading people and feeling, more so then hearing. Perhaps this is why seeing Chucky robbed of his self-esteem left my own self broken inside for him. Then felt that in others as well. It helped me to understand even the most horrific of circumstances. I believe it made me an empathetic person who could bottle feelings up inside and still feel things others couldn't. It was a trait that could amplify other emotions, such as deceit; I could tell just by looking at someone if they were abusive, or if someone was lying, I believe it was why the feelings of edginess and fakeness were starting to wear me down and make me actually gauntly, sick.

I couldn't just put a quick smile on my face after he slapped me just because someone showed up, or the fact that he thought it was okay for him to degrade and belittle me. If that wasn't enough and I didn't agree with him or my facial expression didn't convey that I deserved it, he would than give me a lesson on how to look and speak; it was just all becoming too much.

My life was literately and figuratively messed up. The control was revolting and nothing but a bitter taste inside. It was anything but the glamour he claimed it to be or others may have thought.

Even cops thought, wow, look at all that money, the jewelry and the houses, thinking it was *purdyyyy*…I heard it in passing whenever there was a pull over or conversation from some off chance that Damien pissed them off or gave them a reason to approach us. (now perhaps it wasn't that and in fact they were mocking towards it all as I was)

However, you could see the envious looks from other people, all around us, it was pathetic and really it was getting quite old. I watched certain old friends, or unsuspecting individuals treat me differently, on a daily basis, thinking I had it all when they never took the time to look within my eyes and see the dull, bottomless depth of them. (Like the woman in the store-prime example)

I found the humor in all of it, often sharing those emotions with Desiree and her agreeing with me. She told me how even her friends have been treating her different because of the kids she would babysit and working for a Hell's Angel, as his babysitter'.

Or when she wore a support sweater that Damien had given her. She said it made her own feelings amplified because no one knew the pain of living like this and no one knew the truth. She couldn't understand why he was allowed to do these things to his family and would relay to me regularly, "how did he get away with it". She was messed up, with this treacherous life as well. I knew it confused her, because while she became uplifted within her circle; I would talk her away from it, as I did with my own children.

It was a double edged sword to me and I was being stabbed at both ends. Except that I was older now, even wiser and knew that it wasn't as "cool" as some thought. I was at the top of that food chain and truly the bad asses when I was young were far more amazing to me than him, or what I was living now. I would wish for even that many times, over this now living hell.

I knew I had to try my hardest to shelter her from anymore incidents of abuse, even if I had to push her away and fake aloofness. I couldn't, I just couldn't see my precious girl fall victim to this lifestyle, nor could I have her hurt by him. I had seen her cracking under the pressure and watched one to many tears slide from her innocent eyes. I loved Desiree as a daughter, perhaps a sister even and her upbringing did NOT entail this!

It was close to the time we had to move into the big house and I was stalling, digging my feet into the ground not wanting to move but having no voice to say it. I knew if I stepped foot in that house, I could very well end up never coming out alive. I could feel it, his aggression was becoming too much, my body could only take so much more, and if he carelessly threw me the wrong way I could die, never mind the words he used towards me daily.

I was starting to truly dislike him and I have always cared about even the worst souls and that scared me. I felt I was betraying my own self by allowing the hatred that was slowly building up inside. I could no longer see any beauty in our lives together; only pain.

That was, I guess, where I needed to be to pull myself back up but at that time it was scary, it hurt and it was now foreign to me, not being the victim.

I thought he was turning me into him, I thought I was picking up his habits when I spoke mean words about him to myself, behind his back and when I whispered to my boys late every night.

Telling my sons, "never to be like dad, please never live his life" begging them even, "please it is wrong my baby boys, oh so wrong" only to continue "I promise, babies, I will get us away". I felt like I was erroneous for doing that and maybe I was, as you shouldn't treat another parent like that, but I had to for their sake and their very impact on this world, with their lives. I still however felt I was the problem.

Treasured Thoughts

*"To think I gave it one more chance, or looked for
another shred of hope, when all he did was spit in my face
and laugh at me with his friends"*

It was just past the supper-time hour and Damien had just walked in the door. My dining room table was located across the path of the kitchen floor and I had his food laid out for him when he arrived. He looked to be in a good mood, brilliant even and not all fluffed up in leather and scrubs. He had started dressing a bit better than when I first met him; with Hawaiian shirts and Levi's from the construction warehouse. Now he wore designer jeans, a white tank- under a long sleeved, or short sleeved shirt. He was spunky and more my age bracket I guess. I mean a suit with French cuffs, casual jeans or even a leather/modern jacket would've been better in my eyes, than the Hawaiian shirts. But that was his era, his time and he liked it-so did many others, but now however he dressed more modern and upbeat.

I asked him that evening, after he was done eating if he could sit down with me at the table. I wanted to talk to him and told him that I had something to share with him. I casually and slowly tested the waters with him as he sat down. I wanted to not just hit him with "statement form material" or did I want him to think that in least.

I wanted him to see compassion in my eyes and not go or take it to another level and importantly I never wanted him to think I was hiding something from him. I was an honest person but he was someone I had to be weary of, he didn't make me feel I could truly trust him; let alone with my inner most thoughts, but I had to try. I had to and I remember being very, very cautious as I garnered up the nerve to tell him about my diary. The journal that Stella said I should *NEVER* show him.

I had to read and show it to him. It was something, I felt he deserved to hear, 'me, Kerri Krysko' being my actual self.

I had to start being true to myself and I knew I wrote those feelings down because I was hurt inside. I had to get it all out, I was suffocating. I never knew, until part way through writing it, that it was for/to him. When I bared my soul on that paper; I had done it to release those pent up emotions and with the purest of intentions. How could that be used against someone, and there I found my conviction to be honest with him. I also knew I had to let him see the hurt and tears he inflicted on me, for him to see the truth. Why I needed to read it *to* him. I needed him to see the truth. I NEEDED TO KNOW if it had any sort of an impact on him. or if he even cared.

I was so upset about all he had done, from the set-up of first trying to meet me, to his vendetta with Kane, the words he spoke to me and ultimately how he treated me like a dog. I needed to see if these were just moments for him or if all of this *was him* and his true intentions.

I needed to know and I had to, before I ever moved out of my apartment and into the mansion AND most definitely before I married him.

My very life depended on it but even with emotion and feeling what would I really accomplish? Verification that he didn't care or that he was so self-absorbed, that I actually meant nothing? Could my chest really take anymore hateful snide remarks and could I find the strength to finally severe the tie that bound us? Or was this showing him my weaknesses for further torment and abuse. Could exposing the truth mean freedom? I had to try.

I had no idea going into this, what would happen but I thought or hoped for something nice, beautiful even. I thought maybe he would actually hear me, he would throw his brutish arms around me and hold me, as he said he was sorry. I thought and wished for that with everything I had left inside me. I needed to see the human side of Damien. I was searching for hope, a promise and even maybe a future. I needed to believe in us again and I was willing to give him the benefit of the doubt- that everything, the lifestyle, his previous drinking anything and all of it had gotten to his head. I needed the human shell, to be exposed to what lay beneath.

When I asked him to sit down because I wanted to share my very heart with him and bare my soul, I honestly thought he would be nice and even compassionate towards me. I really wanted to prove Stella wrong in some regard and I also wanted what I had written to be out in the open, not to be some hidden papers somewhere. I just wanted to be me and I felt I could this night. I felt he would listen to me and even if he did get upset, my tears and hurt would stop his eruption and perhaps he would finally, truly, hear me. I just wanted to try my hardest to fix things and I no longer wanted to hide who I was. I wanted to be me, so I didn't have to be his mannequin any longer or step ford wife.

I thought everyone had a heart in them and it just took different ways to reach them and in my lapse in judgement, a moment of weakness, I let the wall down. I was allowing The Beast into my world of existence and worst of all into my inner thoughts.

I let The Beast into my sadness and my high hopes for this outcome were smashed down, thrown in my face; as he lunged at me. He ripped the papers, not even three pages into me reading them, from my hands as he insultingly mimicked me, accompanied with his snarled lip, voice of mockery and hateful stare.

The tears poured from eyes, as I pleaded for him to give them back; I wanted to read to him what my heart was saying. I tried and begged like a fool to give me this chance and for some reason he handed them back to me, as we sat at the cherry wood table in our dining room. He sat across from me as I slowly continued reading him my words with every true emotion I had, he tilted his head back n forth like I was nothing more than a freak.

I was humiliated and to me he was heartless. I tried to keep reading and he just shook his head saying I needed help, it was there I stopped, rose and went to just walk away; but he had other plans for me and what I hoped for by trying to do this, ended in a another night of horror.

Damien liked to pull my hair and drag me around, it was his way of rendering me useless and having control. I tried to run to the bathroom and lock myself in but I didn't even make it remotely close. I knew the only way to pacify The Beast was to listen and never, ever show emotion; but that's hard when he hurt you, that's even harder when you have heart and his words sear you, as if you're being branded, like I was.

It was his method for total domination and I knew this night it was my fault, this night was my own stupidity for hoping for the best. This night I would be put in my place without a black eye but a mentality of utter control and supremacy by Damien, my soon to be keeper and husband.

"You just don't learn do you pig? You don't learn to just shut the fuck up and listen. You need a lesson on how to speak to me, don't you whore? Don't you?" was all I heard as he sat me down on his knee and pulled my hair back to look at him, in the living room.

This is all I remember as the night dragged on and on and he taught me how to talk in the right tone and answer the way he directed. It was tedious, it was sick and between each lesson I weakened. I became tired and numb, submissive and a robot. I felt as though I was fading and going to collapse, only for him to pull me up and throw me back down, just to carry on; so he had my full attention. This night lasted until the early dawn, when light was peaking in the windows and the birds sang their glorious songs and he was done with his savage temper. It wasn't the choking, or slapping my face to get me to start all over again when I faltered that broke me, but his interrogation and treatment.

His mental abuse was so extreme that it annihilates and destroys every part of your being or that is what it was doing to me. I was simply a body of emptiness and his continuous taunts, words and teachings became my hell.

My words were practiced over and over until he felt that I had said it right, with the perfect amount of pronunciation and enthusiasm (something I will never forget). You don't ask him to stop or it will continue longer, you do not do or say one thing wrong or your body is lifted skyward and thrown as if your trash. Then held in a position of complete agony.

I had just learned to do as he said and only hope for it to end. This never let up until dawn and I was officially broken and mere shadow of the person I ever was.

I do not know how I survived after that. I don't get it; it was the type of personal agony that would and could break the strongest souls. I was less than nothing by the time he was done and my sons were protected once again, by their mommy not crying out in pain, by their mommy silently taking what was given and listening as she was told.

They will never know they gave me strength while they slept and many times I would let my mind slip to them as he tormented me. I would take myself to a place so deep within just so I could endure his treatment. His mentality was as twisted as a soulless demon towards me. He would know when I was fading as he would tap my face saying "wake up, wake up " in a taunting voice hovering over me, or oh so close to me. He wanted me to jump, he wanted me to be scared, and he wanted to control me. It was sick, my only reprieve was that it wasn't sexual this time; it was purely asserting his place as master.

I had only slap marks, red spots around my neck and bruises on my arms; this time. I appeared to get away unscathed but the mental abuse will forever stay inside me; the bruises that aren't visible to the naked eye, the bruises no one carries now, but you.

It's like choking you until you're about to pass out and then bringing you back; only to do it again and again and again. With the light slowly seeping into the windows, he was done or was finally tired. I tried to just stay on the couch because I knew my sons would be up soon and my oldest had school , but he forcefully brought me to the room, the room I hated now, the room that was my once sanctuary and now with the bad tainted memories, was my dungeon.

He tried to carry on in there but just for the sake of prolonging; hearing in his voice that was no longer enthused by his teaching methods; he finally wanted to sleep. As he was drifting into sleep he ended with the final words that would have an everlasting sting, like lemon juice rubbed into a cut, "You will be perfect when I am done with you, perfect." It was a remark he said with candor and such conviction, that I could taste the acid like vomit in my mouth and feel the worthlessness, of being nothing.

I was lucky though because he didn't try to push himself on me, he just went to sleep. If I had a knife I would have buried it deep within his chest that early dawn, I know I would've. It's like someone is abducted and finally they have a chance at freedom , a chance at life again but they have to kill the person who took them, in order to truly get away; this was I, this was how I felt and this is where he awoke to see me staring down on him.

I was going on day two without sleep and was a queasy mess. But I never allowed my baby boys to see it. After dropping my son off at school; I once again went straight and directly to my doctor's office. I knew I had do whatever I could to keep my sons safe, in case something ever happened to me; the night that had just passed, made me more sure of that, then ever before.

I still never knew, that in some way I had stood up for myself when I expressed my thoughts because I never said them in a crude way. I may have succumbed to his pressure but I spoke the truth in that journal and I exposed it. If there was ever a time of illumination it was then. My now only thoughts were of safely preparing my sons for the inevitable, so sharing with my doctor gave me a notion that they would be safe....*I never told him that but my older son knew only to go to him, if something happened to me. There my notes and file would be opened; for my son to use and protect him and his brother.*

However, from this point on things were a thick haze and I was barely existing. I was no longer living. That was life as this Hells Angel's 'girl' and it wasn't pretty in the least. I was on survival mode, auto-pilot, even I knew it was no way to live but I stayed.

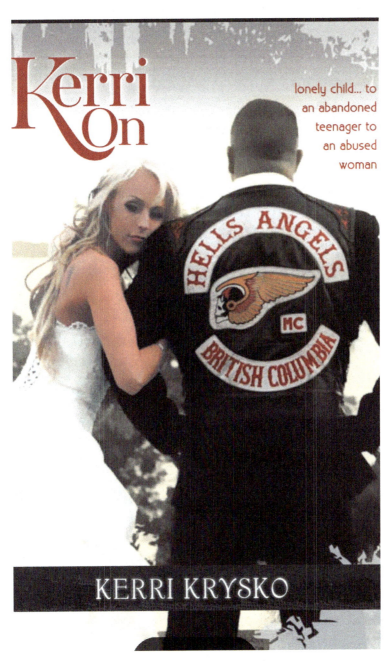

Picture of Kerri On Book

The TRUE wedding photo I used for cover of my first book, **Kerri On**

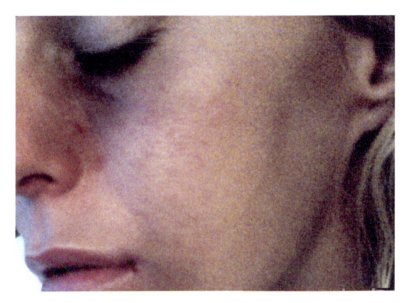

My once-run for safety the island.

Damien taking a picture of the look on my face.

Damien following me with a camera to snap a picture of the look on my face.

Mexico, 2007 - Damien holding my arms back for the camera

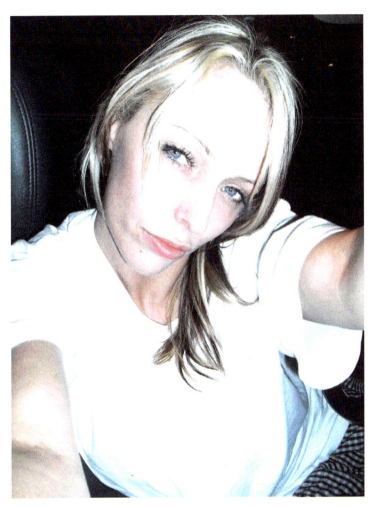

My emotional and and mental demeanor was crumbling 6 months before marriage to Damien.

Right before my wedding by a month - look how utterly beat down I was mentally and emotionally.

The truck I had to always smile in "for the pheasants" as he called them- the people I truly cherished.

"Shangri-La" the very house, that took precedence over all else in his life and was at the root of my very fear- cement fencing and fear of captivity

Kerried Away *cover, original*

Kerried Away cover, original

Damien posing for the camera.

Engagement photo shoot, August 2008

Best men at wedding

Wedding photo, August 8th
"The pier in which I
would one day run for
my very life, from"

My sons and I; 5months following separation.

Blake and me after I had left Damien and I found out the truth to why Blake moved out.

6 months after I left Damien with my good friend & bodyguard who kepy my children and I safe.

My nanny, best friend Desiree (left) and her friend she brought to babysit for wedding - they never came.

Sable, Jacob, Tristan, and Ashton… 8 months since freedom.
Healthy boys having fun.

One year following me leaving Damien

Broken

"It was easier to listen to the falseness of excuses, than acknowledging the evidence of abuse"

It was evident to all those around me something was wrong with me, no matter how much I tried calling for help , begging for it , the truth was never heard. Only the newest escapade, not the extent of stone wall I felt was barricading us in. I needed care, I needed validation and all I needed was to be heard. Like countless others had but just not my treasured family, not them.

I heard the snickers from loved ones and even associates. I heard the rumors that I was on drugs. I don't even do drugs, I couldn't even smoke a joint of pot, without having a full on paranoia attack. Had it occurred to anyone of them that I was being systematically tortured and abused, or to help me?

NO, because they couldn't or they wouldn't and by this time I couldn't care less. No longer was I reaching out for help, their words hurt me, their laughter stung me and their accusations were devastating. I knew the truth and I had the only person I needed to make sure my children were going to be okay long after I was gone. That was now my only thoughts, from awake to asleep.

I had nowhere left to go and the one place that seemed to accept me was our family doctor. I knew he could prove the truth of their lies and I also knew I could trust him, by now so much had already been said and seen. I knew my son, Ashton, could go to him and he would keep them safe. I even planted that into my sons head, over and over. "If something happens, just leave school, go directly to our doctor, he will help you get your brother and you to safety" my son would be strong and "say yes, mom, I love you". He had his best-friend Tristan and that kept him sane I believe.

Somewhere I had given up. I didn't have what families had, a sister or brother to call, a mother or father to run to, a best friend I could trust. All I had were my sons and a sitter who had already been exposed to far too much.

No one will understand this, or what I felt unless you have been there. I had such debilitating anxiety, years ago, from feeling alone and I believe it got its start because of my family and my feelings of abandoned. I wasn't yet ready to face that, mind you, but that's the truth. I seemed to be okay with being alone as long as there were no fists flying my way or words of hate swung at me, I was okay.

I tried once after that to run away and leave only to be hunted down and taken back home. The children were so shaken, I vowed never do that again, unless I called that private number I had hidden far away in my step-fathers office.

My step father was a source of friendship and support for me because he had lived life, too. He had overcome so much, going on to succeed in life. I thought of him as my father and the only one who ever raised me. I knew I could never hold a candle to his real daughter Sam, but I would soak up any love I could get and for him I was grateful. Even his new girlfriend was driving that once sacred bond and safety I had with my step-father away from me. She seemed to focus solely on Sam as his daughter and that only implemented my step-father, to start hiding our conversations from her. But driving the wedge that separated us a little more.

Damien seemed to zero in on my stepfather's money a little too much for my liking, always mentioning it as a derogatory remark or a passing comment. It kept me very aware and on watchful guard to protect the one family member, I held sacred above all else, except to my sons, of course but my step-father to me was my dad and my savior. I guess I felt as though he didn't judge me and that made him extra special to me.

Sam was his treasure and to me, he was mine. I would often think, "I wish I had that type of attention or that chance at life that she had received." She was able to take every course she wanted to, further her education and when she needed money she wasn't pleading in shame like I had to do. She was able to work for his company and get paid a regular paycheck and fly here and there; with the promise of a trust account to secure her future. She or him didn't know that the thousands she received a month could've truly helped me, but also what he gave me no amount of money could hold a candle to and that was someone to trust. It didn't bother me, but became only a wish I couldn't acquire. I loved Sam but not like I treasured our dad.

I would have given anything to give my sons, that type of secure upbringing, if I could have. I would use a little of that as a base to dream from and a base to know what I needed to offer my children. Different pieces of everyone gave me that type of relief and even hope.

I knew that I didn't stand a chance of having a relationship like my little sister and her father had. But he gave me a sense of belonging and friendship. I loved him as a real father and daughter could. I also knew it was only a matter of time before, one day he and I would go our separate ways. It was inevitable, as everyone else in my family had already given up on me. There was already a fiancé jealous of our bond and my mother had started a rumor a little while before this in one of her states, "That my step-father and I were sleeping together" It was sick! That rumor hurt me and my soon-to-be used it as a weapon to throw at me, continuously. My step-father was MY dad and it was okay to love him as a parent but he was also the only one left and time was ticking.

I stuck up for him with fierceness against my mother and in a way that bugged her. He was able to share his own personal thoughts with me and I wouldn't judge him; even meeting a lady in the office he was now dating but still being in love with my mother. He wasn't a person to give up on a marriage just because of rocky roads, and I believe that was hard on him, knowing my mother continuously pushed him away, with playing games.

I believe he needed a friend he could talk too; in turn I needed a person I could rely on. It guided me towards the truth and a belief that I was worth something more than the judgements placed on me, far too early in my childhood. He and I were just two people who could lean on each other and be honest about life together. It gave us a special bond.

My step-father would tell me that he observed the way I was treated and left out. He told me that the family who has lived so far away, didn't know who I was, and that I had a heart too big at times; allowing my once friends, many times take advantage of me and walk on me. He kept telling me that my kindness was a weakness of mine but that kindness can be one of the greatest strengths in world as well, he said be strong Kerri, you know what to do and do it in your own time.

He understood me and he also supported me, quietly and secretively without Damien's knowledge and his now girlfriends. He made sure his grandkids and I had food, even school supplies because he knew that Damien had never provided for us, until just recently that is.

Watching Damien mention my step-father and asking him to invest in some project made me livid. I only shared with my step-father the vehement truth; "do not do it"! I do not trust it and with this I see certain failure. I know that I was the one who placed that seed in my step-father's head but he was smart enough anyhow, not to invest and he didn't.

It was around this time, weeks before our sham wedding that I started wondering if maybe this was only moving forward because my step-father had money. I know it was a petty excuse and a delusional reasoning, an explanation as to why we were getting married; but I was now grasping at straws.

I never actually knew if my sister would even come to be my bridesmaid, as all I only heard, through the grapevine that *they* weren't coming. There was never a yes or no response; there was no definite answer and only ridicule and remarks. I cried, wept, and sobbed often to my dad about this. I trusted him to sit back and be rationale about the whole matter; a voice of reason, if you will.

The bridesmaids, Bella and Stella were asking about booking nails, hair and make-up appointments for the wedding party. I knew not where the money would come from or who would be there to actually book. But I did at and with the regular people I go to. As for paying I had no idea about that now that Damien had found out about my four months of savings in the bank. He drained my account, not even a day after finding out about it; saying he needed insurance or some other shit like that.

I felt as though it was inevitable that would happen and knew eventually the day would come. I knew that once he found out about it; it would be gone. I was squirrelling it away, saving it for the rainiest of days, to ultimately free ourselves from his clutches. His demand and just taking it, robbed me of my plan for freedom and safety.

I had grown more confident around people knowing he wouldn't attack me in front of them. I felt it was the only time I was safe enough to talk back, have a voice or be strong. It back fired horribly at times and I looked bad; I looked wrong and his words, as calculated as they are, only made me out to be as unstable as he was already planting in everyone's heads.

I had only a small amount of truth inside me, and an even smaller support circle, my step-father, my doctor and his nurses and Desiree.

I couldn't trust Stella. Stella had, once too often, proven to be on both sides; I had caught her speaking privately with my sister from Alberta and scheming, in a clucking hen sort of way and just to act perfect to her. I saw her siding with the family and now said things about me, behind my back and to my face. It was if the savior Kerri, who was always there for everyone, had been weakened, so now is my chance to look the leader.

I felt it more as a sting and a hurt or break of trust. I didn't care they were friends, as they were allowed Facebook; of course they would connect. I liked that but sad because I didn't or wasn't allowed it.

Desiree couldn't stand her and told me repeatedly to get her away from me and the boys; to push her far out of our lives as she is not to be trusted. "Look at her with Damien, speaking in ways that were flirtatious and sexual, over the top inappropriate and just plain ignorant. She doesn't have the heart you do Kerri, I don't trust her, I just don't. She wants what you have ..."

It was those type of remarks that perhaps made me start doubting my Stella, but loving her was a different matter altogether. I would always, and I mean always, protect and care for that girl. She had wedged a way into my very heart long ago and I do not just let go of people like that. Step away perhaps, but my love does not just go away. She owned a piece of my heart, always would. But that other side of Stella was becoming all too evident and that sexual side- even jokingly- only fed the beast in his teachings towards me and Stella knew this.

My small support group or network, as you have it, was only a very, very few. I had nothing to go on except their praise, and their opinions. My foggy survival goals were only to live for the day, survive the night and try to search for the happy ending I so dearly longed for; without Damien.

I went to my doctor's office and he asked if I was excited about getting married. I tried to say I was, and then I remembered I didn't have to put on a façade with him. I could be me, but being so fake and false with the smiles and the right tone was slowly just becoming second nature with me. It had been so long since I was able to be myself, that I thought darkness was a part of me and loneliness. I was forgetting who I really was. I was programmed to behave a certain way and my face, body and eyes reflected it.

I had lost so much weight, I was naturally tiny, no more than one-hundred and ten pounds normally, but I was dipping below or just hovering above the one-hundred mark.

My face was almost grey with sucken in eyes that used to be a bright blue and were now only grey. My body always, and I mean always, had the remnants of old and new bruises. That no matter how much I tried, I couldn't even cover it up anymore.

In passing I would hear Damien say I was anemic, his newest excuse for my constant multiple bruises and I think I even started believing him. My doctor, years later, would tell me that during that time when I would go into his office I was almost skittish, on edge, worrying him. I am sure there were times he thought long and hard if he should notify the police of Damien's abuse.

He may not have ever have said that, but I know and no words needed to be said on the matter. I would have respected him no matter what. I asked him for his trust and secrecy the first time I told him of what I live through on a daily basis and he gave me his word; I can only be thankful that he had given me the time to leave safely and proper-ly. Regardless, he had not a clue as to even a half of what I had been through; in that I couldn't share or perhaps Damien's words would've rang true and the club actually would've killed me, because of Damien being locked away without a key (because of his abuse). I had no idea if that was true or not; I decided to play cautious as any wounded person would've done.

When I tried to act, just nervous but happy, my doctor gave me a look that said, "Hello it's me, speak the truth, and don't forget who I am and I have the records." Or that's what I thought he was thinking, because he is wise and smart.

I was most likely his only real gangster or Hells Angels' girl he had as a patient and that tends to leave an impression on anyone. I still get judged by who I was and not who I am. I see it with credentials and other people who think, because they study or read a few books, that they all of a sudden know the life and can speak on it; when in fact, I have lived it and survived it. There is no greater credential than that.

But I am also not that self-absorbed that I cannot acknowledge what a trained professional can do as well. Fact: my doctor. But can a trained professional look past their title and see what another can do as well? I am proud of everyone and give people credit if they are helping others.

Just like I do not judge the police because they are police, they are human beings, they are doing their job, that is their profession, even though some can let the badge get to their heads a bit. Just like a Hells Angels patch, it can bolster and inflate any ego; add an abusive nature in an already powerful individual, and people get hurt; men, woman and children.

I instantly fell apart and crumbled in my doctor's office with his one remark and the look he gave me. I hated that I was marrying The Beast! I had no money to get away! I had to move into the house in a few days! My family who only belittles me is coming down to now attend! Even though they weren't going to come until the last minute. I was sure they were going to say innuendos and comments, that my already beaten down soul just couldn't take it.

I was a mess and I told my doctor the truth; he was my safety net and it helped me to be honest to him, because of my children. I never once told my doctor any of these things to try and sink my soon-to-be husband, I told him these things so that I could protect my children because I had no one that could protect them other than him.

Let me be clear, right now; I never told my doctor anything that had to do with street shit, thug life, money, cars, or bling; I told him of my own personal hell and the violence that smashed me in the face every turn I made. I told him of my pain and sadness. I told him the truth, because he was all I had; he was all I had that truly cared and no one, not one person as powerful as Damien came to rescue us. My doctor was all I had and he held a truth not many would ever have the compassion to do!

I spoke candidly to him, as I sat their mere weeks before my wedding. I hated that I was getting married and I never wanted to in the first place. I was stuck in a vicarious situation that was suffocating me. I was honest with him about that and in that moment.

But elsewhere, inside of me and every breath I took, I knew I was being trained to be a mannequin, a show piece and his own personal whore. It was sick and I would never tell my doctor the full extent of Damien's twisted personality that was taking me on a ride through the very depths of perilous moments you could not even imagine. I was ashamed of myself and I was scared to share it all, but I said enough, showed some of the marks; that I knew could help my sons.

I cracked slowly from the inside and I was slipping. This burden or these burdens were becoming much too big for me to handle or my shoulders could carry. I knew the moment I stepped into that sinister house I was gone; I just felt it and I felt as if the once sanctuary I had built for us, was being taken away. I was losing everything close to me and felt more alone than ever. I had no room for anxiety or panic attacks I had only myself and my own built prison walls. Having to move soon spiked my nervous behavior.

My doctor didn't want me to get married but he gave me hope that I could back out, leave, if you will. He said I should speak with my family, since they will all be here soon. He gave me options in that regard but I kept so much close to my chest and had yet to see past the fact, that it never started with the guys I dated…not like I had been told and believed. My head ached to see Action in these moments before my upcoming nuptials but still no word or call.

I hoped desperately that maybe my doctor was right. Maybe this is a good thing and when my family did start arriving I would have a little more of a support system in place; if I wanted or needed it. Damien wouldn't dare hit me in front of everyone. Or would he? This was where he needed to shine, above all else, and I felt having my aunties, cousins and others, would perhaps give me a little more strength I had been missing.

I still had a need to be accepted by my sisters and immediate family. I was blinded maybe by the fact, that no one would want to see me actually hit, would they? And when push came to shove, they would be there, right? I knew they branded me 'no good' from when I was young, but they didn't really mean all the words they spewed, did they? They would support me and help me.

I know I would help them in the same situation and I loved them. Were they only upset at me because I was with him? If I left they would once again come around? Maybe they just needed to see me, or once they knew the full extent then they would help me or even love me? I felt I had no one and I cannot express this enough. It was those thoughts and maybe a little optimism and flicker of hopefulness to hold onto.

I left my doctors feeling depleted but encouraged. I always left his office feeling better but this time I had options or maybe a renewed sense of reasoning. I let myself hope for a better day and answers to all this turmoil. I left there feeling like it was now or never and within a few short weeks we would be married. This may just be a chance to back out.

Maybe my family was exactly what I needed, the strength to fight for what I believed in and the solidity of support I craved. My resolve was met and when everyone arrived, I would lay my cards on the table, be honest and show the scared girl I had become to them.

I really thought I had a chance; I really did, and walked through the next week with such life. I was excited to see everyone; I was excited to finally be me. I still heard through the limited conversation with my sister and mom that I shouldn't get married and other ignorant comments but I would placate them and say, "You never know", kind of pushing it aside, blowing it off, and agreeing at the same time.

I thought once there here, they will be happy because I agreed with them and needed their help and lift to freedom. I just needed them here; I needed my family to help me get through this and give me the strength, I needed.

But Damien surprised me, two days before everyone arrived and 6 days before our wedding. He walked in one day, late morning, sun shining and said, "The moving truck is on its way, the house is ready just in time for everyone to see it. We can have the party or gift opening in our new house now, baby". He was bubbly with excitement and my insides hit the ground with a thud.

He was radiating and so happy. He had all his own dreams coming true with this house and I knew it. I knew he was excited to show it off and I am sure he pushed it this way so everyone could see it and in turn, stroke his ego, but I didn't want to go, or move. I just didn't.

Now my very nightmare, apprehension and thoughts came to the forefront in a crash. I wasn't making it until my family arrived, the time was here.....

Tightened Noose

"Every time you think, that you just might have it all figured out, life throws you another direction or path to cross"

The house wasn't *really* move in ready; there was still wires hanging from some of the walls and the driveway had nothing but gravel, not a big deal. The guest house was only framed, not yet sided or rocked. The pool was heated and running perfectly, but still did not have a proper safe cover. There was so much left to be done, needless to say the inspector didn't pass the inspection for "move in ready".

Damien didn't care, no one told him what to do; he had other plans and they were not by abiding by law or the code of safety, put in place for builders/owners and otherwise. Nor what this inspector stated or wanted.

I was left choking on my shock. Everything made me timid and everything set me on edge. Even if it was supposed to be normal, simple stuff. I questioned everything now right down to the hand gesture and tone, even feel of it all.

I tried to think straight and I tried to speak with him that perhaps we should wait. It was August 2, 2008 and we were getting married on August 8, 2008. Only six days away and we were moving! It was all too much, too fast and way to sudden. This was not something I had wanted.

Not a single penny to my name, and this was an expense we could do without. I needed time, and Damien wanted it done, now. This was a joke and I was grasping at straws and reasons to delay this.

I couldn't begin to explain what I was feeling, I thought we were months away from that and I thought just maybe I could stay in my apartment, forever. I didn't want to go and he was starting to realize it;

I couldn't break his heart and disappoint him, I just couldn't. I am not a mean person but you could clearly see I was not as elated as him, nor was I pleased about this.

He was beaming, excited and thrilled, the boys thought this was perfect and they were excited to. It being summer-time and now they would have a pool; they were just children, seeing the fun they could have and looking forward to seeing everyone in the family.

I was officially upside down and somehow making trips back and forth to the moving truck, numb. I was in a cocoon of shock, apprehension and uncertainty. I seen past the glamor and seen the future, it was bleak at best.

I took a moment to call Desiree and asked her to come over, she was supposed to stay with us for the week of the wedding so her, and a few friends, could make some money and help with all the kids. I needed her fast and she knew that some kind of shit had hit the proverbial fan when I said we were moving into the house, today. I could hear her voice shake on the other end of the line and she said she would be right over. Like I said, this was as unexpected as a snow storm in the middle of summer.

When she arrived, we packed up the kids and went to get refreshments for everyone; it was our excuse to re-evaluate the situation.

She was my rock and I was her mentor; a shitty one at that. At least I had stopped her from hanging out on the streets with certain crowds and smoking way too much pot. I had helped her transition well from delinquent teenager to a much more balanced individual; who thought about the friends she was choosing and not just falling into a life style that could take years to break free from. I could give myself that credit but not much more.

I had finally had a plan of action for when my family arrived. I was so hopeful but that hope crashed and burned as I saw our beautiful apartment being gutted of all our furniture. I was panicking and I wouldn't be able to hold it in much longer; Desiree could feel my tension without me saying a word.

The boys were protected from our talk, as we learnt long ago to shield them from anymore unnecessary 'grown-up chats.' We also had learnt to take our batteries from our phones and leave them sitting on the table as we would go outside to talk, or in this case, left in the vehicle as we went outside. We knew all to well the surveillance we were under, and not by just the cops, but Damien himself.

The alertness of having to live like that, was the only way I knew how and I had cautioned Des, long ago, after my mother and I were caught on recordings talking about his abuse. It was a technique he used to know all that was going on, or so we thought. It was being one step ahead and always keeping the knowledge and secrets bottled up inside, which isn't good or healthy for anyone.

She wrapped her arms around me when she came to the other side of the SUV after we had parked. We sent the kids into the playground and we both shook, we both cried and we both knew this was judgement day. This was it; we knew that once I went into that house, it was likely I would never get out, alive. We knew this and she was the only one who truly cared about my children and I; she was the only one who knew the truth. She knew the horror we had already faced and she knew the truth behind how abusive Damien could get. She was all I had and I held onto her for dear life in these moments. She a mess, just like I was.

My knees went weak and then gave out completely as I collapsed into her arms, slowly falling to ground as I wept. I was scared, I was so scared and I was losing our home. I felt sick and my legs couldn't hold me up any longer. We were in a state of shock and this shock rocked us both, to our core, this hurt like nothing else because it was already so embedded inside, that I wasn't going to make it out of this one, this time.

I was terrified, petrified, and all I could do was watch every moment I had with my children; they were my paintings, they were my light and they were all I had to now look forward to. They were my lifeline and only hope to keep fighting for our futures.

Desiree and I knew how bad this was, it was worse than bad, this was destiny colliding and dreams taken away all in a moment, a flash and without warning; but I didn't have many warnings did I? I felt betrayed and I felt wronged, I felt scared and I felt panicked but most of all I felt my looming death.

Do you know the power this man wielded over me? He took running and hiding away from me, he hurt me but he also broke and destroyed my soul. As a person, a mother, a friend and an already survivor, he took all that was me and spit it out. Only to be in the form that suited him and his perverse ideas on how I should be.

This man was worse than running from the *policia* in Mexico; he was a Hells Angel with connections worldwide; he was a man who had a vendetta against the father of my first son and he was the father of my youngest son. This man was beauty and the Beast all rolled into one and it was a deadly combination. He was my own living nightmare and he never thought he did a thing wrong.

This man, just announced I was moving from my home into a mansion that had an eight foot high, cement, brick fence and iron, gates for an entrance (not to mention-by remote control access). A house that had cement floors; that would hurt to land on, and a pool with no cover that was unsafe for my sons. This man was ripping, the only thing I had to ground us, my own home, with neighbours away from me, as a mother. Fudge me, I was scared!

Devastation doesn't describe what I felt, nothing could.

Everyone thought I loved the life, I was so lucky or they thought I deserved what I got from him. I don't know which hurt more, the fact that some thought I deserved his treatment or the ones who couldn't see past the glitz and glamour and didn't notice the hollow person I had become.

I never got upset over other girls, there wasn't a jealous bone in me for him, there was just "as long as it wasn't me, inside". I was a person who deserved normalcy and a person who kept the darkest of ALL your secrets and I was alone, with only a teenager who held me and my children for hope. It was a sad day and a day, I had all but almost given up.

Desire heard me crying as I begged her, I begged her with every part of my body and soul " don't leave, don't leave me Desiree, not for a minute , please Desiree, please don't leave me, I will die , I know it, I know it, my babies need me, please, they need me, Desiree. " I begged her with nothing less than the true pain in my soul. I begged to the gods and I begged for mercy. It was lights out for me and nowhere else to go.

I know she will never forget that day, as I never will, either. It was a day of great sadness and ultimate defeat. I tried my hardest to be brave and strong like people said but I had no more steam and nothing left to give.

Desiree promised me she wouldn't leave me and she enlisted her friend, to come along too. I knew it was only a matter of time before, eventually, I would be alone and the nightmares of my reality would once again take over. But for now at least I was somewhat safe with her there and promising to be around.

I just needed to sort myself out and I just didn't know where to start searching; I was officially lost and the survivor I once thought I was, with a brilliant heart of kindness and understanding, was no longer worth the fight. I was ready to succumb to the anguish, but I wasn't ready to leave my sons to him. That was the only thing worth fighting for.

As I watched them play in the park, so happy, full of joy and carefree, I couldn't even begin to imagine when I was once like that. They were so excited for family to come and had not a clue as to what our life was about to turn into, all because their mother was as weak as a newborn kitten, not strong enough to stand up to the bully, not strong enough to walk away.

Yes, I had that number to call but that was a huge step and one that took complete clarity. I didn't have that, all I knew was being asphyxiated by fear. All I knew now, by this point that I may be problem. That somehow I inflicted everyone with disappointment, by why was it only the ones who have been doing and saying that to me for so long and that sliver of reason had me hold on longer.

It was my own self-doubt that was allowing his taunts to officially take root in my head; that scared me. I was now putting myself into the category he had already placed me in and agreeing with him. I was unconsciously repeating his comments and saying them to myself; that was how I felt and that is what I did.

I never once thought, during this time, I wasn't these nasty labels, not at all, if anything I agreed with all the names he called to me. I looked in the mirror and only saw ugly; I could see every disgusting, volatile remark reflected on the skin of my piggish face and body. I thought I was gross, I thought I was fat, I thought I was nothing.

I only felt nice when my doctor or someone who actually liked me said I was. It lasted all of the moment and no further, but it placed little tiny glimmers of light in me and those I passed to my children; those were my gifts to them, to make up for how pathetic I really was.

Desiree was blank, lost in thought, and I was simply a hollow shell of a person. I knew once we left this park I would have to face the music. I had to compose myself just enough to put on my front and façade for him.

His crew were at my house, moving my life away and touching my things; I didn't want or like them touching anything but they didn't care nor did they even notice it bothered me. They all knew the truth of his brutality towards me and others but somehow they justified it to themselves and turned a blind eye. They were intoxicated by the power he had, the *unwavering power of the patch*.

The only thing they would ever know or accept was Damien's truth and justifications. He was their undisputed leader and they supported him a hundred percent, in all things; even then it kind of made me sick watching it all because he would never allow one of his crew to climb the later to where he was, they were his puppets as much as I.

If he said it was *"Move In Day"*, then that is what it was and not one of them would've stopped, no matter how much or even if I begged them to.

His crew were his workers who he commanded and could enlist on any given chore he wanted; he paid them, he housed them but really, he just owned them.

Some were family, like legit blood relatives and others not. In a crew you get the sense of family solidarity and that's the lure of it all; the feeling of a place to belong and the strong hold of "strength in numbers".

Today my home was being packed and loaded into the belly of the Beasts domain. This house loomed menacingly in my immediate future. The deathblows and control he would now exert over me; was nothing like how he treated his crew. He may smack them around if they get out line, which is fact, but they didn't have to live with him. I did.

I didn't know how much more I could take.

Desiree helped pull me together, for the sake of sanity, and get the boys back in the car. We picked up Ashton's best friend, coffees, take out and headed back to the apartment. Again putting on a invisible Band-Aid to cover up what I was truly feeling, suffocating all I felt was wrong and all I felt I couldn't fix.

I didn't expect what I walked into. While I was mentally preparing myself, my house had been gutted. My precious home touched by the very people who laughed at me mockingly and transported away from the residents who surrounded me at this apartment. It scared me now with no one around or going to be around when at this big house. I was sad, very sad. Terrified and broken.

I went into a corner and just slid down the wall and cried, all alone for a few minutes. When Ashton came in he asked "Mama, what's wrong?" I told him it was about leaving and moving from our home that was upsetting me, but I would be okay, my son, I will be okay. I always addressed my boys like that because they were mine.

It was a great cover up and even a perfectly honest explanation. Like always my boys gave me all I needed, to pull myself together and put on the brave face I had mastered. Today however, I allowed the solemn expression, for there was no way to extinguish it.

Damien was with the moving truck dropping off a load and I had a few more minutes to get it together before he arrived. Because when he came back, we were all heading over, for good!

I couldn't take his mental cruelty, if he seen my clearly visible distress. Having him sit me down, just to tell me how to look and speak, was a degrading feeling, like no other. I wasn't up to it, not today. Nor in front of his crew.

He even explained to them and me once; as he laughed that he had grabbed his *ex* and spanked her, with her pants down, in front of every-one because she was "acting up"! When I heard that story, I felt every raw emotion of humiliation for her and with her. I still feel sad to this day, thinking about it. That is WRONG!

I tried to call my step-father just to hear his voice; he'd said he had just spoken with Damien and asked if I was getting ready for our wed-ding; he then said, out of the blue, he had an early wedding present for us and asked if tomorrow _we_ could meet him together, both Damien and I.

I couldn't open up to him like I normally would've about what was going on and Damien beat me to the punch with calling him. Why? My step-father was being so supportive on the phone and I could sense that it wasn't the right time; I'd look like an insufficient human being if I did. Plus if I got to see him, I was happy.

I was excited any time I could see my step-father and so quickly agreed. He made life happier for me and always gave me something to look forward to. My anticipation wasn't for the wedding present, it was for seeing him. I told Damien when he arrived, my smile was back on my face, and he said that 'yes' he had spoken to my step-father, too. *I had yet to put two and two together, that maybe something was up until much later.*

Knowing that Desiree was now staying with us until after the wed-ding, made me more at ease and a little calmer moving into the house. I was willing to try and like the new place but I was cracking and the only reprieves I had was knowing my family was arriving soon... It gave me the 'oomph' I needed to *Kerri On...*

I never once prepared myself for the simple fact that they treated me in the same manner as Damien did, with their words. I had yet to see the familiarity so colorfully decorated and my only comparison at times, was how they made me feel. I didn't clue in that maybe, just maybe, I didn't have them in my corner.

I didn't know I had so much riding on them. Or it would take that one look to set me off, or one remark to throw me over the edge and one laugh to actually rip my very heart out.

I didn't know that, after so long of the back-and-forths with my family, he was able to make it look like I was the problem because they had already thought that anyhow, most of their lives.

It set the stage for the worst day of my life. Worse than any fist that had been swung my way, or any long tortuous nights of lessons. My family was my hope and that's all I believed in for the time being.

I had so much of that hope, riding on the words of my doctor that I didn't for see the colossal disaster heading my way. My doctor knew that my family had always thought of me like the blacksheep but he never knew the extent of their opinions and thoughts, neither did I.

In most cases, no matter what, family is always there for you. But, in my case, I didn't have a sister who would drop everything, if I was being hurt, to help me; I didn't have a mother to wrap loving arms around me, unconditionally, long enough to heal or wash away any hurt I was feeling; I didn't have a father who would really truly protect his daughter. I had run away so, so long ago that those ties were severely damaged and I had never actually repaired them because I didn't feel I had to or tried countless times. Only to have that one comment, by them throw me back down, as I walked away. It or us, were damaged by years of bad judgements, opinions or otherwise wrong assumptions.

If I had heard, even one percent of what I had been through happen to anyone of them, I wouldn't hesitate to offer my help but they wouldn't do it for me, not at all.

I believed having my whole family here, would've somehow saved me, in some way. I thought I could open up to them and somehow they would help me; I don't know why, but I thought that their arrival was going to allow me to finally be me. I only had them as my saving grace and I thought that was enough. I put all my eggs in this basket; that I didn't think anything could break their shield around me. I didn't make a second option nor did I think of that lady on the phone, not so long ago. I was riding on them and them alone.

I felt safer knowing they were coming and I felt I could rely on them enough to hold me up, if I fell, because I was about to. I had so much hope in them, finally coming down to BC, after so many years away from me, that I never prepared for the what if's. I only prepared for them.

I was far too busy, mentally and physically, trying to protect myself that I hadn't allowed myself to envision my family not saving me. Nor did I prepare for the head games Damien would play. I was on survival mode, not exactly my more intelligent traits or times.

My life choices are not their fault, not at all. Those are mine and mine alone to carry, bear and share. But there is something to be said, about humanity and being humane.

I would find out, soon enough, exactly how much support and love I really did have in life; that realization came the day of their arrival. It was three days later, another two sleepless nights, in a house I swear was haunted and much, much too large.

A place not even my own beautiful furniture could make warm and inviting. A house built on blood money and greed!

A house I never respected, warmed up to nor liked. A house that was not mine, or ours but truly in every sense *his*.

Days before the Wedding

Day 1 in the house

Damien was radiating with true glory and pride living here. I could understand how much easier it would be for him to finish off the house while living there; I had no choice but to agree. But I could understand his reasoning.

I watched how he would languish and luxuriate, in the four-person tub; in the morning, just soaking it all in. Damien was on top of the world. He was finally settled and I was anything but settled, or remotely felt at home.

It was bound to cause another disconnection but it was fact. I never needed a huge mansion and all the toys in his life. I need stability, warmth and love. We all do. That's when I truly glow; that's when no matter the bumps in life I know it's okay, and everything is going to be fine, just fine. That was all I ever needed.

Every morning for the last year I had drawn a bath for him, served him my cooking and cleaned our home to more than any person could want or hope for with their spouse. I liked to vacuum lines in the carpet, gleaming shiny floors, polished wood and streak free, clear glass. I relished in making a home. Quite possibly, I enjoyed being able to control the chaos in my life the only way available to me. Cleaning.

I loved making my surroundings aesthetically pleasing by using creative talent I was gifted with. It is talent that still brings me much joy. There is nothing wrong with being that type of woman. It was me and many men enjoy that, kids they thrive on the balance of it all and friends enjoy the benefit of it. To in turn, give them something brilliant, made me in turn, shine. That was me, the Kerri I loved to be.

Our new house had twenty-three televisions, a theater room, three living rooms and a two level master bedroom. Every bedroom with again, full bathrooms in each one, plus a nanny suite fully equipped with the up to date appliances.

It had an office down a rock hallway, with a mahogany wood door that had a metal-shuttered window, so you could request entance. At the base of the rock hallway, beside the office door, was a tall, steel, old school vault and safe.

All the crown molding, surrounding every inch of this mansion was a dark mahogany, which glistened with rich wealth and stature. Our home also had a guest house, with a dual loft suite and any man's dream of a garage.

Our pool was a twelve foot deep, kidney in shape, with a diving board and two running, waterfalls on each side. Yes, to an outsider we had it all, but in reality we weren't even scraping by or I wasn't anyhow.

I was being swallowed whole and Damien was living to the potential he wanted to be classed in; not realizing there was more to life and success than money, walls and toys.

I had no idea, exactly, how much money Damien went through but it was hundreds of thousands of dollars. I couldn't understand or even begin to figure out, where it all went. I know there were some days he had forty to fifty thousand, sitting in a bag by his feet.

So to be so close to the wedding date, only four days away, I still didn't even have a hundred dollars in my own pocket and just drained out my private bank account, for him. I felt it was controlling and ruthless. It was as if I could now add 'beggar' to my label and role. I couldn't even begin to describe the abject humiliation of it all. I had so much bottled up inside of and it only made my head hang painstakingly, lower.

It was evident. Everyone who was around me noticed it, especially Desiree. She, too, was still waiting for the promised few-hundred dollars to watch all the little ones arriving and mine. It was horribly rotten of Damien to blow us off like this, but he did; we had to pool together and count through change, just to go to the store.

I decided that I would take some of my jewelry to the pawn shop if I wasn't able to get any money by the next day. They were good to me there and always gave a good price, they knew my story and knew my name. It was demeaning and degrading as Damien had his pockets full to overflowing and me I was on a first name basis with the pawnshop a city away.

Damien and I had to meet my step-father in the afternoon as we weren't able to see him the day before. I thought if I had a moment I would ask him privately for a few hundred dollars, even promising Desiree that.

My step-father had asked us to meet him at the halfway point in the afternoon and we were about to head out. So as Damien was ranting that I needed to hurry up, I was quickly reassuring Desiree that I would ask my step-father for money. Maybe he could help me with money just for her- I wasn't too concerned for me. She deserved it, she was owed it and she had already helped so much with moving and other stuff. She never actually babysat the kids alone all too often, we were mostly together now. She was more like my paid companion then anything and I absolutely adored her. No this was for her, I was used to scraping by and there was no way the children would go without.

When I jumped in Damien's truck, which was the size of a semi-truck, he was raring to go. He blew through the gates and blasted the music, not once reaching for my hand or pulling me close like an about to be married couple would do mere days before their wedding. I noticed these things because love was what I craved for above all else, love and gentle care. I searched for it in every gesture.

Damien was going a hundred miles an hour, within his everyday activity, let alone as we were driving to meet my dad. He was busy and today the way he dropped his normal routine, just to take me to see my step-father was out of the ordinary. I mean I could've driven myself and met him, as I usually did. Why did he have to come? It actually kind of bothered me.

I would've taken the boys and had a few minutes to visit just to get away from the house but he insisted on being the one to take me. He was adamant, in fact. And I, hoping to do anything and everything to take the pressurized load off of him so he didn't combust, was thinking he maybe had wanted to just be alone with me. I was left feeling confused with the way he just stormed out of the driveway and ignored me most of the way. This day was different and very hard to explain, other than to say it was all off. Everything just felt off.

Just as we approached the location, of where we were to meet my step-father, was the only time he looked over at me and grabbed my hand, his smile with his perfect white teeth gleamed but his attitude was lacking, fake in fact and I could tell. His luminous smile never reached his eyes, but his grin did. That left my eyebrow raised and with questions I felt deserved to be answered.

I had learned, long ago, the price to pay when out in public and putting on an "I have it all attitude and 'I love it look', as he was now doing. I could tell from the way he walked into a room and the way his voice would change when saying "Hi there, or Bro" to his kingly gestures of bobbing his hand in the air as if to get the party started because he or what he stood for, entered the room. It was the same, it was the false show of' we got it all' crap and he was all over it like nothing else.

I now figured out where we had to meet my father and my heart plummeted, I saw the HSBC bank come into view. I knew this spot all to well; this is where I would often meet him when I needed a few hundred dollars just to get by.

I looked over at Damien and asked "Is this where you and he discussed meeting?" I was searching for any type of clue as to what their discussions had been about. He answered with a "yes, and hunny your going to be so happy, this is a surprise, for us baby."

I didn't know what to make of it, but all I could wish for was that my step-father hadn't invested any of his money in one of Damien's newest venture I'd been hearing about. Mexico Land from the Nato Indians. I didn't like it. I didn't like this at all.

First of all Native land is sacred and to me, you just do not screw with sacred ground. Energy and heritage have deeper and stronger roots than any piece of paper ever will. My own blonde haired, blue eyed son was part native, and his grand parents treasured (on the fathers side) that. We all did and I brag often about this fact; that his great grandmother was a RCMP on the reserve.

Second, the type of money people had been investing in his project- that, from my understanding, never had a title or proprietorship- was astronomical and it was the one endeavor I wasn't remotely close to accepting. I felt very, very strongly about this.

I had spoken already, to my step-father about this and something didn't seem right. He was not to invest- from my advice and to "please dad, trust me, just don't do it". He had agreed and ensured me that it wasn't something he was interested in. He would rather buy more equipment for his company, than land he would never have the time to visit.

But now, seeing where we were, watching how Damien was smiling and play acting, I couldn't help but question his intent or objective in this. I couldn't help but wonder. Why are we, at his bank!

I knew my step-father had a wedding present for us but why meet at a bank? Why leave work in the middle of his workday just to meet us? I mean, really, we could've gone to his office and picked up the wedding gift. I knew that my step-father didn't want anyone in the office to know his personal business and would often meet away from his domain. This felt big. I also knew if he was going to cover anything for the wedding, like booze or food he would've simply given out his credit card. I know him and I know this fact well.

When I saw him arrive, I jumped out of the truck and ran out to him before Damien had a chance to approach. I know I was wearing faded light denim jeans, with a white and light sweater. I seemed to be cold lately, not warm in the least and it was summer. I wrapped my arms around my step-father and whispered in his ear, "What are you doing here?" We had a sort of special bond where only a few words needed to be mentioned and we could pick up on anything.

He gave me a sideways smirk and full smile, then said "Oh you will see". Damien walked up then and they shook hands, we talked together for a few minutes about general things, like the wedding I hadn't planned and arrivals. My step-father said he was ready and his girlfriend had a dress picked out. I was worried about my mother and how this is going to hurt her. She had to attend a event with my step-fathers new girlfriend and of course it would have to be at my wedding. I felt bad for her.

I was also worried about my real father and how he was going to accept walking me only halfway up the aisle and my step-father walking me the other half. I know everyone knows in the family that my step-father raised me and everyone also knew the bond we had but I never wanted to hurt anyone's feelings, that was the last thing I wanted to do; Never mind about getting married in the first place. I loved my real-dad just the bond he had with my older sister is what I had with my step-father.

I silently watched the exchange between Damien and my dad. I leaned against his white ford truck, by the corner entrance of the bank and just took it all in and let them converse.

I had always heard when you got married, you married your mother, or your father and I couldn't figure out how this was true. Because there was NO WAY my step-father was remotely close to Damien inwardly, so nope, to me at that point, this statement or myth was untrue.

Damien had a contained respect for my step-father and he never acted inflated around him. Damien was much more firmly grounded when around him. I enjoyed the casual way they both spoke with each other. I believe Damien never had a proper father figure growing up and I also had heard that his mother never raised him at all, only until he was three. His mother raised his younger brother and his father raised Damien, separating them young because of a nasty divorce. Please don't quote me word for word on that because I know what he told me but I will never know what was true, false, fact or fiction with him.

It was a few minutes later that my step-father looked at me and said that he wasn't much on buying presents and shopping. He had no idea what to get me for my wedding but he knew the house was costing us a fortune. He said that he had spoken with Damien, a little, and wanted to give us something we could use and start out our lives with. He then looked at both of us and said "So, whose name would you like the cheque in?"

Damien, before the question was out, said, "Oh just put it in mine, it will clear faster that way." No word of a lie. He was taking a precious moment away in a blink of the eye and my step father just tilted his head and looked at me. Again no words needed. I didn't care. I just felt so special in that moment. It gave me a sort of ease knowing I didn't have to borrow money on my wedding day and even more of a loving glow knowing that my dad cared. These moments of appreciation and generosity always left me feeling grateful. I felt special and beamed with pride.

As my step-father walked into the bank Damien wrapped his arms around me and told me how awesome my father is. He said I was so lucky to have a father like that and kissed the top of my head. He stepped away, out of ear shot, and went to make a phone call.

I chose to go over into my step-fathers truck and wait for him there- in the driver's seat with the door open. I was desperate to have a few moments alone with him before we went separate ways. I remember leaning against his truck and thinking, *"How do I tell my step father I do not want to get married- I need to back-out?"* He knew how I felt. He knew about the abuse and yet he also knew I wanted to have a married family life more than anything in the world. He knew my yearnings as a child and young adult and he also knew my hurt and pain.

When he came out of the bank he walked towards me with a huge smile on his face. He didn't go towards Damien who was on the other side of the parking lot. He strolled towards me, where I stood waiting. He knew I was in knots and he knew that I had to second guess everything. He actually knew I had never wanted to marry Damien but he also knew it was all up to me. Most importantly, he knew that in order to leave that lifestyle you have to do it the right way and sometimes that took time. He got me and my situation so instead of say negative things, he followed my lead.

He handed me a white envelope and said "This is for you Kerri. This is what I would give all of you girls equally, and I know this is a day you dreamed about, for a very long time. No matter what you decide, I support you!" He hugged me and I cried. Full on tears streaking down my face of genuine touching warmth.

He playfully swatted me and told me to pull it together, as Damien came up from behind. He extended his hand and as Damien said, "Thank-you, Sir," to my step-father and laughed as they shared a firm handshake.

My dad had to go but he promised he would see us before the wedding. He looked at me with such pride and unconditional love. It was a special moment and it felt good. I felt special. This wonderful moment, was my moment. I felt very grateful for the pride that he bestowed on me and the compliment of equality. It was difficult to part and say our good-byes, but I would see him soon.

When Damien and I stepped up into his truck, he swiftly snatched the, still unopened, envelope from my hands and informed me that he would drop me back off at home in order for him to hit his bank. He then tore it open and showed me what my step-father had given us. It was a ten-thousand dollar cheque, made out to Damien as was asked beforehand.

I was shocked and in awe. Ten-thousand dollars! I was feeling such euphoric love for him, my dad in that moment, no words can describe. I knew he did that because of all the times I had asked him for money and help. I am certain that the little loans and gifts, here and there, had added up. He wanted to make sure at least for a little while, the kids and I would be okay.

I knew he cared about me and my children and I knew if anything ever happened to me, he would be the one person in my family/life that truly loved me. I would be lost without him. He was my Dad, not my step-father but my Dad.

People and family members were arriving tomorrow, the next day and following until it was the wedding. I was dropped off at the house and Damien went to the bank. I didn't have a chance to take a picture of the cheque as I would have done, for memory sake. But, Damien just pulled up to the gates and rushed off. He told me that he had more running around to do and would see me later.

I was so excited that I skipped up to the house and told Desire what my dad had just did for us. She swelled right up with me, all excited. She told me that she had met Damien's mother and that she had arrived while we were gone but was staying at Damien's brother's place. Everyone was slowly arriving and I was starting to get excited about just seeing everyone, together.

Desiree was hiding something. I could tell she was holding something back but I also knew that she would wait until it was safely just the two of us before she explained. I also don't think she wanted to take my smile from my face but I noticed her darting eyes and shaken attitude. She may have been happy for me with what my step-father had done but she was visibly distraught. I told her if she wanted to leave for a few hours, she could. That was when she blurted out, "I can't. I can't leave you Kerri."

I took her outside and we sat by the edge of the pool with our feet dangling into the water. The boys were running through the forest and her friend was downstairs, probably unpacking. I asked gently, "Darling, what's wrong, what happened? You can tell me anything."

She nervously lit a cigarette and suggested that I might like to light one too; apparently I was going to need it. She didn't want to hurt me but she something to tell me and it was important. I had never smoked much, then, I had the odd ciggeratte and a pack could last me a month. I rose and ran inside to find my smokes knowing this would give her a few more minutes to compose herself for whatever she was about to share. I was still beaming from seeing my step-father; focussing on that warm feeling seemed to always put a layer of protection and insulation around me. It gave me a clearer head.

When I came back outside, still holding my encouraging smile and sat down beside her, did I notice her face. Looking at her, I saw rivers of tears streaming down her cheeks, only to drip from her chin. Did I stop smiling and grab her in a hug to hold her. I allowed her tears to fall freely, while giving her the courage to speak out.

Desiree's friend was cautiously approaching from the kitchen patio doors. Her friend was someone who had attended kindergarten with Desiree and they were like two peas in a pod. I liked her and her up-bringing was very cushioned, but also corrupt from my understanding. (Again not my story to share)

Desire looked to her for support and beckoned an invite for her to come over and sit with us. Whatever this was, they both knew some-thing I didn't. I was thinking things like, "*did they break something? Did they want to leave but couldn't because of me? Or what?* I didn't understand the way they were acting, but they were now both looking at me like I had to prepare for something, something big.

I said, "C'mon, you guys. You can tell me anything. I love you guys. Whatever it is we can work it out. I understand if you want to leave, I want to as well. I get it. Go for a little while, you really do not have to stay, I will be fine." I thought it was teenage stuff or maybe this had all become too much, they still haven't been paid for any of the help they had given us. But that was not the problem. I had no idea what was going on, but I was now consoling the both of them, they were terrified to say whatever it was and scared to hurt my feelings that much I could sense.

Desiree's friend took the lead and initiated the explanation as to why they were so upset. She said that Damien's mother had arrived at the house accompanied by his brother, walking boldly around and inspecting everything. The girls tried to be friendly and accommodating, even offering to get her something to drink. They felt they had been as welcoming as possible. They were talking while his mother was looking around and then the kids came running upstairs to see who arrived all excited.

Desiree's eyes welled up and tears spilled over the brim again. I immediately was on guard demanding to know everything, these are my children and in that don't mess with me! "What freaking happened" I demanded, again, while I leapt up from the pool edge "Are my kids okay?!"

They pulled me back down to a sitting position and reassured me that and the boys were fine, whispering to keep it quiet, they didn't trust the few around to hear. Their extreme upset was about Damien's mother's total contemptuous disregard for Ashton; barely acknowledging my child, as if he wasn't worth her time.

Desiree said she was floored and offended on Ashton's behalf. She went and told Ashton and Sable to go downstairs. Just to get them away and be with them in a less caustic environment. That's when Desi's friend took over dealing with her, verbally and offered to help Damien's mom with anything she needed.

"Girl, how old are you? Never mind, don't answer that!" she snapped in a nasty patronizing tone, "This house was built for me, by my son.

Kerri will learn this soon enough. This is my son's house and *mine*."
she had hissed, "If I need anything, I will get it myself. Likely, I will be
moving down here." She then turned to her son, Damien's brother, and
asked him to show her around. And off they went. Leaving these young
girls jaws dropped and hearts stung.

Marissa-Desi's friend, said she stood there aghast. She was adamant
that if I had been here and heard how things were said, in the manner
they were spoken in; I would have been devastated. They went on to say
that they had to tell me and that never, in all the years that their parents
had been married, had they ever witnessed a grandmother behave as ob-
noxiously as his mother had to the children. They warned me that this is
not normal; there was something definitely not right. Damien's brother,
Drake seemed to light up when his mother spoke and even laughed in
an obnoxious way.

I still had a little push of strength bolstering inside me from seeing
my step-father; that I took it as another reason to store away and be on
guard as opposed to breaking me in half morally. (That says something
about the importance of having, at least, a little bit of a support network
around you when faced with another stinging and startling truth).

His mother never had liked me and wouldn't have given me the
time of day. I can remember, once, trying to call her after Damien had
thoroughly thumped me again and I had fled my apartment; sobbing
to her that I had nowhere to go and her telling me that my place is
at home and to go home. She didn't seem to register what I had just
shared with her, about the violence her son had just unleashed on me
or maybe, she simply accepted it and thought it normal. But her telling
me to go home and make Damien happy stuck with me. That was the
last time I'd spoken with her.

Mind you, I had only met her once, briefly, and added to the over-wrought phone call, really, what should I expect? But, to disregard any child is wrong but to disregard MY child, as I was now hearing, My son, her soon-to-be-grandson, sneered at in his own home was an epically vicious mistake. This was NOT going to happen and this mother (me) would go toe-to-toe with any mother in defense of my child; I didn't care who her son was.

That was where our relationship started as daughter and mother-in-law and that was where it abruptly ended, that very day.

My eyes seemed to betray my thoughts because instead of hurt I was mad, I was livid. I was a caged animal ready to claw my way out, in my mind. Oh, I couldn't handle much more and it took all I could, not to dial her up and get her on the phone, right now…

I forced myself to sit back and slow my breathing.

I then explained to the girls that they needed to be absolutely sure about what they were telling me. They never faltered, they didn't hesitate nor did they cry again. With dry-eyes, they were vehement and I knew I had done the right thing by being strong and not weeping like a fool; they were following my lead.

Instead I felt the fight come flaring out in me, it just all became too much, who knows. But I do know for sure, that this was only the *first* straw and my will would be tested harshly over the next forty eight hours. I didn't care about her walking around our house saying it was hers, to me, I thought she was older and I loved taking care of people. So really, that part of the tale just didn't bother me. But I wasn't there to hear her tone or how she had addressed everyone.

The girls, on the other hand, kept bringing it up like what she said was "straight from hell." I didn't get it, fully. I thought, *"They're young and will eventually understand that it is the right thing to do to take care of your parents as they get older-mother is laws can be hard to handle"*. So that part I blew off but addressing or *not* addressing my son and blatantly dismissing him as part of the family. He had already been through enough; she had just prodded a wounded animal in me and I protect my young. Now, that my friends, was her biggest mistake.

I filed the comment about "this is her son's and her house" in the back of mind for future reference and quickly went to scoop up my baby boys to tickle, love and snuggle them. They were my precious little friends, my life and my pure loves. They are my absolute living truth. What great joy they have brought me in my dark hours and what a path we have taken together. But what a team we are.

I gave the girls my last twenty dollars and told them to go out for a bit and get out of the house; they had done so much and deserved a break from this life. Obviously, I didn't feel the loss of the twenty (that I always had hidden for emergency) because Damien was coming back with money for me; I needed the few moments alone to find my peace, find a way to relax and prepare myself for my niece and nephews to arrive. Now that brought me a joy like no other, I love kids and this auntie, couldn't wait to see.

When Damien arrived back at the house he didn't approach me or acknowledge me. I was waiting for him to have a few minutes so I could take the boys out and pick up a few things. I patiently waited and when another hour went by, I lost my patience and stood at his doorway to ask for some money. In order for me to go out to buy some much-needed supplies. He looked at me with his curled lip of disgust, grabbed my arm and led me deeper into the room and cave he called his office.

He sternly told me to never interrupt him again. And then he told me, that he had Noooo money for me. I was immobile with surprise; I am sure my mouth hung open and my eyes wide. Truly, I never expected this. The reality of it washed over me and my hurt and sadness was evident. I just looked at him with such overwhelming melancholy; I didn't say a word, I never could.

I knew the way he was digging his fingers into my arm would leave significant bruises and that a lot of people were now going to see. I was always worried about that and I felt ashamed. Why wouldn't he release me? Why does he do this and why now. I let the again tears fall from eyes in devastation and shock. I cry silently and never out loud, ever, so when I started freely sobbing he continued.

"That money went towards bills, Kerri! How the fuck else do you think you get to live in a house like this? Are you fucking dumb? Hello? Hello? Hello" he knocked on my head, as if he was knocking on a door. "Fuck you're stupid" He increased his pressure on my arm until I bent my knees in pain and sunk to the floor in humiliation. He left me there, in a heap, to wallow in my sorrow and self-pity as he walked away shaking his head.

Life as *his* wife was a reality that was sinking in and trapped in this wicked house made me weep all the more. My body was numb and my heart was exposed. I hated his house. I hated this dungeon and I hated my life. I hated myself and all those emotions crashed in at once. The only thing that kept me together that day was anticipating the arrival of my sisters, mother and family the very next day. The rest of that day, I was hidden away, out of sight of him. I had my sons to comfort me and the promise of safety when everyone arrived.

When the girls came back, it was exactly what I needed to take my immediate uneasiness, curdling inside my stomach, away. I pretended I was asleep. I didn't have the energy or courage after the humiliation to mention anything about the money I owed them money and there was no way to get it. He had made his point and left his mark.

I was barely holding on long enough for him to be gone to fly out the next morning; he was going to pick up his son, from another province, for the wedding. I had to be strong, I needed my family more than ever before and somehow I thought they could save me. I relied on it and I thought everything would be okay once they were here.

Countdown Begins

Day 3 before nuptials

I awoke the next morning to painful stiffness, fatigue and a debilitating gloom, hanging stagnant in the balance. The light was seeping into our new bedroom and the only breath taking vison I saw. I was grateful to have that moment, to just breathe it all in and slowly rise. These simple moments were my moments and it helped soothe me in ways not much else could.

Today was going to busy and I knew this but I finally had it all to myself. No Damien, no attacks and soon my very own family would be here. I was actually so excited to see my family, that I had butterflies. I got up to that thought and that alone. I could taste freedom and I could feel the acceptance I had been craving. I just had to share all I have been through, not the astronomical running for safety moments of terror. But it all; then they would hear me and only then would they understand.

I knew the boys were just as excited and happy to see them as I was. We talked about them endlessly together and all the good- never did my own children know, how I felt they didn't care about me. They loved their cousins and no matter how tumultuous the family was, these boys/kids were innocent of it all; all they saw was adventure, fun and party-time.

All they knew was the goodness I had described to them and found in each, plus every one of their relatives. The boys remembered all the times I had mentioned I missed my family. They never saw anything beyond the loving each other to the fullest and as their mother, I had worked at reinforcing that belief.

I let it all sink in and then jumped out of bed in a hurry, to get ready for the coming day. I wanted to look my best. I wanted my family and everyone to be proud of me; I wanted everything to be perfect and positive. I knew I had to have myself all together so they didn't judge me with the scornful scrutiny I had come to expect. I wanted, no, I needed to know they loved me; I needed to know they were there for me. I needed to know we were family and with that strength I could get through anything. I needed them and I thought maybe I just had to share it all with them, for them to truly understand what we were up against.

I had heard the rumblings, from behind my back, of their thoughts and opinions, on my marriage, my fiancé and my life. I wanted them to know the truth; I wanted to share with them what I had only been able to share with a very selective few. I wanted them to know that I acknowledged and agreed with them that the abuse was bad and that I shouldn't be getting married.

I needed to explain why I was still moving forward with this wedding; I saw it as my last chance to freedom; I believed I had to take it through to the end so he couldn't continue to hunt me down and stop me from my life. I was doing this for freedom; and if somehow the gods were happy and shined down on me maybe, just maybe, miraculously, the abuse would stop.

I needed them to know they didn't have to continue saying hurtful things to me, every time we talked; because I was very well aware of my shortcomings, even planning to share their distaste for my weakness.

I wanted them to support me, help me walk through the middle of this, and give me the strength that only family could bring-united. By just being there for me and my sons. I needed them to be watchful and offer clarity, when Damien would twist things up, mentally. I desperately needed their humanity, for once in my life; I needed to feel as though I mattered and beg them to be treat me as a person. As their sister and as their daughter.

I wanted them to know I agreed with them. I was no longer going to be guarded but needed to be completely open just so I had their support; like I had with my doctor, the nurses and only the closest of confidants in my private world of parents. My circle was small in regards to support and I wanted to make them part of it. If they would have me. I wanted them to know they didn't have to rescue me, I had a plan if all else failed but I just needed them to show Damien it was not allowed to treat their sister, daughter or nephews like he did. I needed them to shield me with love so I could grow and support.

I wasn't a fool, though; I knew it wouldn't stop the abuse. He was a different type of abuser, one I had only heard of in movies, newspapers and in extreme cases. There was no yelling or arguing, he could grab you in a blink of an eye, toss you to the ground and beat you with fervor. It was different and he was a toxic form of power and plain deadly. He was a force to be reckoned with and I needed help, their help because if I kept on living like this was okay for me, I was hurting my sons and others.

I couldn't help that somehow I just happened to be his muse, his toy and his obsession; as sick as it was. I wanted them to know I wasn't blind and I wasn't a fool. My eyes were wide open but I was scared because I had tried to get away and somehow I kept taking it, slowly feeling like I deserved it. His title and who he was scared me, no terrified me.

I wanted them to embrace me, give me strength and stand beside me as I took this all on. I needed them to know the whole truth about Kane, the planning on Damien's part, everything. I needed them to support me like my doctor said family did and would. I really thought I had it all mapped out and I had pushed on stoically just to survive until this day. This day they would arrive and somewhere I thought they would laugh with me, cry with me and most importantly just hold me until I was tough enough to stand on my own two feet again.

I was very new to this idea of a support network, a support group, which kept you together and strong. That held your truth even when someone tried to rob it from you. I really had no idea about it all, but I knew it was necessary, and hearing about it made me confidant. Feeling it from others did make me feel better, even for a moment or the day.

I was raised on *"be solid, quiet, don't say shit to anyone"* mentality. I had been on my own since I was fifteen years old and that was the street talk that had been embedded in me. But I had grown and I had seen that side of life, far too long and I liked the good side, with the good life. Positive healthy people, who didn't hurt others or take from them. I always had, admiring it at a distance, yearning for it and relishing every moment I had within it.

I was now officially ready to take another step into the structure of it all, by being honest and looking for the support from the people society said were supposed to be there. I was ready to share it all about Damien and I so this day meant a lot to me, a lot more than anyone would ever know. Showing my family I was not stupid, a fool or even deserved this. I had made mistakes and I own them but I need them now, I need them. I was ready to open my sealed lips and be honest.

It wasn't about cancelling a wedding , or phoning that phone number to go underground. This was a day to show I understood their opinion and that I did agree, but that right now I needed them to be strong for me, so I could be strong. I needed to know they loved me and stood beside me and that no Beast could ever crack my circle of love, my family. I needed them to trust me so I could trust myself to make the right choices. I needed them to understand I had woken The Beast and was with a dangerous gangster that used his power, in all the wrong ways and against me. They needed to understand it was either *die or die trying* with him. I'm not implying that all gangsters are like that. I am saying this man was. Not all, but he was supposed to be my husband in forty-eight hours and either I do call that number or I share with them and hopefully formulate a plan to get him away from us. OMG how I needed their help and support.

I recalled all I had learned so far about building a safety network and today was my day to apply it and use it. I knew that every nice thing said to me, felt good, I knew that strangers liked me and people embraced me when *they all* weren't around. I knew this, but strangers can't help you in the dead of night while you are being beaten and afraid. But family could, right? Family had your back; family wants to keep you safe and family was there for you. I wanted to have faith in them and that principle alone.

After yesterday, it was even more imperative that I seek them out and share my truth in private. He was gone on a flight to Alberta and they were to arrive. I had been eagerly waiting for today, for weeks, because I also wanted them to *hear* other truths from me; that it wasn't right to belittle me in front of my children, or that it wasn't right to call me names. It hurt me and I needed for them to stop, to please stop; I could only be the joke for so long. I deserved the same respect that they, gave each other.

I wanted them to see that I was an adult now, not the teenager they still thought I was. And if all they did was mock me because I needed help then they should start looking at the years in between all that, when I had always done good things for others; stop seeing all the teenage stuff and to quit judging me so brutally. They needed to start seeing the Kerri I am, not the Kerri they thought I was and I needed to take the first step; by being honest with them-not my doctor-not the nurses, but them.

The have all lived thousands of miles away, for fifteen years, so how could they possibly know? "Please see the *me*, I am," was all I wanted to ask of them, never mind PS: by the way can you help me to stand up to Hells Angel who likes to torment me.

I talked to myself practicing what I would say to them, as soon as they were all here. I would do it in a mirror to gather strength, when I was driving or alone in my head. I had to build all that courage up so that I could speak from my heart and ask them to believe in me and help me for the sake of my children's and our future. Those weeks of planning had brought me focus and helped me to survive to this point and they had no idea, none at all. I was going to agree with them but also hoped for them to agree with me and support me, with my slow climb to freedom.

Desiree had said I was a fool to trust them and that over the last few years, she had seen the way they treated me. She said it was cruel and that she'd never seen a family do that before. It was as though she was so wise for her years or maybe that she was an outsider looking in. Perhaps my kindness and forgiving way had only set the stage to get continually walked on, maybe she was right. But, I refused to go there, not now. I shut her thoughts down even asking her to stop.

She was still sleeping while I was mentally preparing to hold a big family discussion once they arrived. I was finally ready to be open, honest and completely put it all on table about what I have been going through, how I got here. I was ready to share how he planned this, years ago, and my only hope of surviving was to get through this. If they could back me and be there for me, in case I fell, or worse, if I died, my kids would be okay and safe.

I needed to do this and my finish line was almost here. Yesterday he had ripped what little smile I had from me, taking my father's money for his own gain and I couldn't take any more of it. My mind only played back, on repeat, over and over all these humiliating moments he put me through. There were no more sunny days ahead for me and I knew it.

I looked in the mirror after getting out of the shower and saw my body mottled with bruises. My face was untouched but my arms and legs were covered. I had no less than a dozen or more across my petite frame. In differing stages of healing, my bruises stood out in a myriad of colours; varying hues of purples, blacks, blues, reds, greens and yellows. They added to the repulsion I felt for myself. Before me, a dark, empty shell of my former self stared back from the reflection with hollow eyes.

I thought I was fat, grotesquely large, even though I weighed no more than one hundred and five pounds. I saw multiple rolls where there were none; I saw layers of cellulite where there wasn't. I saw every imperfection magnified because, to me, I was as imperfect as could be. I thought I was repulsive and the very sight of me, made people turn away in disgust and that is what he told me countless times; only if I put eyelashes on, was I prettier and presentable. I was grateful for the fake eyelashes as they covered the hideous way I looked. For me, the lashes covered the deep, dark shadows in my eyes. To me, it hid the hollowness and pain from my blank stares… to me it gave me a bandaid to hide my emptiness.

I was so worn out, almost defeated and broken. I left the bathroom to go into the kitchen and make a coffee. I saw a note on top of some papers addressed to me. I quickly scanned the contents.

{I have them in front of me right now- inserted into the middle of book}

"Hope you have a great day hunny. See you when I get back. I love you,"

Love Beast

He seemed to sign his name 'Beast', more and more frequently, like it was an alter ego he had embraced

I read the papers that lay beneath the note and something in my chest slid and dropped. I was shaking by the time I finished reading; I was in shock. As I read, it dawned on me that he had purposely intended for me to read these papers, the day before our wedding. It was a direct blow; another calculated move to have complete and utter control over me and everything else in my life.

In my trembling hands, I held a _prenuptial agreement_ that he had drawn up for me. It was two days before our wedding! The careless way he left it for me, shook me to the core. How much more can one heart take? How much more could I take? I felt his grip tighten around my neck in a noose, without him even present.

It was another punch in my gut as I re-evaluated all I had been through with this man. I was disgusted and his level of trust for me was obvious, or so I surmised. He would constantly throw in my face that I was exactly like my mother. That my mother had never deserved everything she'd received from her own divorce, of 20+ years of marriage. I could hear those daily comments pass through my consciousness and I felt betrayed.

I didn't know what was more comical, really. The concept that Damien thought he was some millionaire and needed a prenuptial agreement or knowing how he would chauvinistically boast to his 'associates' how he kept me in my place. Apparently, again, I was meant to feel shame and he gets to feel a further inflation of his status and appalling ego.

He was mistaken if he thought he actually was some hot shot millionaire. I out of anyone knew the truth; his debt load was racked, heavily, through the roof. I was smart but I was also very, very naïve t to have succumbed, over time, I'd let him take everything from me, isolate me, instead of being the strong woman I had seen others be.

This was truly a joke, and yet another slap in my face. I was shaking, and not because I wanted the house but because he purposely meant to hurt me. His mental tactics and cruel displays of manipulation were gouging a deep mark on my heart. And striking a blow to any perception of an '*Us*' or '*We*'.

I picked up the phone, consumed by flames of furious rage, and with my finger stabbed out his phone number. I knew I was a coward to call him on the phone and not confront him face-to-face, but it was the only way I could ever feel safe when reacting to him and his treatment; I felt safer when other people were around or when he was far away on the other end of the phone line. Never, to him privately, never! I knew I would end up dead *(I do not say those words loosely-he told me this countless times, "I'm going to kill you, your dead")*.

He was a fair distance away, in another province; my family would be here by the time he returned, so I had nothing to lose.

When he answered I said into the phone with a lethal, yet quiet tone, actually with a distinct and even clearer pronunciation, you'd be proud. "I would like the money my father gifted us, to give back to him. And I would like it NOW! Asshole! (I can mimic it to a tea). "I'm leaving your piece of shit ass and moving out! Take your pre-nup and shove it up your penniless broke ass! Wanna-be MISTER TRUMP and M"....

As my words hung even lower but disgusted, "I never wanted to marry you, in the first place!"

I meant every damn word I spoke into that phone and thought this was the perfect opportunity to finally leave him.

Yes, those were my initial words, fueled by all those years of abuse had rushed to the surface. The audacity of this man knew no boundaries. He was a joke to me. I had mimicked him; I had been abused by him. I have dealt with so much from him, that the caged woman I'd become, surfaced. Gone was the plan to talk with my family, gone were the fake smiles covering any bravado. I snapped. I was so sick of his outrageous display of wealth that he never seemed to have and taking from others. This was the perfect time to step up and stomp out of his life for good. I was done.

But I was also boldly aware of how invested he was with status, prestige and greed. That the waters I was walking on, were untested and unchartered territory.

He simply replied, "Oh hunny, I will be back tonight. We are getting married soon, relax".

"Baby even if you ran away with the pool boy , every year of marriage is a hundred thousand in your pocket"

I went to hang up, after a truly musical laugh escaped me, but then I heard the familiar tone of deadly seriousness that I had learned, long, long ago. He spoke coldly after my mocking laugh, "Play nice hunny or you know what happens…. It only takes three signatures, to have you committed."

I almost puked as my stomach turned over and now the full extent of his madness hit its peak. I had to get out of here! I had to leave. *"Omg"* screamed inside my head. He was sick and demented. Every emotion cascaded around me.

"Pack the kids, pack the kids, run." That's all that I thought, *"Get out*

of here!" and then it would hit me again, thinking ahead, thinking of now and
thinking,"Get out now"!

I didn't tear up the prenuptial papers. No, to me he could have them
for a souvenir and prove his excuse to everyone. I left them for all to
see, but mostly for him to have.

I packed up our belongings and a few bags. I woke Desiree and her
friend up fast and shut down my phone. My only thought as I prepared
to leave this, cold, lonely house. "I never wanted to be here in the first
place, I really didn't like it and this was my chance to finally be free".

Let him think that I wouldn't sign his hoax of an agreement, this
was my chance to leave but his threats still resonated throughout my
mind. IF it's not death, it's now a mental hospital. What did I ever do to
him, for him to hate me so?

Left I did. I phoned my step-father and asked him *once again* to help
me, get a room for a few nights. I explained in ashamed, frustrated tears
that were choking me, that I didn't HAVE any money. That Damien had
taken it, spent it and I wasn't allowed to have any and *"Please dad just get
me out of here", I can't do this"*. I told him what Damien had threatened
and my step-father laughed. That was the only consolation I had and
it helped me get back to the reality of why that note was comical. His
laugh helped.

My step-father was upset, don't get me wrong, but calm and helped
me see how mixed up Damien really was. After a good talk he booked
me a room. I felt ashamed. I felt humiliated. But I felt at least I have
someone and I had him. Damien took that special moment by my
step-father and stepped on it with a twisted mind and warped sense of
entitlement.

In the back of my mind I thought or wanted to believe my family arriving would be there for me. That hope cascaded into a wish for their approval and support like I had by my step-father. Their arrival would help me too. Everything felt right and perhaps this is how it had to be, in order to leave and I was okay with that.

I drove out of that house while Desiree waited for the boys to get up and secured our room at the hotel . I decided to stop by the kids and our old apartment, until my nerves subsided. I needed time to unravel and calm my nerves. I had the keys and aimlessly walked around the empty unit, until I curled into a corner and just sobbed. My tears were that of devastation.

Was this my time to finally leave him for good, with the family coming from so far away, is this my chance to finally be free of him. Would I be allowed? His tone stated otherwise, so I didn't know. But I did know this; I never wanted to marry him. I hadn't planned my wedding and I lacked those euphoric warm, fuzzy, feelings of certainty I am sure most brides have. My feelings were spent in survival mode, fleeing or loneliness. Oh, such abject loneliness enveloped me as I allowed my mind to go over everything.

It was the greed, this is his motive and I tried to come up with an excuse for his again behavior. I had watched in him over the last few months. The money he had lately, the tens of thousands, even hundreds of thousands, was being given to him from unsuspecting people. This man had a mortgage to the hilt and a truck he could barely afford, but he had his *scratch* (cash) and could afford what I would never be allowed. What is it with this man and his items; his possessions and belongings?

I remember thinking: if I was only his most precious new-house, would I then be treated with respect, dignity and lifted up above all else, forgotten now was the why we were together and only the moments and flights most present in my mind.

He never took the time, ever, in all these years to really know me, none at all. If he had, he would've realized I wasn't my mother nor would I have wanted to be in such a big house, all alone. I like cozy and inviting, not big and intimidating. If I left it would be with my sons and our bags nothing more, he was the one who wouldn't leave us alone. I wasn't begging to stay, nor had I ever. It was him who sought me out, not me seeking him. He chose me and I knew he was up to something worse, I could feel it. This was a manipulation tactic, spiraled with greed and mixed with power. He was all about show and this display with a pre-nup was nothing more than an attempt to demoralize me and feed his ego. It stung, it hurt, no, it burnt me and I knew it was another ploy to show everyone coming I was nothing more than a piece of meat for him to tenderize with brutal force.

In my state of distress, I just tried to make sense of everything and really never realized, I had only been going in circles. Like a round wheel of abuse. I searched for my resolution and solution every day, sometimes frantically, a dozen or more times. Was this my chance and it never being the one. I was holding onto to the newest moment as an excuse, opposed to just knowing it was all wrong in the first place. This is the way an abuser spins you around, only to make you forget your own self-worth, preservation and morals.

In that apartment, as empty as it was, I held onto that very same chance and instant. I became that long-lost little girl clutching and holding any kind of 'good' she could find, like my family is coming and thought, *"YES, this was our chance, he gave us an excuse to backout"* My family being present would keep me safe from being held captive or beaten this time.

In my delusional moment I thought I still had my apartment or maybe I would be able to leave with the kids and move far way, like his first wife did to Alberta. Silently, I had been watching for any chance at freedom away from this man and maybe, just maybe, it was now being handed to me.

I embraced my chance whole-heartedly but the burnt feeling still stung with the careless treatment he had served me, not just with the papers he left casually for any visitor to see but the way he took all that meant the world to me away. My once car, my savings, my dad's wedding present and my very own smile. I was raw. It was his way to mentally spin me in confusing circles, losing sight of what was wrong and what was right. It created doubt in me. I had so much bottled up inside of me, that it combusted, scorched me and left me painfully void of an ever present reality. *I had always been treated this way by people close to me...*

What compounded my feelings and broke my very heart was my knowing family would have something else to add to their ever chronicled list of "flaws of Kerri", to yap about. Why did he do this a mere two days before the wedding or immediate family arriving? Would this reason be yet another saving grace or excuse for him?

It was as if he wanted to leave me the paperwork specifically for the purpose of hurting me and make me look like a fool. Was it crazy that I caught on to him and phoned to tell him he was an asshole- because I noticed his mentally warped game? My mind couldn't see forward, past the incident. But yet it could go as far back as I could remember.

An abused woman tries to leave, she really does but each blow hurts and each emotional blow rocks us to the center of whatever good might be left and this day my inner core was gutted. On this day, I was penniless, without a car, without a home, unless I abided by strict orders, of course. It was two days before a wedding I dreaded and the worst moment in my life. It was a warm-up to what life was about to become if I married him; the authoritarian control of a man, who wasn't just physically abusive but emotionally and mentally as well. Add a Hells Angel patch, to match his already inflated power tripping ego and the result was a dangerous. A very dangerous individual who wanted to own me, NO control me..

It seemed as if he had everyone surrounding him and we (the boys and I) only had ourselves. My faith in my family was something based on a deep hope and a yearning, only a child gets when whimpering from a terrifying nightmare, in the middle of a raging storm.

I needed them more than any of them ever knew. I needed to be held up, or better yet, just held; for I was falling and I didn't know if I would make it another day and I didn't know what was real anymore.

I held on to the conclusion that I would be fine until my family arrived. I could hold it together and there is where my faith and belief sprang from. I got back up from the ground of my bare apartment our once only stable sanctuary and wiped my tears, to walk out that door; with only a plan and wish for ultimate freedom.

I was going to casually pull it together and walk into that house to get my children. One last time, I was going to cover up my pain with a false face and try my best to hold it together in front of everyone already there. We were once again going on the phoney journey of a mini holiday and "fun in a hotel room" for a night, just until family arrived. After that, maybe just maybe, a new beginning in a whole new province…and a perhaps whole new land…..

I locked the door and strolled down the apartments corridors; doing my best to pull myself together and smile at my old neighbours. I'd had a good cry, no I was breathless when I collided with floor and tears poured down my face in hollowness. I had only somewhat of a plan, but now however I had my deep inner conviction. He was as fake as could be and just so totally mentally fucked up!

Don't get me wrong, I think it is one-hundred percent fine to have a pre-nuptial agreement. I understand that if you have things that need to remain in your family, lots of money that was earned beforehand and to protect property that has already been signed or given to someone else. There are personal and individual circumstances, but what he did was different. He had nothing as of yet, and anything he did have, was while we were together (not that I wanted any of it), so it was all redundant to me. This was a mere way to exert more control and nothing more. It was his nasty way of never mentioning it beforehand and flying out of town. Then leaving it for all to see until I awoke and found it, with the added mixture of more than likely using my own fathers wedding present to have it drawn up, add to that that, it was only forty-eight hours before our hoax of a wedding = complete and utter JERK.

Runaway Bride

"The often frenzied feeling of chaos, may not be the negative forces that surround you, but in fact; the very way you, allowed your life pieces to fall into place"

It was his way of owning it all, even me. It was a clever, calculated, way to inflict even more torment onto me and put me in my place. Just so I would know he was master and I was servant. But what he never expected was that I had been pushed too far, too many times. The love I thought I once had for him was already shrivelled and gone. I had given up on *"us"* a long time ago and what was the worst thing about it all, I was giving up on myself in the process.

You see, the docile, quiet girl that had never muttered a word back or even spoke up, was at her breaking point. Sleepless, aching all through her body but shored up by the idea of her family all arriving and she feels she has a bit more backbone than she previously had. Put the simple basic facts together with "she's not stupid, and knows what he's done is morally and ethically wrong". Anyone with eyes and heart, would know she doesn't want to actually marry The Beast, she wants to run and that girl has now started speaking up.

Again, his mistake or flaw in all this. Was he never really took the time to actually know me, or care to know me at all. He didn't realize I never wanted to marry him in the first place; he only victimized me to make me feel I had to stay with him and could never leave or I would be hunted down like an animal and killed.

What he apparently forgot was that he had me an inch from losing my life a mere few months beforehand; when I ran to safety on the island. That took me weeks to heal from and my heart never healed towards him or about him quite the same. He didn't propose in a loving manner but in a desperately orchestrated one and he conveniently forgot because *he got away with it, when I said yes*.

The drive back to the house gave me breathing time to prepare to brave another storm, hold on, one more day. My family was all slowly arriving and going to be here together soon. I had placed such a deep faith into a belief system that I was told would work to rescue me. I was so concentrated on that hope I never prepared myself for an outcome that didn't work; or what it would feel like to find myself not supported. I had one plan, not two or three; I had only one.

That, I didn't see what maybe I should've or I didn't hold onto what I knew as a child; that I was me, Kerri. I had stood alone or apart most of my life. I forgot who I was.

I had this vision of love and support. I had such deep knowledge that I was in real trouble this time and my blood family were the only ones who could save me. I lost me somewhere and I held onto that little girl who knew family should be there for each other, forgetting it was me who had painted that beautiful picture of reunion, safety and forgiveness that I believed in, not them who believed in the same or the same with me painted in that picture.

I should've stopped and made a back-up plan. Or not placed so much faith into people who had never believed in me in the first place. I should've stopped to take a harsh look around me when walking back into that wretched house we'd built and paid attention to the people already there.

I am usually so perceptive; why this slipped my notice was beyond me. I was caught in the middle of a carousel spinning in a circle of emotions. I should've asked myself, *"Why are these people here?*

For me?

For my fiancé or for the glamour and allure of being invited to a Hells Angels wedding; to take pictures amongst the elite of all bad boys?"

Instead I felt utterly devastated and my emotions were taking a stronger hold as the hour approached to permanently be shackled to him. He had already left his mark with so much other things, why the pre-nup, on the counter for all to see.

It was an embarrassment that he had done that and mixed with the simple fact that it inflated his status, of somehow being rich (when he wasn't in the least). It was a rotten joke that no one cared about who he hurt. When I cared about every last one of them and now somehow, as a result of all his tactics, I was deemed unworthy, condemned and deserving of this treatment.

Damien had a way of talking or diverting every conversation to himself, as if it built him up somehow. The simple fact that I was wearing bruises all over my frame, in the heat of summer and no one questioned this? Or even asked! Should've stopped me further from spending so much time licking my own wounds and paid more attention to who was in our house surrounding us, instead I thought, *"What morals do these people in my house have?"*

Damien didn't have to worry about building a support group or supporters; he had a worldwide support group and I had only a few, at best.

I was so busy feeling alone and betrayed that I prevented myself from seeing the obvious or acknowledging it. If I had, I would not have invested so much belief into a safety net of family and just got the hell out.

Secretly snide comments were being passed the last few days, again whispered behind hands and it broke my already fragile being in two.

No, instead I only saw the horror before me. Not what was in front of me. Then on a plan that already should've been in place. Focused on the scary feeling of, what would happen when my family does leave? Or oh my god, what am I doing? I am an idiot only knocking an already broken person in half.

So I ignored the strangely distant looks of wanna-be-relatives, and distant friends. I ignored the narrow-eyed gazes of speculation people were throwing my way. I forgot to be perceptive and use my knowledge I had already acquired amongst these people, to be smarter and on it.

Again, I just thought it was because they could see I was miserable and not the obvious signs, that they might've actually thought I was everything Damien had been telling them. Crazy....

I knew how he worked, but in the moments of abuse, I forgot. Of course he had to cover up his behavior, or even the questions if people asked why I had bruises. Why I didn't seem like the blushing bride. Why I had to now, a day before the wedding, cancel all the hair and nail appointments for the bridesmaids. Because he was up to something far deeper than my instincts even detected, he was capable of a manipulation that is carefully premeditated.

I knew he took the money and hid it away somewhere, there was no way he could have me near it. I might leave. I'd only felt the panic of the upcoming nuptials, the lonely feeling of abuse and the days that would follow after I got married.

I may have woken up to a shocker with his ridiculous pre-nup but there was something far more sinister going on here than I realized. I only knew or felt how I was feeling. I held onto that with such resolve, that I didn't notice the diabolical, twisted mechanisms of Damian, that I would've normally noticed going on around me. It's why I had confided in my doctor and even the nurses over the last year and half. I needed to get away. Instead, my friends thought I was in la la land and that ship came in with a bang.

I had looked past so much already and this was a humiliating way to treat me before all my relatives arrived. It was wrong , if he really felt I should sign a pre nup; why not bring it up months beforehand? Because that's not him, he did this as a way to look rich and to make me look like marrying him was a privilege, when in fact, it was my worst nightmare come true, by far.

I was hurt. Yes, but more than anything I was grasping at straws and just couldn't handle anymore personal blows to my character. I walked away instead of facing everyone. I walked right out that door with my bags, returning only for Desiree and my sons. I left my dress hanging and I left all my belongings. I left it all. It was time to use the gift of strength he had given me with his blatant disregard and petty contract full of macho ego, and leave.

My one mistake in vacating the premises as I did, was I should have spoken the truth and explained to others why I was leaving. I gave Damien a tool to manipulate the situation further by being the voice everyone would hear. I didn't give myself a chance when I did that, or to steer this mess in the proper direction by explaining why I was leaving in the first place. Instead I gave Damien a full clip of ammunition to fire off at will against me.

As a person living through an abusive relationship, man or woman, we often get tied up in the moment; it's all we have. These moments lead us into cycle and why it keeps going around and around. Never actually ending but continues to circulate.

I chose not to play by given fact and instead play by emotion. I should've laughed, not got angry on the phone or even called him in the first place. I should've then made my coffee, sat outside and casually rolled my eyes at arriving guest, and told the truth. "Damien is not rich, we built this house together. Why he goes to these levels to show off and think he is impressing people or goes on his inflated ego trip, is truly beyond me"? I should've planted my own seeds of doubt and absolute realistic truth, into everyone's mind.

I should have taken that one word our teachers teach us, patience.

I should NOT have, gotten upset and packed my things, ultimately leaving. It gave him further opportunity to take control and make broadcasts of outrageous stories to all in residence. I had allowed him the opportunity to sink his teeth in and go for the kill, with his game of millionaire status and dominant abuse.

I couldn't help thinking, *"Is this why some wives look worn out when there only forty? From living with these kinds of games and control?"* I admit that I thought that more than once. I thought a lot of things in the moment and to myself.

I knew I could go back to my apartment but then what if he showed up and refused to leave, again or threw me off the balcony, only to take the children to his enclosed property?

I wasn't looking at big picture but at the simple *now* steps. In my mind, I truly thought my family would show up and wrap their arms around me and my sons; encasing us, like a shield.

I didn't want to be married to Damien, or locked away and tortured in the now built, castle walls of that contaminated house. I thought my family would help me, even be happy to do it and I felt better knowing that. I actually fooled myself enough to think I was doing the right thing, not the exact opposite by leaving everyone to listen to and accept whatever Damien might say to cover up his wrong-doings.

I hadn't gotten that far with him, I just wasn't like him, the pre-mediated man with a plan. I had no idea he was already filling stories in peoples minds; to me I just thought it was all about the power of his patch.

I couldn't even bear to try to speak with the few people who were present. I felt so ashamed that my family was now going to walk into all of this and yet, I felt better knowing they were en route. I felt like I was going to let them down yet again but I was finally going to gain their respect to.

Alone with Desiree, we called movers and made plans for them to arrive at the house the next day, grab our furniture and move it back into the apartment for the time being. We had it all figured out and my step-father said he would help pay for it. I still had my phone off as I didn't want to speak with Damien or hear his deviant nonsense. To me, I was doing the most logical steps possible. To me I was showing my family that I was serious and I really thought they would be proud.

I left a voicemail on my sister's and mom's phones, with the contact information for Desiree's phone number and our room number; so when they arrived through the mountains they would know where we were and the directions to the hotel. They were only booked at the hotel right across the street (a five minute walk from ours) so I didn't think it would be much of an ordeal to find me when they arrived.

I was hoping once they were settled we would meet up and even imagined them cascading into my room with huge arms filled with love to hold me. I thought they would show up because they cared. But once nightfall settled in and I had heard from no one, I started wondering. Desiree and her friend were watching me closely and I felt so vulnerable that night. I was chronicling mentally the miles/km and hours and the fact maybe they stopped somewhere along the way, in my head because they hadn't arrived yet.

When I went to sleep two nights before my wedding, alone with no family in sight, I was sad. But I stayed firmly where I was because I knew I was doing the right thing, by not marrying Damien and fighting for freedom the only way I knew how to.

I tossed all night long, even getting up to go to the front desk just to talk to the gentleman there. He knew me now, the why's we come there and so forth. He seen the bruises and knew our flight. So we talked as we always do when the boys are sleeping and that gentleman gave me a feeling of security. I went back upstairs to finally sleep.

We all woke in a panicked rush. We only had a few hours before the moving truck would be at the Big House. It would be arriving at noon, so I had limited time to mentally prepare to see Damien. It was the day before our wedding and I was still trying to stomach everything that had happened the days before and I was trying to remain strong.

Desiree and her friend did their best to console me and show support. They never once told me I should marry him. And after they tried calling my family half the night, with no response, they were apprehensive about them too. I heard/saw it in their comments and demeanor.

I also seen them whisper about it. That hurt but I couldn't blame them, not at all. Having them beside me helped but having to now face Damien and go to the house, left me visibly shaking and scared. They told me not to go, they would in my stead. I couldn't do that to them, it was my obligation to go and knowing people were around I thought I would be safe. This was not their battle to go up against. Mine.

They told me again they didn't think it was normal that we hadn't heard from anyone in my family. They said that they left numerous texts messages and that they thought it was rude, even disrespectful that we hadn't even received a reply. Des raised her voice to me and said, "Your family should've called right away! All of this, Kerri, makes no sense! It makes me sick." Desiree yelled it out loud, that late morning, before we left the hotel to go. She said "Kerri wake the fuck up!!!! Why didn't *your* very own family show up or call? Why Kerri, think about it, Kerri please let us go over there something is not right, not right at all"!!!!

It was insane because all night and even into the next morning, I was giving or making excuses for why my family hadn't heard, or responded to our S.O.S calls. Or that of my sitters. They should've arrived by mid-day, yesterday!

I was also becoming suspicious, but did my best to put on a brave face. I had to, for the children and myself. That's all I had left to go on and I guess when a truth is staring you so obviously in the face, you try to deny it; as I did for them. I just jumped in our rental vehicle and drove there, not wanting to believe the obvious.

My Very Breath Taken In a Moment of Clarity

"When we love and are robbed of that, we crumble in ways that are unfathomable to everyone else, until they too feel the loss you have"

Once we arrived at the big house, we noticed the driveway was packed with cars, suvs, trucks you name it and a few had Alberta plates on them. My very heart sunk because in that moment I knew where my family had been, with him.

I turned around and told my sons that their cousins were here and they went ripping out of the car and up that driveway so fast, it was adorable. I never allowed them to hear my anguish about any of this, I covered it up with love, kisses and a false smile. That dug at me and why I believe I couldn't keep carrying this false demeanor any longer. When my sons showed their enthusiasm and went ripping up that driveway with excitement it brought normalcy to all of our nerves, for the briefest of moments.

The girls and I just looked at each other and mentally prepared to face everyone. We took our time in the driveway. No one came from around the front of the house, no one. Everyone would know I was here, by seeing even hearing the boys clamber through the house. I didn't want to spectacle, but I guess after about 15-20 minutes, many cigarettes later, it was time to go up and into the backyard of the house; to check on my sons at least.

What hit me when I rounded the corner was something I never expected to see, not at all. It broke my heart, ripped it out and stomped on it. Not by hand, brutal force or combat but by a truth so obvious it's directly in your sight and you feel it like a truth so profound that it's all your left with. The many snide remarks, judgements and abuse, hit with such force, I stumbled and fell against Desiree with a thud.

My family. My sisters. My mother and Damien. Along with a few others, sat there merrily around the pool laughing, having a blast. A few with their heads pressed together, as if to be secretive. I could see their eyes, one by one pass over me; it left me feeling like I didn't even matter, no acknowledgment, nothing, I was invisible. No one cared and I hurt like I had lost all that I had ever loved.

It was a previous night of emotional pain for me, a strongness only barely hung onto and a plan of support I felt I had mentally built up and strategically planned with my doctor, plus others; all taken away in After staring in horror, I spun around to go back the way I had come, around the side of the house to the front yard. I just cried. The girls held me and my resolve splintered in every piece you can imagine. All I had planned and hoped for, was gone with the reality of seeing my family's ignorance.

My life was in crisis and they were all having a poolside party, with the very man who struck his own hand against me time and time again. Des and her friend gave each other looks over my bowed head as I wept. They allowed me to feel my pain, and hurt as I needed to. They gave me a gift that day/moment without ever realizing it; they gave me validation, without scolding me or told you so words. BOTH those girls, gave me *acceptance* and allowed me to feel exactly what I needed to, in those moments.

It showed me that all the nights I waited for my sisters and family to arrive for help, or all the nights I needed my family's arms to cradle me, hold me and heal me, were never going to happen. Only in my *wildest dreams*. Now and even before as a child. I felt the blow with a physical force of shame. No one cared about me and no one ever had. They just sat there, looked over and went back to laughing and talking.

No sister came and wrapped her arms around me, no mother made a move to embrace me and, strangely, none of my nieces or nephews even ran to their auntie for hugs to love me. I was as alone as anyone could ever be. My loneliness was my terror and fear. I had nothing and to me I was already nothing.

Even though I hadn't seen family in over a year, this was my greeting, nothing. It was a huge display of what I really did mean to all of them and I felt as worthless as Damien had been telling me I was. But I wasn't prepared for what was to follow. As the crumbles broke away, with every last disloyalty and judgement exposed, felt like the feel of an open palm slapping across naked skin. It smacked me straight in the heart with a truth, that brought me to my very knees.

Desiree looked at me, when the tears could no longer be stopped and said "they're sick. That I wasn't anything like them and they should be ashamed".

Desiree doesn't speak like that nor have I seen her as upset as she was. I just kept seeing Damien's head turn towards me, on repeat in my mind. Him giving me a smug victorious look before I turned to walk away. It kept playing in my mind what I had just witnessed, and that made me cry all the more. It was unlike any cry I had ever felt, it took the wind out me, knocking my body to its knees. It was gut-retching and humiliating; a dark and empty wail of how alone I really was. Except I don't cry out when I cry, so my cheeks were drenched as I stared without direct eye contact and felt a longing for all I never had.

I was lost and hollow. I couldn't take anymore. I didn't want what I had had seen to be true but it was true, there was no more hope just me. I who was a Nobody. I knew it, now, with every soul shaking breath I took. Why would they so carelessly turn their backs on me?

Quietly I took out my cell phone and called the hotel, they were staying at for the wedding. (I had booked it for everyone so I was able to access the details). I asked the front desk if anyone from my family had arrived yet and who all checked in. When she came back on the phone she told me- they had all checked in yesterday afternoon, as planned. I don't know if I hung up the phone, or just allowed it to drop to the ground. A knife stabbed through the very essence of my heart. There were no more excuses left or to be made. I was very much alone and that day haunted me above all else.

There is no feeling more hurtful than when family, blood and friends you have held so close to your heart, betray you. Or when you realize they don't care about you as much as you cared for them.

All those weeks I had held onto them and their love to help pull me through, I'd held onto in a way that kept me sane and from falling. They had no idea. I felt a devastating loss that day; A grief that happens when you lose a family member, except I lost every last one of them all in a swoop. I was hurt, no, I was ripped apart in ways I only felt as a child. I was as devastated by their disregard as I was with myself for thinking I could lean on them.

They had been here, in town, the whole the time. They chose not to show up or call. They chose to roll their very eyes at the text messages and voicemails they received.

All the times I had assured my sons, (Their own grandchildren/nephews!) that they hadn't arrived yet, was a lie. All the while I am braving a face and sharing with my own sons, that they were just as excited to see them, as they were. It was a joke.

No they didn't want to come say 'hi' nor did they try and reachout to see if I was okay. They didn't miss me, as I missed them. It was a one-sided relationship and that day I felt it and saw it, in more clarity than ever before. That day in my heart, I lost my family and knew the truth.

When my mother came around the side of the house so many minutes later, it was too long already since the brazen truth was seen. I was by know, leaning up against the car with tears splashed down my mascara drenched face. She looked at me with such pity it was wrong. It was the same look as how many years so far in my life, like I did something wrong.

They had no care for my feelings nor what I had been going through. Only their own justifications of what they thought I deserved. I knew they'd heard all they had to "From Damien". You could see it, clearly. I also felt in my bones and heart that they knew everything yesterday. I could envision them rolling their eyes at the drama of arriving and me being at a hotel before our upcoming wedding. I felt it in her bored stare and her tediously slow approach.

No one asked me what happened, no one even bothered to see if I was okay and no one cared enough to even want to. They had all spent yesterday and part of today talking about me and not one of them cared enough to even try and see if I was okay. I felt as little as one could be.

I looked to Desiree for strength because I finally knew all those weeks of hopeful thoughts and visions of my family supporting me were out the window. I could not trust them, with my life, nor my sons. If I did, it would be the same as with Damien; only doing and living as they felt I should. With only their rules and ideas. It almost choked me. I felt I had nothing left. I felt I had no one and nothing. Damien had not only taken my visions as a girl but he also took my family. That day I saw it and felt it, in every part of my soul.

I told my mother to go away and thanked her in a defiantly crushed way, for not coming to the hotel to see me. I told her how we were all so excited to see them and obviously those feelings weren't reciprocated. She looked at me with her own pangs of guilt and said they had heard what happened. That they thought I needed my own time, alone.

I couldn't help and still to this day help, but think, "Haven't I had enough of that, my whole life". If somebody tells you they need you, do they not need you and they casually blew that off.

I yelled at her. I let it all pour out, "I needed my fucking mother, I needed MY family and that's how family should be, there for each other! " I looked at her and carried on with a proven truth and one I carried as a child; endlessly making those very promises, that my own children would never feel that crippling void of feeling of loneliness.

"I will never, ever, allow my sons to feel what YOU all make me do standing in this very moment! I could never do what you've all done to me, NOW, or ever!"

I had said thank you sarcastically and then told her in a sure, steady voice, "The moving truck will be here in half hour to grab my things, and I am not getting married, nor living in this very house. And, by the way *Mother*, your carelessness and everyone's non-action to my distressed calls will *never* be forgotten".

Kind Kerri was gone in flash, gone. Only a protective, alone, frightened parent stood in her place. "You and everyone make me sick! You out of anyone know the marks I carry by that man, and before my very sham of a wedding you, blow me off, leave me alone to only make us suffer more!"

She was terrified with my outburst, I saw it. She was walking on eggshells and that is what pissed me off. Like, *"why is she doing that? Where is a hug or even a hello?"* I had enough of the pain that kept hitting my heart. I wanted, no I needed love dammit, love!

My sister came out and said, "Oh Kerri suck it up, he gave you a pre-nup sign it and grow up". Her voice, that droll tone and know-it-all attitude all these years, rocked me.

I looked at her and said "Really?! You really think that's what this is all about, *Sister*?" The pain and disbelief resonated throughout my tone but then quick as a trigger I spit back out, before she could speak, "No! That's not all, it's not even the half of it. We left you messages. I was so excited to see you and this is how you treat me?! Get away from me, all of you, GET AWAY FROM ME!"

I rushed up the stairs- rampant even just to start getting a few things ready for the movers. I couldn't look at them, none of them. It hurt, they hurt me, and everyone hurt me. What I saw, what I felt and what I endured. It was fight or flight. It was make it or break it.

I needed to calm down, cool off and I needed to vent by packing boxes, cleaning and just take a few minutes to myself. I was upset at the betrayal of seeing them all sit there in their bathing suits, having lunch, laughing as I sat alone in a hotel room counting the hours for them to arrive. It was such a slap in the face and it is a sting I still feel to this day. The Damien thing never hurt like this did and it would never, ever, remotely come even close. I never loved him, like I cared for my family.

He must've heard about the moving company arriving from my family because he tried to approach me. His eyes danced as they do when I am hurt. He tried to say, "Oh baby just sign the paper, it's no big deal". Then laughed, right up in my face, just to taunt me. I walked away and never said a word. I seen his play, displayed like only he could do.

It was not about that, not at all, it was the control, the torture and abuse, the loneliness and the life. It was all of it and I couldn't take any-more. He didn't like me walking away, you could hear it bugged him in the way he laughed about my sudden withdraw. Mockingly triggering him with my disobedience.

I stayed always in the proximity of people so he couldn't get me alone. I had no more esteem carrying me; I was nothing but an empty shell of broken hollowness. I was on the constant verge of tears and anger. He realized what I was doing by dodging him but he kept trying to approach.

"Get away from me!" I finally snapped so everyone could hear. I was idiotic and playing right into his hands. But I couldn't stop it and felt only the emotion of loss, pain and suffering.

To them it just looked like a soon-to-be husband trying to make-up; to his soon-to-be bride. His gentle approach appeared as if he cared but his face said something else altogether, something none of them could see.

He came up close to my ear and whispered, "whore, you surrey fucking whore, keep it up! They all think you're crazy, they all know you're bipolar, c'mon HUNNY show them! You are nothing to anyone, you pig-whore!" Then turned around, all cool, collected and walked away.

I allowed the tears to fall freely, even falling to the ground looking at my family with pleading in my eyes, but they turned away. I did my best to not be goaded by him. I couldn't help but notice how no one cared about my tears or to just wrap loving arms around me, or how no one could notice my clearly visible distress. It was appalling! All my alone self could think was, *"DO NOT prove him right"* all my emotion bottled inside exploding slowly.

I saw his tactic. I was the only one who felt his wrath and knew his games. My poor mind was on repeat; I didn't expect to walk in and see them all so jolly and happy. It made feel truly worthless. It hurt and now because of my absence, he was somehow proven right and his devious stories validated. I was more alone in those moments than any other time.

It wasn't those terrifying, anxiety driven, bouts of loneliness I'd felt but a true deep and chilling loneliness that comes from knowing that *"No One Cares"*. It was a loneliness that stung further just because they were right there, in my face, and laughing. When I was so overwrought with sadness.

I was in the kitchen, in front of the double bay windows facing the patio, over-looking the pool. The island was behind me and the cupboards before me. I was clearing out one of the shelves, putting a few items in the boxes from up top my chair, when I looked up, amidst my thoughts and angst, there he was, smiling at me. He was enjoying this to the fullest capacity that a man of his station could. I snapped!

"Fuck off! Please, just fuck off!" I roared. All those emotions boiled to the surface. The doors were wide open, as it was August 7th, 2008 and sunny, beautiful. Summer was in full swing. The family gasped like I'd called Satan himself, up from hell.

No one knew what he was doing, poking at me, taunting me but I felt safe from his brutal hands that day, or I thought I was. I felt like I had nothing to lose and I just didn't care anymore. I had been shown exactly what I meant to everyone and I was broken inside. The final piece I had held onto just for them, snapped in every fragment imaginable. I had seen in the distance, everyone in the family shake their heads. He just roared in his obnoxious way and joined them.

I only had my babysitters. My sons were off finally playing with their cousins, who had still never said 'hi' to their auntie. Another blow that rattled my insides. I couldn't help but feel victimized by everyone. Knowing that Desiree was there, no longer comforted me. I had to watch and feel, not just him, but my family be as distant as two foreign shores. I had to see them bond with the beast and it robbed me everything I had left, which wasn't much. I wanted to die, I wanted die, instead I fought as animal would do who was cornered.

My Hurt Became My Rage

"The bond that breaks us,
can make us or even destroy us"

The movers finally arrived moments later, or a lifetime to me and came up to the door. I let them in and told them which couches were coming and where they were going. I never divulged more than that, just tried to stay neutral so everything remained calm.

The movers' arrival did however catch everyone's attention so I tried my damnedest to hold my composure. I had not much composure at all. All of a sudden everyone was coming up to me, saying this and that, like I mattered or they cared, even acting concerned about me. It was joke and wounded me further. *Like "don't put on a show because strangers are around and try to convince them of a caring family!"*

Damien is what finally iced the cake with my toxic outburst that was not good for the children to see, hear or witness in any way, shape or form.

His stance, mixed with whispers about how crazy I am into my ear and name calling, broke me in two, I cracked! I exploded!

I looked at my mother with a tear stained face and a solidity I would later see in the mirror. I begged her with the pain in my eyes and the hurt in my voice, "Mom don't you see what he's doing? Please mom, see it…help me mom, he planned this". I begged her, first quietly with pain and tears rolling down my face. She only turned away from me. That last turn that meant so much and in a instance, I cracked.

"MOM! Don't you FUCKING see the way he treats me? Does anyone in this despicable, fucked up family see how he's done this all to destroy me?" I was vibrating with feeling; I was rocked with emotion and broken beyond repair. I again went about my escapade in a manner that shook the very foundations of our family. A moment never to be forgotten and a moment that I have had to live with every since.

"NOW hear me, do you F★#!'N hear me NOW assholes!!!!! He keeps calling me names as soon as you turn your back, did you NOT F★#!'N hear!?" I ripped my shirt off my upper body in a display that showed how hurt I was and how angry.

"LOOK you fucking heartless bitches! Look at my bruises, look everyone……look at what that man, that *you* covet, does to me!" There I fell to my knees in pain. Hurt to the core and cried as a child would. "Please, please just look, please", I whimpered, baring my very body for them to see my bruising….

They all just stared at me like I was mentally ill, no one came anywhere near to help me and once again my weakness became my strength. Someone ran to keep the movers outside, in the front yard and away. On the ground begging to be heard, noticing their actions; I shot up.

I stormed onto the deck, through the kitchen and out the french patio doors. The bbq was in my way; I pushed it over, then the table I threw over in haste and into the pool, I did anything to unleash the devastation inside me. I screamed, crying out, begging for mercy, begging for anything to just stop the hurt raging inside. I begged to be heard, with profanities so extreme it bared my very soul and showed my pain.

Once again I tried looking at them, as they scattered trying to protect the items in my path, the items I felt were nothing compared to *me,* a human being. I was rabid; I was lost but most importantly I was trying to show a truth to people who had, in my eyes, never given a damn anyway.

I cried out in anguish, like really cried out in all the ways I felt, begging them to hear me once again. "Look this is why I am leaving, (as I showed them again all the bruises racked and piled on my body) not because of a paper. NOT a piece fucking of paper; that is a lie".

I laughed in a wicked tone, which made me look wanton and wild. I had reached my breaking point and there was no going back now.

I stared at my mother, as blank as any lost soul would be and pleaded again to just hear me. "MOM please you know the truth, you know the truth".

No one cared!

I could see Damien off in the distance, behind all their backs smiling, smirking smugly. He was enjoying all of it and he looked like he just won every vote that he needed to be cast. His smugness, my sister's disgust and Desiree's broken hearted tears falling down her cheeks, helped bring me somewhat back to reality.

I looked worse than ever and there, I started to get all my feelings back. I unleashed the fury that was inside and had no more steam, no more will. I felt bad. I was sorry but I knew I had lost. I was defeated.

I just needed them to believe me or just show they loved me and that I wasn't crazy. I needed all the things my support group had said they would be, just to be true.

I built it so far up in my mind, my safety plan. That when he pulled his one last tactic before they arrived, I fell apart. I fell apart because I thought I could, because I knew they were all going to be here, finally everyone in BC. I had been carrying so much dead weight inside, that I let it all go on the promise of a hope within my very essence of a woman, mother and child.

Instead of all I had built up, my whole demeanor, all my strength I had privately garnered from the doctor. I felt had our best interests at heart. Came crashing down; a day, a moment and a minute too soon.

I was starting to slowly, level out after my breakdown with my mother's very hand now on my shoulder; until my sister spoke to me like she would to a delinquent child.

In a shameful high pitched tone she scolded me, she couldn't hold it back and not once thought of placing herself in my shoes. "KERRI how could you act like this in front of the kids! Shame on you". And with a lasting remark, "YOU need *help!*"

I cracked into these tiny little pieces I thought I had garnered all over again. My head taunted, no one cared, they had only seen the illusion of what he had weaved with his tales and not the truth. But my sister's tone was as insensitive as a whip. Every semblance of reality I had put together, shattered all over again with her response and opinion. I shook my mother's hand free from my shoulder and lunged at her. She jumped away, almost ran and right behind Damien, then past him a few more feet.

I spoke as she ran out the door in a voice only meant for her. "If you ever went through one minute of hell in, I've endured bitch…you wouldn't be spouting off your bossy tone. I loved you TELLY"! I cried out in a fury meant for disloyalty and for her.

"I would've walk through fire to protect you! Then hunt any asshole down just to save you! That's why bitch you will never understand me! I don't need help, YOU DO!" Run Telly, run and speak to all you can that your sister is messed up, 'cause bitch I have heard it my whole life. I'm surprised you even came!"

My truth ruffled her feathers and she spat the only thing she knew would hurt me, out. Except my truth was in her the names I called her, but what was sad, was that she meant every last syllable that spewed from her mouth. "Get help, Kerri-Lynn! He's right about you; you *are* mental, you always have been!" She turned on her heel and said in a rush, that she was taking her kids out of here. That I was sick and there was no way she was subjecting them to my behavior. Out of anything I understood that but the message was that of another caliber and it shook me to devastation. I hurt.

Damien rushed towards me, acting to the fullest like I was about to come unglued again and he knight in shining armor was going to console me, no calm me down. It was the go ahead to intervene with my sisters' remark. It was his way of getting validation for his manipulations. I ran into the house, beside the same matching patio doors to the kitchen and tried to get past everyone, just to get away from him, through our room now. Freedom was through those doors, to the front staircase. No one stopped him. Instead following him towards me and I was cornered.

When he turned to come at me I darted away, only to be stopped. I was cornered just inside the bedroom doors. He grabbed hold of me and pulled me even further into our room. (Which sat directly beside the other matching patio doors- leading into the kitchen).

I screamed "NO, don't leave me alone with him, please, please, please don't' leave me alone with him!" I freaked and I struggled. Anything to get him away from me or anyone to hear me, from the very inside of my soul. Not in anguish or pain but in fear. I screamed "NOOOOOOO" saying profanities I'm not proud of describing. No one would listen.

No one in my family, or the associates around at the time cared about anything but what he was saying, nor noticing what he was doing. "Come on whore, keep going, hahahaha" in my ear, he quickly spew, then back away; every few minutes when he got close enough.

I flipped like a switch, when he put his hand on me. I grabbed my painting, directly in front of me and threw it to the ground with such force, the frame splintered. (Not my most thought out plan, nor the best way to try and get people to understand me), but at the moment screaming my truth, it was all I had left without seriously falling to the ground and willing myself to die. It was all I had in me to fight for what

I knew to be wrong in epic proportions.

My sister again with her tone, started freaking out. "The PINO" and ran at it to protect it. But it was too late and she snapped at me again, after another tossed item hit the ground, "Kerri, the kids!!!!!" *It wasn't the kids' telly, it was him and he was hurting me. No one would listen, no one would listen.*

No one understood what he was doing; trying to get me alone; pushing me further into the room. They wanted him to be alone with me, not understanding he was going to hurt me, no one could see my panic and they never stopped long enough to even try. My cries out anger, screams of profanities, and epic display of a true a breakdown; went unheard. My feelings ignored in a blatant disregard for my well-being. No one in the heated moment of breakdown, heard my pleas, they only saw the destruction, and they only saw the truth in his words. No one saw or observed the pain and horror in mine. To me, I felt betrayed and that destroyed any reminisce of who I was.

I carry this moment and breakdown as a fault. I am guilty of breaking. I carry every non-ladylike swear and ever shattering moment as a reminder to how I once felt. I was a fool and, yes, I cracked as any person would finally crack after intense pressure and abuse. I am sorry I couldn't hold it together anymore. My only excuse was; I was broken begging for help the only way I truly broken woman can.

He got his way as my mother arranged with the movers, who tried to help me, even one of them throwing off his shirt to protect me in the beginning but backed away once someone there got them outside and away from the house. I vaguely remember them coming in a few times, asking if I was alright but again I was lost as a mess on the ground and Damien trying to say it was about building the fucking house and getting married within the same week!

My mother and everyone pushed me more so to be alone with Damien, as I fell to the ground, beside the painting after it was shattered. I begged them not to and please just get him away from me (when he touched me I reacted and no one seen a thing but my unstable display, not my fear, not sadness, nor my pain or bruises) even quietly now by this point, but again I went unheard. Instead they started getting every-one who surrounded us to exit my bedroom, and everyone listened, leaving me to face the beast.

My body just collapsed after so much anguish and self-defeat; all my strength was ripped from me by their intervention and all for Damien's benefit. I was half-curled in a ball, half exposed, from my shirt ripped off, in my display of fevered emotions. In the corner beside the very same doors I ran into to, my sister just looked at me with shame. I was disgraced.

My sitters were disregarded when they tried to speak up, gluing themselves to me, many times. They tried to talk calmly and explain what Damien was going to do me and what he has already done, but they were spoken to like children and told to go sit down. Directed by firm adult voices of my relatives and a finger only pointing them where to sit, by the pool.

They were tuned out and turned away. They were the only ones fighting for me and they were told to "Stop! SIT down!" while Damien had a word with me. They cried and still no one seen past a thing but themselves.

I was left alone as everyone was told to clear the room and now looked as mental as Damien tried to make me out to be. I was defeated and as the glass doors were shutting and my ignored pleas, begging my mom, were simply, ignored, I was left alone with Damien, for him to supposedly calm me down.

I was already calm but no one seen past the previous display. No one wanted to be around me or just hold me with care.

Taken

"The shattering existence of your worst fears, playing out like a crippling dream now becomes your only salvation"

His face was taking all of me in, as he twisted his head from side to side evaluating what he was going to now do to me because he had me alone. He locked the door, or sealed it in a display of contemplation and excruciating time standing still quality.

Meticulously and slowly he approached, displaying his contempt to the fullest. No longer was the concerned show he tried with family, but the wicked look that voiced his whispered thoughts in my ear previously, to further belittle me, during my breakdown of mass proportions.

I looked at him, depleted. I tried to speak but instead my disgust came out, "stay away from me, D, leave me alone." But seeing him tilt his head and the way he taunted me before came forward in a rush, "I hate you, you're a sick person for what you've done" and I did.

All he did was laugh in a mocking tone and strike fast. He yanked me up by my hair, grabbing my throat and smacked me right across the face with the back of his hand. He no longer had his own control. I shared too much and goaded him in ways no one does.

I called out for help but no one came. No one would come, no one ever did. I was with The Beast of all Beasts and I was on my own. I knew it now, more than ever before as my last ear defying scream was let from lips. I almost landed with a thud against that wall; directly behind me facing the deck but he had me now by my throat. He had somehow twisted things on such a level that I could never understand. I fed right into it by trying my hardest to hold it all in and exploding.

I cried out and pleaded for anyone to help. They chose to ignore me. I couldn't understand how they couldn't hear. They were right outside the doors. Cleaning up my previous mess and I am quite sure talking about my display just moments before.

I begged him to stop and let me go. He never did, he liked having that much power. He told me as he held me a few inches up the wall by my throat that I was nothing and no one wanted me! He hurt me with that truth unlike any fist, hand or brutality ever could.

Damien carried on saying things like, I was a stench he could never quite clear from his head. I was a pathetic whore of a woman who would never satisfy a man. I was to be used and discarded. Then in a twisted way, he looked at me with the mascara running down my face and said he was going to show me once and for all my place!

He grabbed me with both hands and threw me the few meters onto the bed.

I wailed out as I hit with a thump and onto whatever hard was on the bed at the moment. I cried out in anguish to Get away from me,

GET AWAY from please someone…HELP ME, anyone please…It fell on deaf ears and I looked at man who would do anything to hurt me and show me who was boss.

I tried to crawl up and away, only for him to yank me back down and mockingly spit in my face. His saliva dripped from my eye and made me feel ashamed. He threw his body over mine and pulled my head to the side yanking it brutally. He whispered in a vile tone, "I am going to break you, Kerri-Lynn Krysko, break you!" He tried to kiss my cheek as he whispered," then I will re-build you into the perfect little fucking whore, everyone will want. YOU whore will be all mine." then he laid his mark, the mark I feared and had only heard about. "I own you bitch and your going to listen NOW! No more outbursts, no more running, no more talking to everyone about how bad I am and listen like a good wench."

He started to talk as if he was playing out a fantasy, rubbing his body against mine. I shuddered at his words, and quivered from his touch.

"You're mean, so mean" and my tears just fell one after the other from my eyes. I tried to get up, I tried to call out and then he grabbed me with such force, I thought my neck was going to snap and choked me.

I struggled, all alone, trying to get away, oh how I struggled, but there was no stopping the dazed feeling that was engulfing me. He was holding my neck with pressure that brought the stars to the surface while he rubbed his perverse sick body against mine, spitting venom as he choked me. I was fading thinking I was actually *going to die."* Then he released me, and I barely struggled to the surface from that brink of blackness. It was scary.

I felt him grab at my pants and rip them off of me. He was brutal and distant. I tried once more screaming but my voice was raw and hoarse. I did it anyhow and banged on the headboard to try and get anyone's attention. When no one came I broke into every imaginable piece a woman could. I allowed the tears to pour silently from my eyes as he slammed his sweaty body close to mine. I squirmed as far off the bed as I could, trying to get away. To no avail.

Then he pushed me over the edge, off the bed and onto the floor (the opposite of wall from the doors). I was meshed between the wall and the bed now as he continued his charade. No more cries for help came out, only tears of humiliation. I was only further destroyed with his groping, every time I tried.

I tried to look away but he held my face with one hand, trying to make me look at him while he took what he wanted. He spewed every volatile thing you could imagine as he grabbed at my breasts and pinched them, just to get a response. He wanted me to fight back and there I gave up. I tried to get him to stop but he was intent on inflicting his will. My cries for help went unheard, over and over I tried to scream or call out, until I just stopped. No one would ever help me, not my family, no one. He Damien, was intent on destroying every part of me. I was alone, left to deal with the sickness that thrives when evil is born.

He raped me beside the bed, while everyone was just outside the doors casually visiting, ignoring any signals of distress they might've heard. I don't know what hurt more them outside or him.

When Damien was done taking what he wanted, he rolled over, pulling me up beside him, as I lay limp. He held onto me like he hadn't just violently, violated me and said the words that often repeat themselves, within my mind. "Now your all better hunny, see just what you needed to smarten up!" I felt hollow.

He reached over and plucked the eyelash, which was now on my cheek, off my face because of his spit and said, "I'm going to let everyone know the wedding is still on and tell the movers to go." Just like that, he got up and walked out the door. He was satisfied with his punishment and I was broken.

I heard him laugh outside the door, not mean, not rude, not tauntingly but full filled and that is the day I knew for absolute certain I would never , ever ask anyone for help again, I was alone.

I grabbed my stuff to cover my body and crawled to the bathroom where the toilet was. I locked the door and slipped further away into my sadness than ever before. The silent tears just took over as I lay in there for what seemed like forever, quietly ashamed, reliving what had happened, on repeat.

The one time I finally snap and he gets away with his abuse once again. What hurt the most was they were right outside the doors and could've helped me, but didn't. I didn't just flip a BBQ over or a painting because he was whispering indignant words in my ear, taunting me and then lying to everyone. I snapped because he powerfully controlled all I did and who I was.

He was poking at me to make me snap and he brought it to a whole new level when he touched and abused my body with my family right outside the doors. When he was done, he had pulled up his pants and told me to now be a good girl; as he walked outside. Telling the movers to leave, I sat there alone, afraid, used and shattered.

My mother tried to come in and talk to me a lifetime later and I couldn't talk, I just couldn't. I felt betrayed in every sense of the word. I had more bruises than ever before and wished myself dead.

I didn't talk to anyone for quite sometime. I was numb and when someone did ask me something I just told them to get away from me. I spoke only to a certain few; my nannies, my best-friend at the time, Stella and one of my bridesmaids named Bella. They were my only reprieves to this nightmare and they made me feel like I wasn't going crazy. They arrived at some point during or after this all took place.

My nanny said to me, after I cried into her arms, that my sister Sabrina had no need to mention the kids because they weren't even around. They were playing somewhere far away in the house. She was on top of that when I had cried out in anguish.

My voice was raw, from screaming for help. It was hoarse, rough and barely coherent. You could see a bruise around my eye now visibly showing and marks on my arms where held me down. Bright purple and blue ones but somehow it was no big deal to anyone, not one person but save my littlest Desi~

It wasn't until she packed them up (my sister) bringing them close to the chaos that they, the children knew what was going on (or mine anyways). Desiree said, "Kerri, I can't witness you get married to him, I can't Kerri, I can't" she cried tears of hurt and I held onto her for dear life. We held onto each other. There was now no way out. Police wouldn't keep me safe, no one would.

My mother had somehow during all this, broke out in hives that covered her whole body. Blaming the stress and what had happened with me and my display. Like I caused this to happen to her, when in fact she didn't just get raped and degraded with her own family outside the doors. I couldn't feel the sympathy for her at this time, just couldn't.

I kept telling her, "I am not getting married mom." But no one would hear me and dismissed it in passing; she had her friends and other family present and I was too much of a burden to deal with.

I was cast out from people's concerns after that debacle, not one of them knowing what had just happened to me or caring enough to even ask. It was taboo to speak about and solely blamed on me. All the while The Beast continued socializing as if he hadn't created a thing nor at fault in the least. He would only approach to display affection like he cared and me well I seized up and would suck in my breath. I was withdrawn and barely there in mind or spirit. I knew they whispered about me but by then my heart had been pulverized. I was numb, but getting married the next day.

When I tried to leave as evening was gracing the sky, I was stopped cold. Damien came rushing out of the house, probably alerted by everyone's concern. I supposedly was "unstable". He growled at me to "get inside, you're not going anywhere!" He had no idea Desiree and her friend were right there. They had heard the way he spoke when he thought no one was around, abrasive and rough. They came out from behind the truck, but he didn't care, he thought they were just kids. He'd already displayed his aggression in front of them, countless times. I believe he was relieved to see that it was only them and not family.

He didn't like that I was leaving but I had to. There was no refusing, he had to let me go. He turned with a huff and walked back into the house. No longer was there fake concern or the care he had tried to enact in front of everyone else, like I was a patient at a psych ward. But he wouldn't let me take my sons, he had a grip of a vice around them with his mental control.

The girls and I left. We drove back to the hotel that we were booked at and once we walked in there I crumbled. I shattered into a million of pieces that no one could mend back together with any amount of sheer will if they tried. What was done was done.

I told them everything that had happened and Desiree gagged and puked outside the door. She wanted to call her mom. She couldn't take anymore. She told me about how they were treated by the family and everyone there. She mentioned that a lady that was at the house was stirring the pot, saying one thing, guzzling beer since she woke up, and then saying another to every different person. They felt she was at the root of some of the goings on, since we stayed at the hotel the previous night.

They then told me about how sick it was to watch how no one helped me, hearing my distress and when they went to, they were stopped in their tracks. Desiree cried for herself, for me and for the whole of all of it. She was a mess and I knew from that day and many other days I wouldn't have survived without her genuine reasoning and outsider view. I did feel crazy.

 I was starting to lose my own balance of what was right and wrong because how could one person get away with all this? How could no one in my family, not wrap loving, caring arms around their blood sister, daughter or family member that was clearly in distress? It was all very overwhelming and I knew that day forward, IT WAS WRONG but all my fault. I had no more fight left inside.

I showed the girls my body that was now racked with more bruises than ever before, every limb - 4 or five of them. The took pictures , only one or two but couldn't they were shaking we all were. I needed to document what he had done, but felt to exposed and covered up fast.

I could no longer speak, my voice was hoarse and barely above a whisper; I had been choked senseless and all the cries out for help, with anger, had only added to that. We laughed for the first time since that morning deliriously joking that it didn't matter about getting married the next day, because I couldn't say my vows if I tried. Although, that laugh only lasted a moment, it did give me back, a small piece of my humanity back.

At the hotel, I called the movers to apologize for any inconvenience. It was who I was and when they greeted me on the other line, I was so relieved I had called them. The one guy asked if I was okay. He told me if I ever needed help in the future he would drop everything to be there. Then right before I hung up, he said to me that he almost barrelled into the room when everyone shut me in there and he said he heard me asking for help". He asked me again if I needed any help, he didn't care who my fiancée was; he had clearly seen the memorabilia of club stuff around the house. He would help anyway he could and he wanted to cement that in my mind.

The man I spoke with, from the moving company, (whom I will not name) gave me another piece of humanity that day. When I hung up , it did make me feel at least, a little better.

"To those two movers, I bless you for that day. It was one of my hardest. I really thought I was going crazy and your words I needed in those moments. Forever and always grateful ~ Thank-you".

Hanging up the phone and seeing these girls peering at me waiting for information was priceless. I also believe it gave them backbone to stand up for what they believed in, especially hearing it from someone else. I told them what was said, with tears in my eyes.

It was yet another revelation to me how much of an outcast I really was within the eyes of immediate family and Damien's world.

His mother's words still seared through my mind once in a while. I asked her once, what to do about how physical her son gets with me. She had said. "OH go home and do what he wants Kerri, no sense in running." No wonder he feels justified in his behaviors. Perhaps he wasn't taught properly, like right from wrong.

Desiree and (her friend) heard my gratefulness in how I described the phone call I had just had and they realize how truly important it was. All they saw or heard was that someone validated what they had already been telling me. If anything it created more frustration for them and a juvenile perception of what they knew was wrong.

I could see that Desiree was reaching her breaking point, especially after the way they were treated by all my relatives and Damien's family. I panicked, I couldn't lose her and have her abandon me; she was more my anchor then anything and what kept me afloat. But she was adamant that they were getting picked up once we got back to the house. She promised she would return, but the sinking feeling I had was in the pit of my stomach.

I quickly switched to my composed face and tried to be strong, even cool for her but it wasn't enough. The way they were disrespect-ed was far deeper then even I could comprehend at the time. Desiree kept mentioning, "Kerri, we can still move you back to the apartment, you don't have to marry him." Even, pleading with me not to. It didn't matter, he would just kill me there or hunt me down, following where I went. I was barricaded into a 4x4 box and no way out.

I felt stuck or weak and still do not know why I didn't run at that point. I know this however, having everyone in my life, blood relative and otherwise, side with him made me doubt my individuality. I still somewhere inside never wanted to be a disappointment and knew even deeper down I was worthless. I felt it in every way a woman could. From looking in the mirror and knowing *"god was I ever ugly,"* to gazing over my body every moment and seeing *"How I am utterly repulsive"* dug a feeling of empty so deep and scared. I felt I couldn't do anything anymore, I tried my best.

The words of my sister in that heated outburst echo inside of me and to this day, I know she was the only one that stopped me from my breakdown. "Kids, the kids, the kids! It was my saving grace and I am quite sure even Damien's. If they could've just stopped for two minutes and wondered if what I was saying was only a true or gave me a hug, maybe it would have helped. But regardless his torment never would, it would've been another day when no one was around of that I knew for sure.

I know the gentle love of care would've had me fall to my knees and cry hopelessly in whoever's arms heard me at that moment. Instead fate dealt me a blow and then handed it to me on a silver platter.

This was a day in which I started to look at them all as people and not family (that would come years later, but the die had been cast and seed planted). I needed what my mother knew to be truth and I needed validation. I needed someone to be strong for me because I was no longer that courgeous, outspoken girl I used to be. I needed the hopefulness in my doctors words to be true, I needed all my planning to be for something and not so brutally displayed to be false.

I was a broken woman begging with everything she had left in her, to be heard and cared about. It never worked and my plan for freedom was gone in a flash, taken from me along with everything else, myself.

My life seemed to take a different curve and a destiny in which I knew I now, only deserved this.

Half Truths and Secret Agendas

"Your truth does not always need to be told, but instead carried inside you with soft glow"

The girls and I left our hotel room and decided to go to the other hotel to see if any of the Krysko family and my real father had arrived. I really just needed to see him, I would never tell him what Damien did to me but I knew somehow he'd rib me and make me laugh.

Or even my aunts and uncles, seeing their faces would bring light to my life. You see, I soaked other people's lives up as a way to bring joy into mine. It's a habit I created young and simple things always passed such positive energy onto me. I also needed Desiree and Alyssa to see that not all my family is ruthless and judgemental.

When we walked into the "Pacific Inn" in White Rock, BC it was like entering into a whole new world. It's a place that resembles a hidden hot springs with rocks, plants and the muggy or stuffy climate. In the center of the entrance you can peer over a rail and see directly down into the pool and sauna area. It is beautiful and it's also old. A mixture of pure awesomeness and then a lingering thought of what a person could do to a place like that.

This is the same place Damien took me the night he proposed and it brought back the same feelings of being trapped within in me and disgust for saying yes.

I never wanted to marry Damien; he tactically pre-mediated a proposal in front of the kids like that because he knew I was done with him. But, he also knew I was petrified of him. It was a conscious decision I made in that moment, now one I regretted to the fullest. His abuse never stopped once he proposed, if anything it became a mental way to control me even further. It was sick and it was wrong. I never once thought otherwise. I wasn't that far gone, I just knew the lengths he would go and that was scarier than the abuse itself. I remember it clearly, walking in and going back in time, I had to forcefully push all those emotions away and face family, it was hard because it kept popping up in my mind.

I asked the front desk if they were here and that's when I heard my aunties laugh echo throughout the building. I instantly felt a rush of peacefulness. I almost ran to where the restaurant was and then I saw them. They were all there and their hugs were that of genuine care and affection. I couldn't nor wouldn't bring them down. They drove thirteen hours just to come and were having a drink.

My aunt stands as tall as my shoulders and is the one who puts on the Christmas Eve dinners for the Kryskos every year. She is a true delight and a librarian. I love her and her arms felt like heaven. We all chatted and visited. It was so nice to see them and when we all hugged and said our good-byes. I just smiled and thanked them for coming.

I didn't once, not once, think of how dishevelled I looked or if any visible bruises were forming. I didn't have to; they never gave me that insecurity or let on that they had noticed. But afterwards, I felt it and afterwards I felt ashamed.

It was time to return to the house, in my rental car. My step-father rented me a vehicle for the wedding because so many people were coming from out of town that it was necessary. It gave me a security that I could leave if I wanted to, at any time, if things got tough. Its how I was able to leave to go to the hotel.

As I was pulling out of the Pacific Inn, my anxiety spiked. I drove back towards the hotel where we stayed and made an excuse to the girls that I had left something inside. I don't know why or how I knew to do this but I did. If I didn't have the support from my family, I still needed to protect myself and my kids if something happened to me. I had been documenting Damien's abuse with my family doctor for quite some time. I knew the children and I had stayed at this particular hotel a few times already when we were running. I had become acquainted with the owner; we had an unspoken truth between us. He kindly offered me discounted rates.

So, I walked into the lobby and asked to speak to him; he smiled as he usually did and invited me into the office. In there, I broke down and I thanked him for always being open to us coming here under fake names so The Beast couldn't find me and so forth. He reassured me that my room would be here for a few days and not to worry. It was an off the wall thing to do but I did it that day. *(Down the road this very same hotel would actually help save my children from Damien's clutches- book 3)* I just felt I needed safety, or I felt I needed someone else to know the extent of fear I had for my life. This was another day and moment when I opened up to another stranger, just to feel sane.

When I jumped back into the car I remember Des looking at me like I had taken way too long and so I hugged her. I mean really hugged her and begged her not to go. She said she had to but she would be back in the morning, she reassured me.

As we pulled up to the house my hollowness returned. I couldn't walk back into the house, I just couldn't. It was pure panic. I would be at the doors then retreat. It was lunancy but my true state of mind. I just couldn't do it. Des had already called her ride to pick her and Alyssa up.

Damien came right outside, when we arrived and started mimicking me, my dishevelled and reluctant spirit. He tried to tell me to get inside. I just couldn't, something stopped me, a few hours away helped me but this was fear. I stood there and cried. I mean really cried and said I hated him. "This is a façade Damien, what you have done is wrong just wrong and he snapped. He grabbed me by my shouldars and yelled at Desiree to look in my purse to see if I had any Ativan (A tranquilizer I do not take but carry for emergency panic attacks. It's a safety net knowing it's there without ever taking one). He used this as a way to point out my mental issues or later I would hear about my "supposed pill addiction".

I turned on him and said "do you want to hurt me, beat me, and rape me?" He was shocked and instantly noted my level of stability. I didn't have the grotesque fight in me from before, I just had nothing. I was not mean, nor yelling just absolutely broken.

He went on to say "don't cause a scene cunt!" "I dare you." in a deadly tone. He'd stop masking what he did to me in front of Desiree. He didn't care anymore, to him she was a child and someone who knew better than to say anything. It was a fear he instilled in others that he thought were weak. It was his way and that to him, was the only way.

There Desiree broke, crumbled with all she had. She started crying, telling him, "There is no way I am coming to your wedding, I can't do this, I just can't do this!"

She was pleading with me to leave with her. I know she was; I saw it in her eyes, but my kids were inside with people I no longer trusted. I felt as gross as any human being could feel. I could do nothing. This was not 5 hours since he so forcefully took me in that bedroom. Twelve hours until our wedding and a moment of pushing both your feet in the sand to stop the force from pulling you in a direction you just don't want to go. I couldn't go inside, I couldn't do it and I was weak, with nothing left.

I fell onto my knees, trying to show him or them how distraught I really was. I grabbed both sides of my hair, pulling at it while moaning, "I hate myself, I hate my life, I hate myself." I begged to God above, "Why are you doing this to me? Please make it stop, please." I wanted to die, rocking back and forth.

Des and I just cried as I begged for mercy, from anyone. She wrapped her arms around me, begging me to come and I was at a parallel because my precious babies were inside and I knew my family would never, ever be there for me. Even taking my children as the spewed their justifications at me. Today proved it. Damien won and that killed me because all my hopes were crashed. He watched the spectacle with uncaring heart, mixed with indignant comments. Then, I heard his cold laugh.

He looked from me to Desiree clutching each other as she held me and said, "See she's crazy, the fucking little whore is crazy!" I turned on him and all I could spit out was, "I hate you Damien, you're mean, you're just so, so mean" as the tears continued to fall from my eyes.

There was no 'crazy' scene like earlier. I knew better. He was standing idly in the driveway of a gated cold stone house. Neighbours couldn't hear me if I cried out for help. My thoughts engulfed me all at once.

I crouched into a ball and just trembled and shook. He laughed at me. I think he had finally had enough of Des and I, or maybe in case someone noticed but he picked me up and shook me. I went to yell out but he was faster than I could've imagined and he threw me up against the house, feet dangling above the ground, and choked me. His breath was against my neck as he threatened me to stop, "If you don't shut the fuck up and get in the house, you know what will happen!"

At that moment someone pulled into the driveway and he dropped me. Desiree ran up and hugged me, pleading in my ear not to get married and telling me she loved me. He put me down as the car fully pulled in. He held the back of my neck, preventing me from doing a thing. I hugged my little Des and told her to go. Just go, I understand.

As I watched her walk towards the car to get in she turned around one last time. Tears cascaded down her already soaked face. She mouthed "I love you Kerri, I love you" and I just bawled.

I knew she wouldn't come to the wedding, I knew within every part of me. Just like Blake had said there was no way he was coming because he doesn't think it's right, either. The two most loyal, treasured friends I had, made their stand. I was alone with people who actually thought I was delusional.

After Desiree had left he once again turned his focus to me. Like a snap he changed into a counselling tone for the soon-to-be, "Hunny, I love you and the two most stressful things in the world for couples are, getting married and building a house. We are doing both!" I stood against the rock he had just choked me against, numb. No longer shocked by his twisted mentality. He felt elated that Des was now gone, of that I am sure, with that statement it said it all and me. Now he truly had me at his bidding, for I was amongst the very people who turned the backs so noticeably and heartless.

Those headlights of Desiree diming in the distance and felt numb. Absolutely numb.

It's as simple as a statement and an analogy with him.

I still didn't want to go in but I had to my two most precious sons were in that house and I needed to be able to feel them within my arms. It wasn't right or fair to put my healing hopes onto them, but I never told them about the bad things. I whispered hopes and dreams, stories of wonderful lives and adventure. Not once did I belittle their other parent or any of my family members to them, not once. What they had seen so far, was enough for their innocent and beautiful minds.

It was quiet when I walked in; everyone was in the backyard visiting. Damien's mother had arrived, while I had been out and when she was shown the grand tour of our newly build house, she spoke aloud to all that were present. Apparently, she had explained in a matter of fact tone, "This is my son's house, he built this for me." I almost choked when I heard she'd said that again to someone else. It was salt on an already open wound. Not that he built it for her but that there was no inclusion of me and the boys in there. It was all him. No matter that the wood I had asked the builders to darken, or the carpets I chose and the kitchen that was built. No sign that my décor was evident within the monstrous structure of it all. I take great pride in what I build, decorate and make. It's about seeing the potential beauty in any broken or discarded item and allowing it to shine once again.

It was nightfall and Stella was spending the night. Damien didn't believe that he shouldn't see me the day or night before the wedding, he made that clear. He wouldn't leave nor did he think it was necessary to. He parked himself directly at the bottom of the stairs by the door.

I was numb by the emotion and shock of it all. I tried to sit down at the table in the kitchen and just couldn't focus. No one would speak to me, not a word. It was supposed to be my wedding day in less than twenty-four hours and I might as well have been a ghost for all it mattered.

My mother was in my master bedroom lying down, her body swollen with hives. I felt horrible for her. But that didn't stop me from hoping at least tonight I could curl up beside her and know that she was there. I tried to brush my hair but looking in the mirror became unbearable and I remember sitting down against the side wall. I was nauseated and numb. Stella had arrived but she just took it all in and did the socializing for me. I knew she sided with everyone, I could see the concern and watchful gaze from her at a distance. I had already learned how manipulating she could be within my family and also knew she conversed with my sisters regularly on social media. I had seen it and felt it. The only person I could truly count on was a doctor that was safely tucked away in his private home with his healthy family and my nanny, Des, who was gone. It left me sickened.

My mother heard my muffled sobbing from the master bathroom and came in to see if I was okay. She sat down beside me and there, for the first time that day, I felt genuine love from my family. I whimpered against her chest and my true inner core wept. Her hands against my heart felt kind but her heartbeat did nothing to stop the tears from flowing. She whispered over and over, "I'm here for you."

My voice was barely above a whisper and raspy with pain. There was no way I could talk, not tonight or to say my vows. Damien's hands squeezed much too tight around my neck today and the screaming and continuous sobbing I had done hadn't helped my throat. She shushed me and held me. After quite sometime she went into my closet, grabbed the nightie I had been saving for this night and a warm cloth to gently wipe my face. All the things I wanted to say and the truths I had to tell but doubted I would ever be heard because my voice was robbed from me that day, in more ways than one. Were left unspoken.

She gently pulled the shirt from my body and gasped as she took in what he had done. She started shaking and said, "I can't do this, I can't do this" then walked to her make-up case and took a sedative. My mother was not able to be mentally strong for me in that moment. She was traumatized and like she did around my other sisters, she was cowering. I don't know why she didn't stand up for me that day and help me. Regardless, that one special moment, I will forever grateful for when she had found me in the bathroom and tenderly held me.

To back track a bit, *when Sable (my youngest son) was turning two years old, she had come over to the mainland for the planned family festivities.*

That day Damien was trying to force me to sign over my car to his brother and I was reluctant to do so. He became enraged when I wouldn't or didn't want to and my car was the only asset I had left. My house in Alberta, just a few years beforehand was now gone and sold. She tried defending me.

He was agitated and barked out an order, which sent my mother, scurrying to the room like a child. She had tried to tell him nicely that I just wasn't comfortable giving away my ten thousand dollar car and that my step-father had bought it for me. It was special to me.

Instead her words enraged The Beast further and frustrated what he had planned. He had grabbed my hair and yanked me downwards to sit me at the table so that I would sign on the line, to hand my car over. My mother advanced to protect me and he jumped towards her and bellowed his demands. She was terrified and again Damien got his way; she obeyed. When I say this I stress it and mean it. He was scary, intimidating, unaccustomed to hearing the word 'no' and an unpredictable force to be reckoned with when angered, and that day he was. It never mattered that it was his son's birthday. Nothing ever mattered except him getting what he wanted. This day he wanted my car.

My sons became scared, began crying and even then, he didn't care.

My mother had never been the same around him since that day. She's been jumpy and timid from that day forward. She felt the thunder in his voice and the dominance in his stance. Not only that, but she has had to witness the countless bruises and bloody lips plus flees to safety.

The day before the wedding from hell, was no different and I was never really upset at my mother's meekness when faced with Damien. I knew she wasn't strong enough to stand up for me, but wistfully I wished she would scoop me up with my sons and whisk us away to safety. Silently, I had pleaded for just that, moments before lying helplessly against her chest and earlier screaming the truth to be told.

"People often wondered what it was like being with a Hells Angel or about to marry one. In front of many, Damien seemed glamorous, devoted, real and utterly captivated by me (which he was, just not in the right way). I have had many woman stop and gaze at my engagement ring which had cost no less than fifty-thousand dollars and say to me that I was one lucky lady. If they only knew the half of it and the price I have had to pay just wearing it.

I beg any young lady who thinks a bad boy is the one, to stop, follow your intuition and think. Is this someone who you could spend the rest of your life with?" Ask yourself that because I knew my bad-boy was never 'the one' and I wished many nights for a simple home and a gentle lover.

Mind you, not all are like Damien, nor every bad-boy is actually bad. Only a few are, but a few too many....."

My mother went to sleep and I gathered the courage quietly to brave the ongoing storm. I knew no one in my family would ever look at me the same, not after my meltdown and anguished pleas to be heard. I was alone and yet again, that was my life. I knew I had my sons but they were to be protected from all violence, all arguments. This was the escape plan that I had developed with my nanny: Under no circumstances was she to try and stay to help me if violence or verbal abuse happened between Damien and I, she was to gather the children and leave. Leave, now, Get as far away as possible and only once it was safe, was I to meet her. This was NOT and unspoken truth but one that we had devised and implemented together, as a team.

Damien was starting to imply he would steal my children and that the day they turned ten years old, was the day they no longer needed their mother. He would blatantly state these sentiments to anyone around, that "no mothers of his were needed after his children turned ten" but for me, it was a directly aimed threat and I knew it.

Desiree's boundaries' were being tested daily with what she knew to be wrong. I saw it in her more than once. But a seed had been watered today, and sprouted within my thoughts; I knew it was only a matter of time before I lost her too. To me she would never be gone, because I held her so deep within my heart. I loved her. Love to me just didn't go away.

It was that love that kept me going and living. Those treasured moments of fleeting happiness and security gave me hope that good was out there. That hope, I held onto even as my light was slowly going out. Today she may have physically left but today however how scary this night was, she would forever remain in my heart.

Desiree I was never mad at you for not coming to the wedding. I wouldn't have supported that either.

Wedding Day

"Fear can motivate the weak to then become the strong"

I woke up the next morning to see the sun was shining, but my chest was heavy. On August 08, 2008, my skies dawned bleak, in a thick, smoky-like darkness. I didn't have a schedule for today, none; I was unmoored. I didn't and couldn't get my hair done or my nails, not for myself or the wedding party. I was told there was no money and to get over it. It was made clear to me the days before and I couldn't re-open those wounds, it wasn't worth the additional pain it would cause.

My mother was still sleeping and I just rolled over and looked at her, like really looked at her. I could clearly see she had broken out in a rash and I felt bad for her. I went slowly to the bathroom and grabbed a cloth to run under warm water to bring to her. I wanted to wake her up with kindness and so I did. I didn't speak, I couldn't speak. My voice was raw and raspy so by actions alone, I wanted to wake her with gentle love. I felt bad for yesterday and I always blamed myself, even though I was only fighting for a truth to heard and help. I have always been kind, it is my greatest weakness but yet one of my most treasured traits.

She jumped awake with a start and tried to gather her bearings. My mother is a heavy sleeper but to see how she awoke with alertness; I could clearly see how shaken she was.

When she focused on me and the sadness in her eyes was evident. She pulled me back on the bed to hug me. That was when I felt the true love of a mother I had once known. She didn't use the cloth for herself she used it for me. We had a moment together that was bittersweet, for the both of us.

The house was already full of activity and all I wanted to do was go to my sons, hold them close and kiss them awake. But I hadn't looked in the mirror yet. It would bring every last emotion back and I would crumple.

I tried to ask my mother how bad it was but I didn't have a voice; it was too sore, grated and hoarse. Barely above a forced whisper could I be heard and understood. So I just got up and finally went to look in the mirror and what I saw shamed me further. My right eye was bruised with blue and purple lumps where his fist had hit me on the side of my face and my neck had the visible marks of fingerprints, where he'd choked me.

I wasn't prepared for the sight of the rest of my body and I quickly went to the bathroom where I could shut the door and be alone. I barely made it in before my stomach heaved and I vomited bile into the bidet; having not eaten properly for days it was acidy and hurt. Stella came in and just rubbed my back, over and over. She told me, "I'm not fooled, Kerri, it's going to be okay."

Stella was pregnant and also one of my best friends but I knew she stirred up a truckload of trouble because I had heard her talk with my family, playing both sides. I slowly realized this as emotions and thoughts surfaced. I put my best foot forward and I never showed her my weakness. I was very hyper-sensitive to who I could trust and who I couldn't now.

I look back with new eyes and I clearly see who was my friend and who wasn't but in the moment I latched onto any lifeline I could find with someone familiar with my world. She was no longer my trusted confidant but I needed her none the less.

I had a dark-haired Russian girlfriend as well, who was also dating a member, to confide in and she understood the pressure of dating a Hells Angel. She could see the girls who played both sides. Her name was Bella and she was a true beauty. Her face once decorated the magazine cover of Playboy Vixens.

She had an air about her that exuded confidence and she stood up for what she believed in. I knew Stella was jealous of Natalya but also knew she couldn't get close in there or she would poison my new friendship. Natalya was one of my bridesmaids and someone I truly liked.

My excuse to Stella for why I was leaning over the bidet was that it was just nerves and wedding day jitters. I croaked to her that I needed a few minutes; I needed her to make sure no one came in. I could barely talk, it was pathetic.

I wanted a shower but if Damien came in he would see my nakedness and that terrified me. I did a double check of my room and all the doors to make sure they were locked. Once I knew I was as safe as could be, I discarded my clothes and took in every last inch. The impact of what I saw was gross, and vividly noticeable. I was marred with bruising in places that no one should be and anyone could see even with my clothes on.

My wedding day was a nightmare and there was no way out; I couldn't call the police. He was a gangster and the control he had on others was evident in all he got away with. I was doomed. (Picture of the actual photo, from the cover of book 1- Kerri On- in middle of book)

I quickly showered and wrapped myself in a robe. As I walked towards the kitchen in a fog, I could see a few people sharing stories as they sipped their coffees; each with their own agendas for the day. There was maybe about ten people milling about and passing through. They all bestowed a, rapidly fleeting, fake smile on me. I did not talk. Stella however made a joke about my lost voice to take the edge off and break the awkwardness.

While in the bathroom, they all formulated a plan that the girls in the wedding party would pay for their own hair and nails, then we could still make it go and make it happen. I still didn't have any money to pay for myself and had to hope maybe a sister of mine would help cover it. It was humiliating and only heaped more weight to my shame.

I hadn't thought to cancel the make-up artist. She was scheduled to come over three hours before the wedding at 3:30 pm. I was hoping she could still do my make-up and I could somehow pay her later.

As soon as those plans were confirmed, I was whisked out the door and ready to go within minutes. It was sick really, but actually quite nice of all the girls to pitch in like that; I knew I would hear it for years from my sisters about this day and anything related to it. They never knew the half of it or what I had endured after they allowed Damien to lock me in the room and have his way with me. A day never to be forgotten and a day that reminds me why my relationship will be severely damaged with my family, forever. Not out of hate but because of two different sets of morals.

Herded, en masse, into the hairdresser's, I could see my stylist take all of me in. Sara had been doing my hair for years, she knew about my tumultuous relationship with Damien, my heartache and she knew about the abuse. When everyone was settled she leaned into me and said she felt so sorry for me. Then when I was leaving she hugged me and whispered if I ever needed her she was there for me.

The nail salon, another place I had been going for years, "Envy Nail" was thrilled to see us all. They had a wedding gift for Damien and I. They never mentioned a word and this was a place I could actually sit back and not have to answer any questions. I watched and heard all the girls laugh and have fun. When asked if they were excited about the wedding, by a nice couple. I heard my sister say, "Yeah, excited to get this over with." It hurt. I was so raped of self, sitting amongst them but remained silent and empty. Because of my voice, I just sat back, listened and let them all do their thing.

We arrived at the house to find no family was in sight. The wedding hour was approaching and the make-up artist had arrived. She was a true gem. She was beaming and so excited to do all of our make-up. I believe this was her first true house-call and for a wedding. Her smile faltered when she looked at my face. I just shushed her, and pleaded with my eyes not to say anything. She was shocked and took a deep breath without saying a word but cocked her head to the side, in a gentle manner.

All the girls swarmed her to do their make-up first; I was grateful to just fade away into the shadows. I needed to catch my breath and think, be alone. There was no way out and to top it off I was given a message that the wedding decorator had sent someone else to set-up the venue. She was not going to be there. I felt horrible for her because the one time a few months beforehand I was eager to make the wedding special to me. I had set up a meeting with her. She was a positively genuine and wonderful lady but after our consultation appointment everything changed. Damien started being controlling, never answered her calls. Then he agreed to her price and when the time came wouldn't pay her. It was so wrong- and I was left thinking I didn't or no longer had a wedding decorator, again in the dark.

I knew because of whom he was, she was scared. Plus, she had already spent a heap of money and to be told NO he's not paying for that. She was scared for her life and most likely pissed off, but how do you tell a Hells Angel to pay up? It is especially hard to collect for an individual or independent contractor. I felt so, so bad for her but I was already buried in helplessness there was nothing I could do. I wasn't bothered that she had to cancel and wouldn't be present; I was more bothered that he had bullied and taken from another innocent person. It still bothers me. I did send her a message but received no response back. I believe she thought I was like him, but I wasn't, not even the slightest and I no longer knew that this had all gone ahead.

"Again, if you ever read this book, please know I am so truly sorry and I appreciate all the thought you put into everything."

I was looking numbly at my dress when Damien's mother came in, she was smiling and exuberant; you could see she was very excited. I think she liked being coveted as Damien's mother by everyone, yet she was a Christian woman.

I would never understand how she couldn't notice what her son had done to me. How was any of this right, even in the slightest? I thought she was a Christian woman and that they were supposed to be kind, forgiving and nonjudgmental; the hypocrisy was unsettling but never hurt deep. I allowed her excitement to wash over me and let her give me a hug. I tried talking but couldn't and I believe it only added to her belief in why, allegedly, I was the "Crazy One". When in fact, I had been choked, slapped, thrown and raped while screaming to be heard. By this point I was so numb to everything going on; it was a blur. It was like I was just a piece on a chess board and everyone was moving me here and there.

She said "Kerri, can I help you with your dress, since your mother isn't around"? It was the kindest tone I had ever heard her use with me and I blankly nodded yes. Damien's mother helped tie my dress, with the corset up my back and then she gave me another hug, I have tried to remember that many times, over the years, just to keep my emotions in check. She still pretended not to notice. Once the dress was on, you could only see the bruises on my arm, neck and face.

She rushed me to the make-up artist who pushed everyone else away, even though there were two other woman or people who wanted their make-up done. I tried to say just go ahead and they would have went if not for the artist who said, No firmly. This is Kerri's Day. We were now alone.

This young woman, who was looking forward to her own wedding, had tears in her eyes. I looked at her and allowed my own tears to flow freely down my face. We went into the bathroom and I hugged her, just repeating, "I am so sorry, so sorry."

She said to me, "When you decide to leave, I am here for you. I will never forget this beautiful bride's face with so many bruises". It was another moment of finally being acknowledged for what he had done to me. I caved in ways I had never done. I wept so profoundly, I ushered her out of the bathroom so she could do one more persons make-up before mine, I had to pull myself together.

I wanted to run, flee and just get away. But I had not a cent to my name, nothing. It had been stripped from me the days before. Not even a car for very much longer as the rental had to be returned. My sons were with Damien somewhere and under no circumstance was I leaving without them. He had planned this and I was trapped. I was trapped in a surreal fog of sleep deprivation, physical pain, and lack of nutrition. Depression, panic, abuse, abandonment and a learned helplessness. My body was there but my soul had separated from me; I was there but I wasn't present.

I started hearing loud voices and listening closely I could make out that the limo had arrived and my make-up was still not done. A glance at the clock told me that the wedding was within the hour. I was stalling and I knew it. When I came out of the bathroom and walked up to the make-up artist's chair another person flashed past me to take the seat. Her eyes flared as she said dismissively, "She has to quickly do mine first." It was appalling but the norm. It was another example of how I was walked on by the people that surrounded me, and again, it was noticed by a stranger.

This day was never for me and the sad thing was I had known it from the start. It was hell.

My make-up took a lot of time. She was forced to abandon everything that had been planned for my face. We had agreed to a dewy natural look with a dust of moonlight sheer, eyelashes and nude lips of sheen. Now however, we had to use triple the concealer, black eye shadow accented with greys and lips of bright pink and red. She applied heavy foundation up my neck to match my face. I looked like I was going out for the night and hated it but that was the only way to somewhat hide the bruises.

Everyone was already loaded in the limos, and the gentle, young make-up lady, then walked me out to the car. She hugged me and looked dead center into my eyes and said, "You are beautiful no matter what. Please do not forget me!" She plunged the money she had received from everyone into my hand and said, "You pretty lady keep this. You need it far more than I do."

I began to tear up, threatening to destroy my make-up and she said, "Enough of that! I know what I saw; I also know one day you are going to need me and I will be there for you miss Kerri." I held onto her, even from the car in the backseat and until she shut the door and leaned in for one more hug. That girl was as beautiful as an angel; I felt my God, whoever he or she was, showed me the way and gave me enough courage to Kerri On.

Really, I don't know what was more appalling that day, the ignored bruises or the fact that I had no one to turn to, no one who would help me. I had adamantly shared with those close to me, that I didn't want to marry him; I had shown them with my bruises how desperate I was. No one seemed to hear me and continued to push me through the motions. I felt, so very, disassociated from myself and what was happening around me.

Gratefully, I had the whispers and hugs from almost-strangers. Those people were my only saving grace other than the love from my children. I felt more alone than ever before. I felt more love from virtual strangers, than my own blood family and my twisted, diabolical abusive soon-to-be husband.

The limo slowly backed out of our long driveway, away from her outstretched hand and gentle concerned stare. It left me more shaken then ever before. It's not as if I didn't know any better, or was blind to the fact I was about to marry The Beast.

I knew I was inevitably setting myself up for this, horror show as his wife. I knew I would be hurt to a whole new level. I didn't want to marry him, I told them but the plans rolled on without any way to stop it. No one and I mean no one supported me or helped me when I screamed bloody murder or begged for help. No one! He had them all convinced it was my invented hysteria, not him; somehow had them believing it was the pre-nuptial agreement that had upset me. This man was living off everyone else's money, barely any of his own. I knew this and that's why his piece of paper was a joke. He was not the hard working man my step-father was, or the man next door was. He was not successful in business in my eyes, he was the extortionist that hurt others to get ahead, not worked for it himself. I wholeheartedly believed this as what he had already done to me was painstakingly obvious.

I was ashamed and broken that I no longer had any strength or the voice to stop the limo from driving towards my pain filled destiny, even stopping it at the gas station on the corner, arriving late just for a moment of strength I could not find.

As we pulled into the Hazelmere Golf Course for the ceremony and nuptials, I saw many people and couldn't help looking amongst the crowd of strangers. I maybe had twenty people from my side in a sea of one hundred guests; I saw few familiar faces. Even the ones I had thought would be there for me weren't really; they had proven that the days before. My mind had drifted numerous times in the last forty-eight hours to my doctor and even the nurses' safety plan we had all developed for when my family arrived; their faces hopeful and encouraging, that I wouldn't have to marry him or finally garner the support I needed. I had held onto their ideal belief of what family was and how they would help that, I ignored the signs of truth. I should've realized they gave me hope in their ideas of what a realistic life should look like, but I had to be the one to bring it fruition.

I should've trusted more in Desiree, I should've listened to her. A lone tear, that I had allowed to escape down my cheek in the limo, was for the added emptiness I felt by not having her there with me. My anchor, my truth and the only person who I knew I could look to for reason when I was tied into knots by the mental games Damien played. She kept me sane during my darkest moments and she was in every sense my support beam and pillar of strength. Stella wiped my tear away and with the cutest look, she said "Kerri-Lynn be you, be strong and stop that, right now"! "Your wrecking your make-up and your precious eye lashes will fall off", she made me laugh with her joke because it was innocent but loaded with truth.

Everyone was ushered into the clubhouse once we arrived and I remained in the limo, watching and waiting. I was hoping someone would come out and say hi to me but instead the girls jumped out and spoke to everyone. It reminded me again of how much this wedding was for him and for show.

When I saw my real-father, who was waiting outside to walk me halfway up the aisle, only then did I get out and walk over to him. He was smiling and you could see clearly he was proud. I knew however inside he was upset that it was only halfway up the aisle and not all the way, but my step-father deserved that honour as well. It just should've been half way up the aisle itself and not just to the door. I didn't know that was like that.

My father smiled and the tears started flowing again; I swallowed back every emotion I was feeling so not to let the tears wash away all the make-up that was covering my damaged face. My father, good for his comical ways to ease tension said, "I thought for sure, Kerri, you would be the runaway bride". I laughed, a real laugh, a choking hoarse laugh that I needed more then he knew.

I had wished I was that runaway bride; like the movie, I had wished to be that girl with the love and support of her family. Oh how I wished that, yearned for it with all my being. But a naked truth was stamped on all my features now.

I had stopped watching shows about happy family stuff; it left me sad. My father knew exactly what to do, to ease the nerves, be funny.

The music started and I was being pushed into the direction of rules, and mandatory procedure. My real-dad steered me up the entrance, into the reception room, over the bridge and pond of water and fish. Right to the door that lead to the actual runway of an aisle to my step-father. He then handed me over and my dad placed his arm through mine and there I cried. Tears washed over my face and it took all I had not to choke. He said "be brave Kerri, be brave" into my ear and then he let go. My hand I do not believe was placed into Damien's, but I was left to stand in from of him none the less. There I stood as the he looked at everyone else in the audience and not at me.

I thought Damien would look at me, but he didn't. He was busy looking at the crowd and living in the moment of being center stage. It hurt. I kept watching and waiting for him to truly look at me, like you see at other weddings, he barely did. He made jokes, laughed and never really spent a lot of time acknowledging me at all. I remember to a tea, searching his face, waiting for a true emotional gaze and I never got one from him, nope I was standing there as a show piece, nothing more and he was ashamed I wasn't at my best.

I had watched my own feet walk my pretty dress up the aisle, looking down most of the way, barely making eye contact but forcing a shy glance or to stifle my cry of humility but *I really just wasn't there.* It is very hard to describe the disassociated feeling that had numbed me. It wasn't so much against my will as simply having NO will, at all.

I watched myself struggling to say the vows, trembling with my own voice hoarse and rough; it was a humiliating scene. At one point during the vows I had hesitated and Damien squeezed my hand, hard and then looked at me above his glasses. Drilling me with his threatening eyes of control. It was brief, barely noticeable to others but for me, the pause yawned and widened into a long space of infinite time while he glared daggers into my eyes.

When asked if anyone refuted this marriage, it was a roar of laughter from the crowd and even Damien (Or to me that laughter was in my head, echoing a mockery of vast proportions). People knew, what our marriage would be like, what the children I have already went through and again NO ONE stopped it; most importantly, nor did I. The one person who should've didn't stand up, act graceful with clarity and take a mik to say "This man is NOT the man I am supposed to marry". Acting a coward, the ceremony continued.

After signing the wedding certificate, a few *nice* laughs and well wishes, we were led back to the limo for our wedding-photos. This was a moment where Damien and I were to be alone and I dreaded it.

He didn't pull me close, nor did he want to. I felt our distance and so did he. This was about him and not one moment about *us*.

When the photographer caught my true feelings, he tried to reflect all images towards his bro, D. This was Damien's and clubs own personal photographer and who they used, for events ect. He is a professional and shoots many types of images, from weddings to individual stripper photos and photography. It was the methodical way of tainting our wedding further. To me everything was dirty and the feeling wouldn't escape me, inside. I can't explain it but how I just did.

This photographer was not mean, not at all; just that he was Damien's friend and during our engagement photo shoot a week previously, he made a comment that I was pretty and could use me as a model for some of his high-end clients. Damien freaked, privately to me about it. No I didn't feel comfortable with him. I didn't want to further ruffle D's feathers but the photo's to me were not just a joke but a mess.

My eyes stared hollow and empty and into the lens and Damien felt my disconnection with this charade. He started straightening my shoulders before a picture dictating how he wanted my chest out, holding me aggressively in place. Then when we were at another spot and I didn't get out fast enough he leaned into the car and told me, "You don't want a backhand on the day of your wedding do you cunt?!" He didn't expect an answer; it was, obvious to all, a closed discussion just a remark and his now permanent ownership of me. There are some images that show my true feelings and in those, my eyes stare out blank.

Being led down the pier, for photos, at Crescent Beach in White Rock, BC down the road from the original place we were to go; I wished I could jump over the wooden rails, into the ocean and be washed away. It was sad, but my true thoughts. I tried once to say it's getting late, we should get back but he just said, "THEY can wait!" disrespecting a hundred waiting guest. This was entirely his day, again I state not mine.

He advised me on the way back to the venue, that I had better put on a better face and be happy. It was not a suggestion but an order. When we arrived everyone was already eating, being served because we had taken too long and that upset Damien.

The banquet had begun without the king and his caught looks on some photos were clearly visible as to his upset. There are a few dis-gruntle-faced looking photos of Damien that were candidly shot in that moment but he was always quick to put on a smile, just not for the ones he wasn't posing for. There were no kind words and compliments from him; just demand after demand after demand.

Our MC for our wedding was another Hells Angels member, a No-mad and actually a truly nice person. I believe he and the Beast were pretty close and he'd just had a set of twins. His girlfriend was a true gem, with a heart of gold. I sat with her, in the corner for a few minutes admiring her babies. I love children and find them so innocent, pure, beautiful and gentle. She gave me another of those tiny slivers of peace that carried me through that day. She likely never even knew it.

My sister's laugh could be heard and said to someone I was a "Bride-Zillah and she was glad this was over". Hearing laughter join hers, didn't bother me in the slightest. I was always concerned that other people would hear the malicious slander from my relatives, my own family, and it would change their opinions of me, but it was already done by Damien now that I just blew it off.

I had noticed the change in countless others throughout the years and how once they had met my family things seemed to take a shift. I knew better now and I often cocooned my friends now from it. Bella my bridesmaid just gave me nudge, that meant chin up solider bride and that made me feel good. Knowing I had her in my corner.

You see by this time, the ammunition Damien needed was gathered was validated by my sister, mother (unknowingly) and even my real-father.

I never even knew if my little sister, would honour me, by being a bridesmaid, until the actual day before the wedding. She hadn't come to see me before the wedding, not on the day or the day before. Maybe she picked up her dress and I wasn't there, but no phone call or response from her.

My maid of honor was Stella, and she was there but busy hanging with the family. I visibly seen the divisive and righteous way she played both sides, I watched her at my wedding and the days leading up to it.

Bella, my other bridesmaid had my back and the only one in which I trusted. Another Hells Angels girlfriend that understood the fucked up lifestyle and what it was like with a guy like that. Not to imply that she was abused, or to the extent of my own personal hell. She just *got* it;

she *got* the whole disgust-thing with people bowing down to a guy like that; disgust that the girls that were your best friends because of whom you dated and the snaky twinkies who tried to smile to your face, while their blowing your guy the next night or even the day before at some event.

You see, while some girls think life with a bad-boy is fun, glamorous and cool- there is a whole other dark side, which you better be willing to deal with.

Having a poker-face and a smile of convincingly well proportions, will serve you best.

It *ain't* butterflies and rainbows; it's a whole lotta noisy, confusion and takes courage to be with a guy like that.

You better hope that bad-boy isn't a cheater, or worse, abusive because then you are governed by a corruptive power that will chew you up and spit you out for breakfast; leaving you used and scarred for life.

Hence, what I was living through now. It wasn't grin and bare it because he cheated again, it was take, swallow it and deal with it. Because unless you have someone higher up to save you; your screwed. My abuse was thick and governed by a new law with Damien. He had let all that influence and power get to his head.

There is a saying I heard in a spider-man movie my own son was watching, *"With great power comes even greater responsibility"*.

I had been this bad-boy's girl for so, utterly long and now on the supposedly, 'most beautiful day of my life', I was living a nightmare and a fear I wouldn't wish on an enemy. I was now his wife, which brought on a whole new level of pain I had never even knew existed but I was about to find out.

Bella became or was one person, who gave me hope that maybe I could survive this. Bella, would still be raging whenever her man behaved in a flirtatious manner with another girl but she was luckier than I was. He loved her, would never hit and abuse her, like Damien did to me.

The President's girlfriend was treated as a queen and allowed to show her dominant strength of character. She was another I wished well in life, (a good person with a wild child daughter) but in whole, two-good people with a structured moral compass; *I'd only wished Damien followed their example.*

I couldn't understand how the previous president, who was still a member, could even look at Damien, smile, converse and even shoot the shit with him; knowing that Damien was itching to take his place. It was the power, I believe, Damien was hungry for. I can only be thankful that it never happened and Damien never became president. It would've meant harm to many or perhaps just me.

I evaluated a lot of people during this time, it was the way I had to be, to survive and know what was real and what was not. It was never a longing to have what other people had but a wish that I could mirror something of the beauty I was finding in the broader world; a whole-some look, to find good in people, and a way to stay in the *now.*

I was controlled in all I did, right down to taking a shower and washing my genitals front to back, ten times as he dictated for me to do. I felt like I was as filthy and repulsive as a street urchin is declared. It was a sickness in him that he couldn't control with regards to me and most likely a few others; I was quite sure of it.

My wedding was a nightmare and my family departed with haste, all scattering in their separate directions. My real father had stormed out of my wedding when the father-daughter dance was announced and the DJ called my step-fathers name: not his. He blew out of the parking lot with a screech.

My mother and her friend left shortly after and packed their belongings to drive through the night, straight back to Alberta in the dead of night.

Everyone was just gone, departed and barely a good-bye.

My voice still raspy and barely comprehensible when I spoke, I watched everything with a distant, numb stare. I saw my precious Ashton laughing with and loving his cousins; my little monkey Sable following his brothers every step, shadowing him. I kept a watchful distance because I knew my older son would catch on to my shaken and empty demeanor; He has always been sensitive on that level. It wouldn't have been fair or right to take away their moments of childhood happiness that their memories would save and nuggets of happiness to draw on. I watched them through a seemingly long tunnel but I never lost sight of them- not once. They were my sweet, precious angels.

Damien, well, he was the life of the party, enjoying the praise; basking in it all in, while loudly and brazenly stating to his *Bro's* and family members that *"I was his and he would keep me in line"*.

It was a sad day and day I have regretted; not only because of the pain but for not finding the calm strength I knew was in me. I don't know if it would've made a difference to my family.

I have played out the many 'what-ifs' in my mind. The only thing I knew for sure, their feelings and opinions were formed well before I had a chance to learn my voice, let alone walk.

I don't remember throwing the bouquet, or if I even did. I don't know when the cupcakes were brought out or if they were always on display. Nor what time we left. There is a blankness that is void of memories, to this day.

When it was time for Damien and I to leave, he didn't touch me in the limo, or tell me I was beautiful or that it was the best day of his life. We sat stiffly apart, with as much distance between us, as possible. He was on his phone, only occasionally glancing at me to watch me through ignorant eyes. Once he tried to push me over and lift my skirt like a whore, but the drive stopped that, or was it the phone call. I was numb nor a memory of anything special.

I can remember the hotel suite was breathtakingly beautiful. A cousin had decorated the rooms in the most flowing, romantic bridal-suite ambiance; Candles appeared to cascade into a sea of calmness. It was a stunning suite at the Fairmont, with a view over-looking all of Vancouver.

I was nervous and repulsed that he would soon demand his husbandly rights. I knew it was coming, it was the way he was. A sexual preference that wasn't kind, it wasn't meant to be. He was like that more now than ever before. The twisted perverse way he just took what he wanted for his pleasure. There was no respect, nor was there ever going to be. I was his property and to fight The Beast, meant the ultimate suffering. I closed my eyes squeezing another cascade of tears from the corners, and fell headlong into a fate I did not see an escape from, ever. I was no longer a human being but an object. I wished then to die.....

Afterword

Gratitude

My life is a life of paths, choices and decisions that shaped the very outcome of all I have been through. I deserve no pity, nor do I deserve to be treated as a victim.

When approached please don't feel sorry for me but show me care and dignity you would to a person, who you haven't, just read her very heart on paper. It hurts me when I see you search for the scars or linger to long on my arms, visibly seeing the wounds inflicted upon me by myself and another.

Please do not think when you share praise that I look silly or beam, because it is still hard to process. I do not always feel pretty or beautiful and I am only just learning how to take that compliment. I still laugh when I am nervous and even shy away when I hear noises that are to loud, wincing as a memory or feeling strikes me from my seat or stance.

I recognize beauty in all of you, from good and bad. I see what most may never see because that is the way I had to be to survive. That walk or the way you hold yourself in confidence I am struck by because it's amazing.

You're beautiful too, no matter size, color or education. You're gorgeous, as gorgeous as the positive energy that surrounds you, with all your very own unique traits.

I am awe-struck by our world and the leaps and bounds of awareness we have found. It amazes me every day the way we live, the simplicity and the wonder if I myself, may find a true love once again…You, every last one of you, give me these overwhelming feelings of freedom, beauty and bliss.

My sons, my precious most treasured sons, thank-you for being you and turning out to be a quality that any girl, woman, friend would be proud of. Love yourself and know that we fought hard for this life and be proud, never, ever ashamed.

Sable my little baby bam bam; no matter how big you get. YOU my lovely son, will always be the saving grace of foundation in which Ashton and I drew strength from. You pushed me to finish these last 2 books and actually release this one, today. Thank-you for giving me the clarity to do this. For my baby boy, I never wanted to hurt you by sharing what daddy has done, but help you and all our children in this world. To be happy and importantly safe.

Thank-you for telling me to and saying on this day, that I send this book to print; that it was okay, we were hurt too and we will help people now, mom do this. You gave me the freedom to keep going and do what's right. I love you and I'm so proud of the little man you're becoming. One day when you read this, please my precious boy, know that no matter what, we forgive, we let go and we grow. With kindness and with love, to better understand the hard teachings in life, we may have had to learn…I sure love you *my* little guy.

I hope by writing my true story, and sharing my humility and most inner thoughts that I can help others going through something similar, or even sway the most influenced young person, that perhaps the one that seems to be kind or laid back, may be the right choice and **path**; not the latter.

I hope to give and shed light to a parent, sibling, trusted confidant, on what a person truly being abused, is actually going through and what they do feel, because that one kind gesture or praise can indeed help them; carrying them forward on just hope or belief for a brighter day. Giving them the fight for their own justice and freedom.

We have a self-esteem that is **utterly** smashed to the ground that we only have our thoughts; *your* words have to be helpful not harmful, not judging but perhaps the frustration you feel with the going back and forth, has to be set aside or you have to walk away.

Often times, what you may think is hard, is indeed harder for the other person. What you may think is right or wrong, or "how you would never tolerate that and leave", is something they have tried doing countless times.

No one knows what that person being abused is truly going through or how far they have fallen. Be patient and pass hope, or please don't say anything.

I give you advice to help. Please never take what I say in a harmful manner but an expertise that comes with being a survivor. I wrap all of you, (who have had to endure your loved ones, flight to safety and the help you have given to a person, in your lives going through abuse) with loving arms and just to say, thank-you.

I give you mention, because sometimes YOU are the very ones, that save us, from our own self-built prison walls and YOU deserve to be honored. Again, I thank-you, "for them" because right now they're just not strong enough to do it themselves.

To my family - I love each and every one of you, never ever think I blame you for my breakdown and what I endured behind those closed doors that fateful day, we call my wedding from hell. It was my hell and mine alone, no one is to blame and anyone reading this please these were my own thoughts and feelings.

I wish I would've tried to share with you my inner heart, as I did with Damien and at a time I had a clear head. Then perhaps you would have truly known what I was going through. But the stone was cast long before this and we all were up against an inevitable force, called fate and destiny.

I wrote my memoir initially, to give to my sons in case something ever happened to me and I died. In turn my own precious son Ashton told me, "Mom, please share our story, you've helped so many of my own friends and people; you have to do this".

I was scared to and unsure but I kept going. I signed my memoirs over to my sons; so they could have a brighter future and use who they once were, as a way to help others.

Knowing that I whispered the right things into their ears on those dark nights and they are who they are now, makes me proud.

I share with you all a picture/insert of a note my son wrote me a while ago, when I never wanted to keep sharing what I had been through. I felt lost and the only thing that made me keep going was them and all of you fans, who have reached out to me, being kind and sharing your own personal stories. I treasure all those messages and really without you, I would never have kept going. From my very heart, thank-you so much.

To all the wives, and even guys that I made reference to. You all in your own way, helped me; with truths and little comments, that gave me hope and to fight for what I wanted and finally the strength to …. Thank-you Bella, N, J and C. You're all so truly beautiful with essences of strength.

Awareness is key and until we all learn to be strong, the cycle will repeat and the change we long for, will never happen.

I truly love people and if not for *all* of you, I would not be here today, so I stand strong and with the gentle pushes from both my sons to release my books, I now have. I will continue to be that firsthand testament + voice of reason to help everyone to better understand or to just be a ray of hope to other survivors or the victims- I love you and your not alone..

This book is only part one of Kerried Away. As I mentioned on a recent show, this part of my book had to be split in half. It was 700 pages and just too big. So the rest of my story for this half of my life anyways, will follow shortly.

Love N Light,

Kerri Krysko

PS: Yes, I walk back-down the very same roads that lead me to where this all began, and the ones I felt I needed to see, were the answers I sought, as we clawed our way to freedom — seeking and searching for the truth , sleeping in a car or running to a woman's shelter, *only* to be turned away ... the book, "Kerri" part 2 ... released, December 2015

"The note written below, by my son, when he was 15years old"

To: Mom

It's November 18th today and I just thought I should write something to you and I want to start by saying I can't tell you how much I love you and appreciate everything you've given to me and Saxon. I feel terrible that I can't get you anything but I hope this will work. You do anything and everything for us and I can't imagine being a single mother dealing with two asshole dad's and raising a child and a bad kid alone and having no ~~hope~~ ~~of them.~~ fucked us both

leaving you with physical and emotional pain and how much I wish I could stop it. I live everyday being proud to be your son. I feel like a baby crying threw writing this right now. Thank you for all the love and staying strong going threw all of ~~the~~ everything and ~~me being being~~ being the best Role Model to me, you inspired me to be stronger and ~~it gets me~~ I knew that I had to be your Guardian Angel and help you get threw everything. I don't know what to say now but I'm going to keep writing. ~~But because~~ I know my dad wasn't there for me or paying child support and I'm blessed that Saxon ~~didn't~~ have doesn't ~~have~~ grow up to see ~~how we do.~~ Agree or Disagree. My favourite part of every birthday and Christmas is you and Saxon smileing and happy knowing we are away from him. I love you mom and no matter how many nightmares from the past ~~on~~ that _____ gave me, I'm happy that I ~~get~~ have you with me and Saxon everyday. ~~the~~

Your book will inspire people just like how you inspired me. No matter how m__ _____ hy ~~any~~ Screw James and Trevor, you are my best friend. You have no idea how hard it is being the man of the house but I try. I love you ~~████ Mom ████~~ and I'm proud to be your son. Thank you for being ~~███~~ my inspiration, my best friend, my mom and dad, and my hero. ~~Your~~ Your the coolest. I love you so much mom. Happy birthday mom.

Love: Your Son Ashton A. Krysko

Kerried Away

Part 2

December of 2015

Chapter 18

The Weeks Following Marriage to The Beast

There were days I sat in the back forest of our property and just watched the house from a distance. I loved nature and found solace in the whispers of the trees and songs from the birds. I didn't like that Damien wouldn't allow me to order a cover for the pool, it was dangerous for the children but he was firm on that. I couldn't seem to say anything, otherwise. My step-father had even offered to pay for it but it didn't make a difference. The forest felt safe.

I continued to watch him warily; I watched everything about him right down to how he acted and how he spoke to people on the phone. It no longer blinded me, I was no longer able to find excuses for him, that was long past and the only thing I felt for him was disgust and loathing. He knew it; in the way I was limp against his chest or barely there during converstion.

I wasn't able to paint a brave face for certain club functions anymore. The women knew something was wrong with me, even privately probing me for information trying to find out but I wasn't comfortable in going to half of them I couldn't smile for them and couldn't sit amongst them with my face and arms constantly covered with bruises. Damien knew it would spark questions he couldn't answer. I had no idea he was orchestrating a plan to have me look unstable and a lunatic to everyone; a cover-up for the fact that he was beating me or hitting me on an almost daily basis. It was a tactic of his that I was only just starting to zero in on.

My son was showing signs of strain at school and that gnawed at me. I was honest to everyone there; it was a place Damien rarely went to. It was my haven and mine alone.

I had yet to see my doctor, but after a few weeks of being married I needed to. I always felt a need to protect my kids if I died. I think back and know deep in my heart I didn't plan that, I just did it because I had to. It was survival without premediation. I could never, and I mean never, go to the police, not only my husband would kill me *but I thought the club would be gunning for me too;* he whispered those threats to me all the time now. It was his way of governing me with fear and it worked.

I was under a dark cloud; a vacant, worn out, hollow, thin shell of my former self that people were starting to question.

One day I exploded in a parking lot to Stella saying, "If one more person asks me if I do drugs I am going to flip out!! I'm no drug addict." I crumbled into a million tears, right there. Damien called and was pressuring me on the phone, about something or other, and it turned nasty really fast. I always felt more confident around other people and know Stella standing right there was what gave me the nerve to hang up on him.

What I didn't expect was him to come to where we were, in a rage. He started flipping out, and I tried to roll up the window and lock the door but he was too fast. He grabbed me by my hair and ripped my head halfway out of the window; he bit my ear. I cried out in pain, "Please Damien just stop, please."

Stella and I were complelty shaken by the incident and left wondering why he just felt it was okay to show his true colors. How he was starting to act it out in front of others more and more. She told me to get away from him, it wasn't good. But what she said to me was complelty different then what she said to others and I knew it was only a matter of time, before Damien ripped my hair out and tormented me all night long because Stella told him I was planning on leaving.

It was his way to break me then re-make me into what he wanted. He told me he had to hurt me, so I could get better and be the perfect person. Those tactic and words hurt me more than anything else. It was the mental abuse that robbed me of myself before any physical blow he could inflict. Words don't go away, bruises do. I never thought about how people I knew and what they were starting to think about me, I didn't look at that nor did I care.

I hadn't heard from any people after the wedding, it was like good riddance to me and my children. Let him have her.

I felt more alone then ever before and constantly wished for Deseriee, but she had been through enough and needed her space. It was too hard for to comprehend how family treated me and coveted Damien.

It was hard being alone, but the best thing for me as well. It gave me time to find some of my own strength and courage. I had been raped of it and in its place was a self-doubt so profund it almost swallowed me whole.

CPSIA information can be obtained
at www.ICGtesting.com
Printed in the USA
LVOW01s1538160216

475345LV00010B/27/P

9 780996 633055